Remembering Revolution

REMEMBERING REVOLUTION

Gender, Violence, and Subjectivity in India's Naxalbari Movement

SRILA ROY

OXFORD
UNIVERSITY PRESS

OXFORD
UNIVERSITY PRESS

Oxford University Press is a department of the University of Oxford. It furthers the University's objective of excellence in research, scholarship, and education by publishing worldwide. Oxford is a registered trademark of Oxford University Press in the UK and in certain other countries

Published in India by
Oxford University Press
YMCA Library Building, 1 Jai Singh Road, New Delhi 110 001, India

First Edition published in 2012

ISBN-13: 978-0-19-808172-2
ISBN-10: 0-19-808172-3

Typeset in Adobe Jenson Pro 10.5/12.6
by MAP Systems, Bengaluru 560 082, India
Printed in India by Rakmo Press, New Delhi 110 020

Contents

Portelli, Alessandro. 1998. 'What Makes Oral History Different', in Robert Perks and Alistair Thomson (eds), *The Oral History Reader*. London: Routledge, pp. 63–74.

Punjabi, Kavita. 1997. 'Probing "Morality" and State Violence: Feminist Values and Communicative Interaction in Prison *Testimonios* in Argentina and India', in M. Jacqui Alexander and Chandra Talpade Mohanty (eds), *Feminist Genealogies, Colonial Legacies, Democratic Futures*. New York: Routledge, pp. 20–45.

———. 2002. 'Between Testimony and History: Interpreting Oral Narratives of Tebhaga Women', in Supriya Chaudhuri and Sajni Mukherji (eds), *Literature and Gender: Essays for Jasodhara Bagchi*. New Delhi: Orient Longman, pp. 241–70.

Puri, Jyoti. 1999. *Woman, Body, Desire in Post-colonial India: Narratives of Gender and Sexuality*. London: Routledge.

Puwar, Nirmal. 2004. *Space Invaders: Race, Gender and Bodies Out of Place*. Oxford: Berg.

Radstone, Susannah. 2000. 'Introduction', in Susannah Radstone (ed.), *Memory and Methodology*. Oxford: Berg, pp. 1–22.

Radstone, Susannah and Katharine Hodgkin (eds). 2003. *Regimes of Memory*. London and New York: Routledge.

Rajasingham-Senanayake, Darini. 2001. 'Ambivalent Empowerment: The Tragedy of Tamil Women in Conflict', in Rita Manchanda (ed.), *Women, War, and Peace in South Asia: Beyond Victimhood to Agency*. New Delhi and Thousand Oaks, CA: Sage Publications, pp. 102–30.

———. 2004. 'Between Reality and Representation: Women's Agency in War and Post-Conflict Sri Lanka', *Cultural Dynamics*, 16(2–3): 141–68.

Ram, Mohan. 1971. *Maoism in India*. New York: Barnes and Noble.

Ramphele, Mamphela. 1997. 'Political Widowhood in South Africa: The Embodiment of Ambiguity', in Arthur Kleinman, Veena Das, and Margaret Lock (eds), *Social Suffering*. Berkeley and London: University of California Press, pp. 99–117.

Ray, Manas. 2002. 'Growing Up Refugee', *History Workshop Journal*, 53: 150–79.

Ray, Rabindra. 1988. *The Naxalites and their Ideology*. New Delhi, Oxford: Oxford University Press.

Ray, Raka. 1999. *Fields of Protest: Women's Movements in India*. New Delhi: Kali for Women.

———. 2000. 'Masculinity, Femininity, and Servitude: Domestic Workers in Kolkata in the Late Twentieth Century', *Feminist Studies*, 26(3): 691–718.

Ray, Raka and M. Katzenstein. 2005. 'Introduction: In the Beginning, There was the Nehruvian State', in R. Ray and M. Katzenstein (eds), *Social Movements in India: Poverty, Power, and Politics*. Lanham, MD: Rowman and Littlefield, pp. 1–31.

Acknowledgements

I owe the greatest debt to the women and men who participated in this project—who welcomed me into their homes and lives, gave valuable amounts of their time, hospitality, trust, and patience. This book has collected other debts along the way, from its inception as a PhD thesis at the University of Warwick under the astute and creative guidance of Deborah Steinberg and Parita Mukta. They have both contributed to the shaping of my intellectual life well beyond the bounds of this project. Sudipta Kaviraj and Carol Wolkowitz have been wonderful mentors since they examined the thesis. I am particularly grateful to Carol for taking the time out to read and provide extensive comments to the Introduction and Conclusion of this book.

At Warwick, the faculty of Sociology and the Centre for the Study of Women and Gender—especially Steve Fuller, Robert Fine, Joanna Liddle, and Terry Lovell—provided a creative and nurturing environment for the writing up of this project. An Overseas Research Student Award along with a Warwick Postgraduate Research Fellowship provided the main funding for the thesis. A Feminist Review Trust PhD Writing-up Scholarship aided the final stages of writing.

The field research in Kolkata was facilitated by a number of people I met, some of whom I am fortunate enough to count as friends today. Mithu Roy helped locate and access crucial sources besides conducting archival work and translating data. The many sessions of *adda* with Alakananda Guha and Anirban Das have filtered into some of the ideas presented in this book. I am particularly grateful to Anirban for acting as an informal mentor. Gautam Bhadra was instrumental in identifying key sources and references, most of which would have remained unknown to me without his astute guidance. Numerous others provided sources, references, and contacts, and I am extremely grateful to Pradip Basu, Arun Ghosh, Rajashri Dasgupta, Saumen and Latika Guha, Kalpana Sen, and Gita Das in this respect. Ratnabali Chatterji proved a continuous source of support in the field, and I am especially indebted to her. My thanks to

Sharmishta for her invaluable help with some of the translations from Bangla. The staff at the National Library and the Centre for the Study of Social Sciences in Kolkata was especially helpful.

Colleagues at the University of Nottingham, especially of the Identity, Citizenship and Migration Centre, provided a supportive and friendly environment for this thesis to be written up as a book. I extend my thanks to Nick Stevenson and Amal Treacher Kabesh for reading and commenting on draft chapters, and to Christian Karnerfor for his warm interest. As the only South Asianist in the Nottingham village, Stephen Legg has been a model of collegiality besides being a true friend. Julia O'Connell Davidson and Jacqueline Sanchez-Taylor have made Nottingham home for me in ways that are not easily acknowledged.

The ideas and arguments presented in this book have benefitted from discussions at various stages with Jashodhara Bagchi, Samita Sen, Partha Chatterjee, Jayoti Gupta, Kavita Punjabi, Pradip Basu, Tanika and Sumit Sarkar, Rabindra Ray, Sumanta Bannerjee, Bela Bhatia, David Hardiman, Rajeswari Sunder Rajan, Alpa Shah, Molly Andrews, and Rajarshi Dasgupta. Special thanks to Rajarshi for the use of his unpublished thesis and papers on the Bengali communists. In the run up to publishing this book, I found encouragement from unexpected quarters; warm thanks to Craig Jeffrey and Laura Sjoberg. Oxford University Press brought this book to light quickly and efficiently, and for this I thank them. Sandip Ray allowed the use of a still from Satyajit Ray's *Pratidwandi* with little hesitation, for which I extend my heartfelt thanks.

For cheering me along the way, I thank Atreyee Sen, Rubina Jasani, Niharika Dinkar, Shalini Grover, Rashmi Varma, Luke Robinson, and older friends, Maud Perrier, Amrita Ibrahim, Konkona Sensharma, Jaydeep Sarkar, and Ankur Khanna. Friendships that have deepened over time and shifting locations with Kaavya Asoka, Susan George, and Elisabeth Simbuerger have sustained me through the writing of this book. Elisabeth read the entirety of the project in its earlier manifestation and has been its champion since. My biggest debt is to Disha Mullick who read several chapters and offered detailed advice unabashedly, often at a day or two's notice, and with little patience for academic jargon. This book is much stronger thanks to her generosity and attention.

At the final stages of writing up, the arguments presented benefitted enormously from the incisive comments of friends and colleagues given at very short notice: Stephen Legg, Deepti Misri, Jonathan Dean, Nicolas

Jaoul, Becky Walker, Swati Parashar, Henrike Donner, Alf Nilsen (who offered references and encouragement), and Srimati Basu, this book's ardent advocate. Shraddha Chigateri and Pratiksha Baxi have have been ideal interlocutors in addition to being inspirational friends, and this book and I have gained much from our conversations over the years. Pratiksha has been a virtual presence throughout the writing of this book in ways that have deepened my understanding and restored my sanity. My thanks to Ishan Tankha for being a mensch and letting me use his haunting photograph.

My family has been critical to the execution and completion of this project, from their hospitality to the sharing of memories and stories, to their enduring love that makes me the person I am. My extended family—Didu, Ninou *mashi*, Gina, and Bon—sustained me with good cheer throughout fieldwork in Kolkata. A big thanks to Ninou mashi and Shormi mashi for facilitating my use of one of the images for this book. It is a pleasure to record my thanks to my sister, Mishta Roy, for designing the book's cover. Together with *didi*, my brother-in-law, Anirudh, and my in-laws, Simone and Jean-Pierre, have created homes for me wherever they are, and this book owes much to their generosity and affection. I owe the greatest debt to my parents, Reeti and Debashis for their 'ordinary' and 'extraordinary' acts of kindness, support, and encouragement right from the inception of this project. Without them, this book and I would be a great deal more wanting. And finally, my thanks to Rafael Winkler, who has read each word on every page, for his love, his wise counsel, and his example.

Parts of Chapter 3 have been published as, 'The Everyday Life of the Revolution: Gender, Violence and Memory', *South Asia Research*, 27(2): 187–204, 2007; of Chapter 4 as, 'Revolutionary Marriage: On the Politics of Sexual Stories in Naxalbari', *Feminist Review*, 83: 99–118, 2006; of Chapter 5 as, 'The Grey Zone: The "Ordinary" Violence of Extraordinary Times', *The Journal of the Royal Anthropological Institue*, 14(2): 314–30, 2008; and of Chapter 6 as, 'Testimonies of State Terror: Trauma and Healing in Naxalbari', in Manali Desai, Piya Chatterjee, and Parama Roy (eds), *States of Trauma: Gender and Violence in South Asia*, New Delhi: Zubaan Books, 2009.

Spivak, Gayatri. 2002. 'Breast-giver: For Author, Reader, Teacher, Subaltern, Historian…', in Mahasweta Devi, *Breast Stories*, trans. by Gayatri Chakravorty Spivak, Kolkata: Seagull Books, pp. 76–137.

Sreenivas, Mytheli. 2008. *Wives, Widows, Concubines: The Conjugal Family Ideal in Colonial India*. Bloomington: Indiana University Press.

Standing, Hilary. 1991. *Dependence and Autonomy: Women's Employment and the Family in Calcutta*. London: Routledge.

Steedman, Carolyn. 1988. *The Radical Soldier's Tale: John Pearman, 1819–1908*. London and New York: Routledge.

Stree Shakti Sanghatana. 1989. *We were Making History …: Life Stories of Women in the Telangana People's Struggle*. London: Zed Books.

Sturken, Marita. 1997. *Tangled Memories: The Vietnam War, the AIDS Epidemic, and the Politics of Remembering*. Berkeley and London: University of California Press.

———. 1999. 'Narratives of Recovery: Repressed Memory as Cultural Memory', in Mieke Bal, Jonathan V. Crewe, and Leo Spitzer (eds), *Acts of Memory: Cultural Recall in the Present*. Hanover, NH, and London: University Press of New England, pp. 231–48.

Summerfield, Penny. 1998. *Reconstructing Women's Wartime Lives: Discourse and Subjectivity in Oral Histories of the Second World War*. Manchester: Manchester University Press.

———. 2000. 'Dis/composing the Subject: Intersubjectivities in Oral History', in Tess Cosslett, Celia Lury, and Penny Summerfield (eds), *Feminism and Autobiography: Texts, Theories, Methods*. London: Routledge, pp. 91–106.

———. 2004. 'Culture and Composure: Creating Narratives of the Gendered Self in Oral History Interviews', *Cultural and Social History*, 1(1): 65–93.

Sunder Rajan, Rajeswari. 1993. *Real and Imagined Women: Gender, Culture and Postcolonialism*. London: Routledge.

———. 1999. 'The Story of Draupadi's Disrobing: Meanings for Our Times', in Rajeswari Sunder Rajan (ed.), *Signposts: Gender Issues in Post-Independence India*, New Delhi: Kali for Women, pp. 331–58.

———. 2004. 'Rethinking Law and Violence: The Domestic Violence (Prevention) Bill in India, 2002', *Gender and History*, 16(3): 769–93.

Tal, Kali. 1996. *Worlds of Hurt: Reading the Literatures of Trauma*. Cambridge: Cambridge University Press.

Tambiah, Yasmin. 2005. 'Turncoat Bodies: Sexuality and Sex Work under Militarization in Sri Lanka', *Gender and Society*, 19(2): 243–61.

Tarlo, Emma. 2003. *Unsettling Memories: Narratives of the Emergency in Delhi*. London: C. Hurst & Co.; New Delhi: Zubaan Books, 2009.

Taussig, Michael. 1999. *Defacement: Public Secrecy and the Labor of the Negative*. Stanford: Stanford University Press.

Thapar-Bjorkert, Suruchi. 2006. *Women in the Indian Nationalist Movement: Unseen Faces, Unheard Voices, 1925–1942*. New Delhi and London: Sage Publications.

Remembering Revolution

An Introduction

One of the earliest memories I inherited from my mother was of the home, the *bari* in which she had spent much of her childhood. Situated in south Kolkata,[1] this house was the fruit of my grandfather's entrepreneurial skills; a house he had built 'with his own hands'. Yet, it was a house he never spoke of. His silence was rooted in a certain event that had led to the immediate abandonment of the house, a week before my mother was married in 1971. A group of young boys—boys of the *para* who had played cricket with the children of the household—had held the family hostage and robbed my grandfather's collection of guns and revolvers. Their intentions were never very clear to me but I knew they were not petty criminals. Before the event itself, my grandmother spoke of the men trying to hide in the garage. My mother spoke of the army coming into the house in search of them. I was also told of their violent deaths at the hands of the police, which the family had heard of some months later. The family itself never returned home after the incident with the guns. The loss of our bari was one that I, along with the other children of the family, inherited and mourned.

By the time I joined university, I could locate this familial memory in a wider cultural narrative around a pro-poor revolution led by young students in the late 1960s in Kolkata, a time when the world was rife with anti-state, rebellious bursts of utopian energy. The 'Naxalites' were our very own home-grown brand. For me, the story of the Naxalites was one of youthful rebellion and romantic tragedy, rooted in the imagery of the city of Kolkata and its most representative voice, the middle class. The class element became increasingly important as I graduated from school to university, given a newfound disdain towards everything that was 'petty bourgeois', including my own familial and class background. When I met Anant, a fellow student whose mother, a Naxalite, had been imprisoned for four years, all my suspicions were confirmed. I belonged, indisputably, to the 'other side'. I no longer identified with my mother's pain at the loss of her home. Now, I yearned to belong to the counterculture that the Naxalites together with my university peers represented. The figure of the Naxalite and all the elements that it included—youthful rebellion, social justice on behalf of the oppressed, tragic death—were thus bound up with my attempts to fashion myself at a particular juncture in my life.

My shifting identifications with the figure of the Naxalite are relevant for the central issues that are at stake in this book.[2] Most obviously, *Remembering Revolution* concerns the late 1960s radical Left Naxalbari movement of West Bengal, one of the most violent sociopolitical upheavals in independent India whose ramifications continue till today. This book is about those middle-class women (and men) who told me their stories of 'being a Naxalite', of leaving homes and attempting to politicize the Indian peasantry, largely through violence, at a time of New Left upsurges around the globe. It is also about the wider cultural repertoires that constitute the figure of the Naxalite in diverse ways, as symptomatic of youthful dissatisfaction, of revolutionary valour on behalf of the subaltern, or even of the terror and violence that have become indelible to the history of South Asia, and towards which the movement under discussion has contributed in no small measure. Naxalbari—the shorthand I use for the movement which began with a singular iconic episode to which I turn in Chapter 1—can be understood as a repository of these popular mythologies that comprise its continuing significance in collective memory. The evocation of the word in relation to recent events against land expropriation in neoliberal India signalled the legacy of violent state repression but was also deeply reminiscent of a long tradition of people's protest, nowhere more obvious than in the Indian state of West Bengal.

Theorizing Memory

Memory is a central tool employed in this study, analytically and methodologically. My own memory of the movement shifted from an inherited familial memory to one that was mediated by different narratives associated with the peer group. Identification with these cultural narratives was also part of my attempt to construct a recognizable self-identity that would enable me to belong to a certain social group at a particular time in my life. A few years later, the meanings associated with the 'Naxalite' would change further as I would relinquish my claims to revolutionary grandeur, and settle on something more manageable like academic research. 'Naxalbari' would figure, in the course of my MA research, amidst questions of subaltern struggle and feminist politics. It would be considered less an object of fantastical identification than one of critical enquiry, tinged with a degree of nostalgia for a self-identity that I had now outgrown. Identities, however, are rarely completely discarded, and I would attempt to locate older, inherited stories of my mother and Anant's mother within a newly acquired sociological narrative. Once again, the meaning of Naxalbari changed, as I identified more and more with feminist politics and felt the absence of women's stories (like those of mine and of Anant's mother) from the historical record.

Remembering Revolution began as an attempt to 'fill' the gendered gap of this archive, conceived as a broad (oral) her-story of the movement. To this extent, I sought to locate it within a tradition of feminist historicizing on radical movements in India through a focus on women's personal testimonies. However, I soon realized that the work of memory could not be employed to unearth 'lived experience' as the ground of female subjectivity. Memory cannot give us access to some pure past unmediated by culture—by cultural discourses, narratives, and practices (as well as unconscious desires) that shape our memories and the narratives through which they are transmitted. This makes memory itself a discursive production, a product of historical and cultural construction, and not a mere record of past happenings—neither 'pure experience nor pure event', as Kuhn (1999: 189) puts it—but a form of representation. Memories, Verma writes, are 'interpretive reconstructions' that are products of 'local narrative conventions, cultural assumptions, discursive formations and practices, social contexts and commemoration' (Verma 2004: xxxiii). We could say that memory mediates culture itself insofar as it produces meanings and interpretations of the past that can influence and even transform the present. Memory, thus, performs important interpretive work besides constituting the ground for the consolidation of individual and group identities. Taking from this recent scholarship the concept of memory as mediated by (and also mediating) culture, the research on which this book draws shifted its orientation from the content of memories per se to the cultural work that these memories perform, that is, 'the culturally mediated acts, schemata, and stories' that 'comprise our memories and the way we think about them' (Antze and Lambek 1996: xv). The discussion in the following chapters engages with memory as an 'inventive social practice' (Sturken 1997), as constitutive of subjectivity, and part of the production of cultural meanings and interpretations (Passerini 1987: 195)[3].

While such an idea of memory resonates with current understandings of 'cultural memory,'[4] or what it means for a culture as opposed to an individual to remember, it evokes a relatively older, somewhat less fashionable popular memory approach on whose conceptual tools and methods this book draws. Developed by the Popular Memory Group at the University of Birmingham in the early 1980s and influenced by a small cohort of international oral historians like Luisa Passerini and Alessandro Portelli who pioneered a revision of oral history method, the Group was part of a radical critique and redefinition of historical production beyond the confines of academic historiography to '*all* the ways in which a sense of the past is constructed in our society' (Johnson 1982: 207).[5] Significantly, before the rise and overuse of the concept of cultural memory, it developed a cultural approach that ties the work of personal remembrance with wider cultural forms and meanings. The relation between public representations and private memory, and their theorization as different moments within a larger process or a 'cultural circuit' (Johnson 1982: 207) of memory production, lies at the heart of this approach, and one that crucially moves beyond a conception of personal memory as purely authentic (as has been the case in some forms of oral and feminist history) or as being entirely determined, 'from above', by public memory. Instead, the idea of a cultural circuit suggests 'that personal accounts are in their own ways fictive or constructed, as are public accounts, because they are woven from available ways of understanding which suit the individual in relation to his or her own sense of self, and his or her audience's expectations at the time of telling' (Summerfield 1998: 29).

An emphasis on the ways in which public representations of the past are negotiated at the level of the individual—what is sometimes said to be missing in the study of collective or social memory, as Hamilton (2007: 5) has more recently noted—is the explicit focus of oral history projects like Penny Summerfield and Alistair Thomson's on women and men's wartime memories. As in these studies, memory is here defined as having a subjective *and* social dimension. Accordingly, one of the key questions that propelled this research was: how are memories of Naxalbari culturally produced, received, and contested? How do they implicate the work of gendered identity, in particular, at the interface of personal narratives and wider culturally mediated ones? How are female (and male) subjectivities constituted, in other words, through practices of individual and collective memorializing? Methodologically, the research field was extended beyond personal recollections to include historiographic, official, and popular representations of the movement, even as most of these would be considered 'gender blind' (see Chapters 1 and 2). That said, the analytic core of this book comes from the personal narratives of middle-class women activists obtained through in-depth interviews, some lasting over several meetings.

Narratives of Society, Self, and Other

Like memory, narrative too is an interpretive device through which individuals (and cultures) make sense of the past, and ascribe intelligibility to the world at large and their place in it. One approach to narrative that has developed in popular memory theory can be identified in the work of Graham Dawson (discussed later), which complements Plummer's (1995) analysis of narrative within a 'sociology of stories'. Plummer's study of sexual storytelling goes beyond the structural or textual work that narrative performs to the social, cultural, and political role of stories in everyday life, in the constitution of both personal identities and wider political ones. Plummer argues that the rape survival story has, for instance, enabled women to 'come out' with their own stories of sexual abuse and to inhabit subject positions such as that of a victim or of a survivor. An important implication of this argument is that without such a stock of stories and an audience to validate them, these experiences would simply not be 'tellable' (1995: 58). As detailed in Chapter 1, a common appeal to the language of feminism rendered certain stories tellable, which were otherwise silenced. Public narratives such as those of the Indian women's movement and the Indian Left enabled certain kinds of stories to be told at the cost of others, validating, in turn, some identities and experiences 'while marginalising or rendering unspeakable others' (Redman 1999: 312; see also Lawler 2002). It is through the telling of stories that individuals bestow meaning on past events and 'produce a world in which the self finds a home' (Kaviraj 1992: 13).

Narratives are always related to and productive of some sense of selfhood so much so that the narrative constitution of the self has emerged as a legitimate area of scholarship on its own (see, for example, Ricoeur 1991; and Somers 1994). Underlying these conceptions is the idea that people construct identities that are relatively stable and coherent through the use of stories.

In works like Plummer's, narratives are also linked to marginalized histories and identities or to Foucault's notion of subjugated knowledges—'knowledges that have been disqualified as inadequate to their task or insufficiently elaborated' (Foucault 1980, cited in Sturken 1997: 6). A tradition of critically engaging with such 'subjugated knowledges' and 'counter-memories' of marginalized, powerless groups has long existed in oral history (Passerini 1987; and Portelli 1991), in subaltern studies (Guha 1997a), and in feminist historiography (Scott 1999). Subaltern narratives do not, as emphasized in these varied approaches, occupy an autonomous realm, against the tendency to see personal testimony as 'protected and separate from hegemonic forms' (Olick and Robbins 1998: 126).[6] Sturken also cautions against the romanticization of popular memory, implicit in Foucault's usage of the term 'counter-memory': 'cultural memory may often constitute opposition, but it is not automatically the scene of cultural resistance' (1997: 7). Like feminists who have called for the historicization of experience rather than taking it as something given (Scott 1992), oral historians and popular memory theorists call for an engagement with personal testimony in relation to and not outside of public narratives and historical discourse. Accordingly, this book locates the work of personal remembrance in a wider remit of cultural forms and meanings; of cultural representations and historical interpretations of Naxalbari. It brings historiographic methods into the orbit of theorizing popular memory processes, enabling an understanding of how these different moments interlink and how these linkages produce historically located and mediated cultural repertoires of identity.

In the pages that follow, we see how individuals draw on cultural and historical constructions of revolutionary masculinity and heroic femininity in making sense of their past and their selves. Such idealized constructs were classed insofar as they reinscripted hegemonic forms of *bhadralok* (middle-class) manliness in the discursive domain of the political. Likewise, they were deeply gendered in that they offered men powerful and preferred identities through the repudiation of feminine weakness and the threat of emasculation, and in the symbolic distancing of revolutionary activity from domestic routine. While the revolutionary hero offered potent forms of identification for the ordinary male middle-class self, discourses of heroic femininity positioned women (particularly middle-class Bengali women) in contradictory ways, expecting them to repudiate the feminine for the sake of political agency but also idealizing feminine (and middle-class) codes of domesticity, motherhood, and romance. These cultural forms of revolutionary masculinity and heroic femininity constitute, as demonstrated throughout the book, important resources in the 'composure' of individual subjectivity. I have suggested in mapping my own subjective investments in Naxalbari that cultural narratives 'summon' and give shape to our personal memories. They also make available a range of subject positions that are invested in and occupied for the particular benefits that they afford—social recognition, a sense of belonging, psychic comfort, and so on. The relations between memory, narrative, and identity are thus some of the larger issues that the cultural memory of Naxalbari evokes, and I explore these in the pages that follow.

Composing Memories, Composing the Self

As in several similar studies (Dawson 1994; Summerfield 2000; and Thomson 1998), the interface between public and private memory opens up a way of understanding personal experience and subjectivity as constituted through cultural forms of remembrance. At the heart of this interface is the idea of memory as composure: 'in one sense we compose or construct memories using the public languages and meaning of our culture. In another sense, we compose memories that help us feel relatively comfortable with our lives and identities, that give us a feeling of composure' (Thomson 1998: 301). The practice of composing memories has thus both a cultural and a psychological dimension to it, emphasizing the manner in which individuals seek to achieve coherency through their investment in socially given or constructed identities. Narrative plays a key role in creating and maintaining coherence amidst contradiction in what some (for example, Mishler 1991) have called narrative's 'coherence function', that is, its ability to produce a coherent life story that smoothens out the rough edges of lived experience. The narrative function of producing a coherent subject position that is recognizable and 'liveable' is a central feature of Dawson's study of adventure narratives and the role they play in the symbolic and material constitution of masculinity. Narrative forms such as that of the soldier hero offer the possibility of composing a coherent self-identity that responds to both inner psychic conflicts and ongoing social contradictions. Individuals invest in these narrative positions due to the 'specifically psychic attraction of idealized heroes as figures of identification' and not simply in terms of their social predominance (1994: 31). In exploring women's personal narratives of the Second World War, Summerfield draws on Dawson's theorization of 'subjective composure' to understand the ways in which individuals 'strive' to constitute themselves within a contradictory discursive repertoire in order to make sense of their pasts and themselves (see also Summerfield 2004). Narrative, for Summerfield (2000), is not a site of coherence or composure but one of 'discomposure', which is to say that while individuals might strive to produce a unified, coherent, stable narrative, there is no such thing as a coherent story, and this is precisely what narrative belies (see also Byrne 2003 and Lawler 2008). She equally emphasizes feminist understandings of female subjectivity as being more fragile than masculinity given the contradictory way in which the former is discursively constituted, and that, too, in the image of a dominant masculinity that 'define[s] the parameters of identity and behaviour possible to women' (Summerfield 1998: 14).

As in the case of the Second World War, the category of 'woman' was contradictorily constituted and put into political use in the context of Naxalbari. The revolutionary domain was a strictly masculine one where women activists were, by and large, 'matter out of place', to use Puwar's (2004) evocation of Mary Douglas' (1991) pertinent coinage. If women are 'matter out of place' in the political sphere, they are even more so in militarized ones that are constructed through the exclusion of womanhood and in contradistinction to the private domestic sphere. Even as the political party that led the movement mobilized femininity to render the violence of 'class struggle' legitimate and honourable (see Chapter 2), it provided little political agency for 'real' women, especially middle-class women who entered the revolutionary imaginary through motherhood. While these modes of representation reflect a more pervasive gendering of political, especially militarized spaces, they are also part of individual and collective remembrance and the constitution of individual subjectivity. Taking from Dawson's idea of subjective composure as the way in which identities are fashioned in relation to cultural forms and psychic processes, the composure of (male and female) subjectivities through practices of cultural remembering and forgetting is one of the core concerns of the analysis presented in this book.

Memory Politics and Identity Practices

The practice of 'composure' is also intensely political. We compose our memories in ways to make them 'fit' with the public world; indeed, those memories that do not accord with public narratives risk marginalization and silencing. In trying to ensure a fit between our memories and with what is publicly acceptable, self-composure inevitably relies on practices of repression and exclusion that nevertheless threaten its foundation. Individuals thus 'compose' stories through a range of discursive possibilities, 'taking-up' some discourses while rejecting others in their efforts to compose a recognizable social self. They are not, Edkins (2003: 54) emphasizes, at will to choose what to remember and what to forget, given the powerful public narrative repertoire of a culture that validates the telling of some stories and the silencing of others. The pursuit of composure thus implies conformity to hegemonic discourses that exert a regulatory force upon individual remembering. It could even entail, as Thomson (1998) suggests, a disavowal of alternative narratives through practices of repression and expulsion.

Historical approaches to memory like that of Thomson's end up overestimating how a dominant memory structures, 'from above', personal accounts. The depth of the individual embrace of such public discourses is thus missing. These limitations can be attributed to the inadequate attention that such studies pay to the psychological dimensions of remembering and to the constitution of identity therein.[7] The latter is, of course, a key concern of post-structuralist and psychoanalytically inflected feminist theory that investigates, what Butler (1997) calls, our 'passionate attachments' to normative identities that render them durable and less resistant to change. The conceptualization of identity through repudiation and loss, that animates work like hers, enables a stronger sense of the specific mechanisms and political costs of attaining 'composure' in the practices of memory. While Dawson suggests that certain forms of subjectivity must be disavowed for the sake of composure, according to Butler, foreclosure and loss predate and constitute the subject itself. Her argument on gender as melancholia concerns the way in which all identities are constituted through loss and by being 'subject' to power relations, thereby introducing a stronger Foucauldian sense of power and its productive capacity into an understanding of composure. Power produces subjects that are recognizable as inhabiting a coherent, normative identity. Indeed, recognition is not conferred upon an already existing subject but forms the subject (Butler 1997: 225). 'Composure' can now be viewed less in terms of the efforts to integrate a fractured and contradictory subjectivity than in terms of regulatory practices upon which the very possibility of continuing as a recognizable social being depends. Butler's logic of repudiation also provides a stronger argument for the achievement of composure in and through practices of exclusion, disavowal, and 'forgetting'. What is forgotten is not simply abandoned or lost but is the means through which subjectivity is produced and shaped. As Sturken (1997) notes, subjectivities are constituted as much through forgetting as they are through remembering. The politics of remembering–forgetting is part of a regulatory economy that renders certain subject positions culturally unthinkable and 'unliveable' from the start, while rendering others liveable.

A growing literature in South Asia points to the significance of memory in constituting national and community identities (for example, Amin 1995; Butalia 1998; Mankekar 1999; Mayaram 1997; Pandey 2001; and Tarlo 2003). Where such practices, especially ones of wilful forgetting, have been pronounced is in the founding violence that accompanied the bloody births of India, Pakistan, and, later, Bangladesh. Feminist historiography in this area (Bhasin and Menon 1998; Butalia 1998; Das 2007; Mookherjee 2008; and Saikia 2011) has shown how the twin processes of amnesia and anamnesis (Gandhi 1998, cited in Legg 2011) that national narratives rely on, have specific implications for subaltern, including gendered, memories of national traumas. Perceived as a threat to internal solidarity, these memories are subject not simply to forgetting but to active repression. The discussion in this book is similarly concerned with what is forgotten, denied, or expelled as policing the boundaries of identities, and imbricated in issues of power and gender. It employs, from Butler, a stronger sense of forgetting as repudiation, and examines the political costs of composing a liveable and normative identity. These costs are generally high for women given the unstable nature of constructions of femininity that make it harder for women to attach themselves to an identity (Summerfield 1998).

The book analyses the ways in which Naxalite women take up an idealized heroic femininity, and the manner in which they narratively 'compose' self-identity in acts of repudiation, abjection, and 'forgetting'. Identification with a fantasy of revolution entailed abjection of those experiences that were rooted in more fragmentary and vulnerable aspects of the self. The abject, for these women activists, included that which was coded as feminine within primarily male fantasies of heroic self-sacrifice. Women's donning of the male political outfit is, in any case, a process that is replete with paradoxes and ambiguities. Puwar's (2004) study on the entry of gendered and racialized minorities into everyday public spaces from which they have been normatively excluded explores the tenuous nature of this process and the management of 'difference' in majoritarian contexts. It makes clear that the entry and presence of marginalized subjects like women in male-dominated spaces does not make them more inclusive; on the contrary, women remain 'matter out of place' and often, internalize their own difference in modes of complicity and denial. The transformation from being political outsiders to insiders also exposes hitherto unmarked identities and spaces as masculine and majoritarian while disrupting the status quo. Puwar's study is relevant in this context because it enables a moving beyond the 'gender blindness' of political movements like Naxalbari (that is key to recent feminist histories of the movement, such as Sinha Roy 2011) to map the complexities of women's entry into spaces which 'have not been "reserved" for them' (Puwar 2004: 1), including the disruption, negotiation, and complicity that this encounter causes. Like Puwar, I aim to provide a much more complex picture of the manner in which gender and class are embedded in the character and life of social movements, including—or especially—radical ones like Naxalbari. Radicality can hardly be measured by the extent to which such movements are 'gender blind' or not without a consideration of the latent ways in which they are gendered and interpellate male and female actors in a series of dis/identifications.

Lacerated Memories of Hidden Violence

The issue of violence lies at the heart of the analysis that is put forth. This might seem obvious given that the deployment of violence as a political tool was intrinsic to Naxalite ideology and strategy, which set the tone for subsequent Maoist struggles in the region. The fascination with political violence in popular and historical memory has not meant, however, a consideration of its more banal and gendered experience at the level of everyday life. So, while the figure of the raped woman is exemplary of the ravages of state terror (see Chapter 6), the gendered vulnerability that structured the underground life of the movement has scarcely been included in historical understandings of Naxalbari violence (for example, Banerjee 1984; and Ray 1998). The identification of violence with its most extreme manifestations is not limited to the historiography of the radical Left. As I argue in Chapter 1, and have shown elsewhere (Roy 2009a), feminist scholarship on anti-state 'liberatory' struggles in South Asia has tended to define political violence as state-sponsored terror alone. From my interviews with male and female activists, it was possible to map a broad taxonomy of violence—political, sexual, 'public', and 'private'—as structuring everyday life within the movement, especially in the space of the underground where the revolutionaries took 'shelter' in the homes of peasants, workers, or middle-class sympathizers of the party. It was within such spaces of refuge and safety that female activists, in particular, faced multiple forms of threat, and not at the hands of the enemy alone. As the research progressed, it threw up significant questions around the complex ways in which such violence was remembered and narrated; of what was evoked and silenced in leftist ideals of revolutionary violence; and the politics of recognizing and of refusing recognition to some forms of violence over others.

Revolutionary movements such as the one addressed by this book mirror wider modes of rationalizing certain kinds of violence while rendering others invisible. Much like the state, they confer legitimacy upon their own acts of militancy, thereby effacing the violence of the self and projecting it onto an other. The psychic operation of projection, whereby unwanted feelings are purged from the self and attributed to another, enables one to hurt the other with impunity. But it also enables a denial of one's own pain, which is recast in heroic light, evident in the sacrificial memory adopted in present-day commemorative practices of state repression discussed towards the end of the book. A repression of the facts of political violence and killing from the memory of those who once supported, even instigated, it has been powerfully termed by Passerini as 'lacerations in the memory' in the context of the 1970s New Left mobilizations in Italy:

> ... the very facts of terrorism were absent from those recollections, as though the violence had actually been repressed ... in a society in

> which violent death is so frequent, is this repression part and parcel of every kind of murder? Hasn't all previous violence, whether committed by fascism or by antifascism, been pushed aside, in a sort of collective repression mechanism? (Passerini 1992: 197)

While Passerini's notion of a lacerated memory has been important to later evaluations of militant movements (for example, Hamilton 2007), it has not been extended to an understanding of the erasures and silences that surround *other* forms of violence: ordinary and not political violence, to use her own distinction (Passerini 1992: 192); or the violence that exists *within* violence as I call it. In the face of the 'extraordinary' violence of armed struggle around which cultural memory is woven, forms of violence that fall outside this totalizing category are rendered invisible, and their memory is equally 'lacerated, strewn with silences, riddled with holes' (Passerini 1992: 198). Women, the bearers of tradition, invariably emerge as the custodians of oppositional or 'risky' memories that require disciplining. The gendered dynamics of such memory politics is salient in the traumatic legacy of the Partition of the Indian Subcontinent given the widespread silence surrounding raped and abducted women. This silence—that some have theorized as a collusion between patriarchal notions of honour and the modernist ideology of the newly-formed nation-state (Das 2007)—is not limited to the discourses and practices of the state. Familial and community-based memory of the Partition is crafted out of its own modes of oblivion, especially around women who 'willingly' sacrificed their lives for family/community 'honour' (Butalia 1998; and Das 2007). In transforming death and even murder into sacrifice, violence perpetrated upon women by male members of their own families is shorn of terror, male complicity, and coercion. Women's 'martyrdom' also serves the function of cultural healing, of reinvesting the victimized community with agency, and of restoring male honour.

In exploring the ways in which violence is structured in the cultural memory of the movement and its legacy, the book shows how some forms of violence are more easily remembered, mourned, or even valorized than others, at the level of the individual and a culture, and the gendered dynamics of such forms of remembrance. It further shows how acts of legitimating, even idealizing, some forms of violence necessitate its misrecognition and eventual 'forgetting'. The imagining of revolution and its heroes relies, as already suggested, on a coercive misrecognition of the violence of the self that is transformed into a locus of heroism and self-sacrifice. But it is also linked to the lack of recognition to, or the 'forgetting' of, the violence that was internal to the revolutionary community; those 'little violences' and acts of betrayal that structured everyday interpersonal relationships within the movement. The book overwhelmingly demonstrates how these memories of violence and betrayal—especially of sexual violence suffered at the hands of one's comrades—could not always be articulated as testimony, not at the time of the movement and not even today. Instead, they were and continue to be articulated in the context of a normative silence, subject to forgetting. I employ a stronger sense of forgetting as repudiation, and not merely as silencing or as erasure, given the manner in which some of the women interviewed *dis*identify with the issue of sexual violence even against their own experience of injury (see Chapter 5). Memory functions, in this instance, to normalize male sexual power for the sake of the 'composure' that some women seek in the idealized images offered by the movement. More broadly, we could say that the cultural memory of Naxalbari functions to highlight or to conceal certain forms of violence, a dynamic that has become significant to the growth of right-wing movements in India (see Mukta 2004; and Verma 2004), and to the post-colonial memorialization of political violence more generally (Tarlo 2003; see also Legg 2011).

Beginning with the Everyday

Countering the mainstream (and feminist) mystification of Naxalite violence, the book turns to the everyday as a starting point from which to understand how the trauma of Naxalbari was lived and subjectively experienced. In their ethnography of the communal violence that took place in Bombay in 1992–3, Chatterji and Mehta (2007: 17) employ the term 'everyday' 'to depart from an analysis of broad structures and bounded forms of political economy' to an understanding of 'ordinary' people's lives and death. Like Chatterji and Mehta, I employ the terms 'everyday' and 'extraordinary' when speaking about violence but do not posit a clear separation 'between everyday life and the non-everyday, extraordinary events'. Violence has generally been theorized in academic terms as being 'extraordinary', as sudden and episodic, and a disruption of the ordinary and the everyday. By contrast, 'ordinary' or everyday forms of violence are marked by their lack of visibility and public recognition, and are quasi-synonymous with that which remains invisible, intimate, structural, or even unconscious. Against the tendency to exceptionalize violence and locate it outside or as an interruption of everyday life, recent histories and ethnographies of South Asia (Banerjee *et al.* 2004; Chatterji and Mehta 2007; Das 2007; Jeganathan 2000; and Pandey 2006) identify violence in its daily, invisible, or 'banal' forms. In positing continuities between the 'exceptional' and the 'everyday', they show, moreover, how the trauma of collective violence comes to be incorporated in the temporal structure of relationships and within the weave of daily life (see especially Das 2007).

In the succeeding analysis that begins with the quotidian experience of women's lives, we see how the 'extraordinary' violence of Naxalbari 'loses its exceptional character and becomes a "normal" and banal phenomenon' (Chatterji and Mehta 2007: 48) that folded into the textures of interpersonal relationships. The lived experience of violence also makes it incumbent to treat violence through the lens of gender. In recognizing gender-based violence as a form of everyday violence that persists through periods of political upheaval and relative peace, the book contributes to approaches that seek to problematize absolute distinctions within the study of violence, and to question the visibility afforded to some forms of violence over others. In analysing how forms of social (mis)recognition contribute to the normalization of violence, especially sexual violence, the study also contributes to feminist analyses of how patterns of dominance are sustained and reproduced. In addition, individual chapters explore women's subjective investments in discourses of revolutionary violence that have a particular resonance for contemporary analyses of gender in relation to violent or 'terrorist' movements. The ethnographic data and analyses offered call for a stronger feminist engagement with the underlying gendered politics of revolutionary violence; one that complicates current feminist appraisals of resistant violence as an expression of women's 'agency'.

The Afterlife of Violence: Trauma and Testimony

The analysis of the book—particularly of the conclusive chapter—is equally concerned with the aftermath of violence, within which issues of survival, recovery, and healing assume salience. As recent preoccupations of gender, trauma, and testimony have noted, transforming pain into something else and thereby reinhabiting the world in the aftermath of trauma is a complex task.[8] More often than not, the memory of collective violence and suffering is built around the narrative of the nation, constituting women as subjects of violence within and on behalf of a *masculine* nation. As Das (2007: 59) asks in relation to the Partition of the Indian subcontinent: What do such modalities of remembrance and representation do to the subjectivity of women? How do women's recollections of cultural trauma complicate, in turn, hegemonic national narratives in which gender is not merely absent but rendered invisible? And how can we think of what it means to come to terms with this past, especially through the everyday work of repair and recovery that women generally undertake?

Feminist historians have turned to women's testimonies as a way of marking the limits of official historiography as well as empowering, if not healing, women survivors themselves. Yet, the task of representing gendered trauma is, as I have explored elsewhere (S. Roy 2010), scarcely straightforward. The act of recovering and 'giving voice' can enact its own forms of epistemic violence on survivors who are invariably spoken for when they enter the historical record (Legg 2011). Women's testimonies of political violence are often said to speak through the language of silence and, on more than one historical occasion, they have also been observed to testify to the sufferings of others while rarely speaking of their own (Jelin 2003; and Ross 2001). While some have viewed this mode of silencing the private voice as undermining the universal (and patriarchal) basis of contemporary human rights discourse (Cubilie 2005), others have linked the compulsion to 'narrate the other' to normative gendered roles of which the testimonial one becomes an extension (Jelin 2003: 83). Even when women's stories have been speakable, they have been received with disbelief, as the historical silence on rape and domestic violence shows. For the feminist historian, any attempt at 'recovery' must then begin with the understanding that women, as Sunder Rajan (1993: 89) puts it, are rarely users of a language that is of their own making. The routinized and chronic forms of suffering that women experience in conditions of war and those of relative peace complicate the very idea of recovery in the aftermath of violence and trauma. Recovery, in post-colonial cultures of memory, has inevitably been tied up with the demands and structures of nation-building through which violent histories have been recalled, represented, politicized, and gendered.

A central concern of the ensuing discussion, especially of the concluding chapter, is to foreground some of the complexities involved in the task of personal and historical recovery and reconstruction, particularly those that pivot on giving 'voice' to trauma. This assumes all the more urgency given the current predominance of the equation between telling and healing, and the assumed palliative and political force of testimony (see, for example, Caruth 1995; and Felman and Laub 1992). Aside from the gendered complexities that render it hard for women to voice their suffering, the implications of traumatic memory when it assumes a narrative form, whether in acts of survivor testimony or in forms of public commemoration, must also be addressed. In underscoring the centrality of the question of representation to individual and collective experiences of violence, Das and Kleinman (2001: 5) observe how particular modes of cultural representation and the subject positions that these elicit 'can lay to waste whole forests of significant speech', robbing survivors of their agency. Like all forms of representation, the representation of pain and trauma can be completely divorced from the lives and subjectivities of survivors, and can serve to reify and normalize their experience (see also Caruth 1995).

Remembering Revolution shows that even when violence is mourned and its testimony rendered publicly 'tellable', memory can act as a form of forgetting violence and domesticating its trauma. Unlike stories of everyday vulnerability and violation that occurred 'within' the movement, the memory of state repression is afforded a high degree of recognition in acts of commemoration and in survivor testimony. However, as I show in Chapter 6, violence is reinscribed in these cultural acts as heroic resistance and self-sacrifice, thereby marginalizing alternative forms of witnessing and surviving trauma. Similarly, the analysis of women's narratives of state terror in the same chapter points to certain limitations of bearing testimony to trauma which are as much to do with individual biographies as with the testimonial act itself. It is also the lives of women survivors that expose an after*life* (Arif 2007) as opposed to the aftermath of political violence and state terror; an afterlife that renders more complex the possibility of resuming 'normalcy' and 'everydayness' in the face of violence and devastation (see Das 2007). The afterlives of Naxalbari equally demand an expansion of the category of trauma in relation to political movements where the term has come to stand in for the 'extraordinary' effects of state repression alone.

What Follows ...

Chapter 1 maps the Naxalbari movement, particularly in terms of its gendered, classed, and caste-based economies, and thereby locates it in a longer tradition of communist and peasant struggles in Bengal and accompanied anxieties around sexuality, gender, class, and violence. This discussion also outlines the conceptual gaps in the feminist theorization of the radical Left, and calls for a stronger theorization of everyday violence as continuous with the violence of political struggle. The latter part of Chapter 1 outlines the ethnographic context on which the book draws, offering some reflections on the kinds of issues thrown up in the field, between my 'informants' and myself. I then move on, in Chapter 2, to consider the representation of 'woman' in a variety of texts such as official, literary, autobiographical, and media sources, besides considering official constructions of revolutionary masculinity, another area of silence in this and comparative struggles. Using inter-textual methods that blur the divisions of what constitutes fact and what fiction, this chapter uncovers the complicated terrain of femininities and masculinities employed in the cause of the revolution as they intersected with class–caste. The implications of these representational economies—especially that of an idealized heroic masculinity that is split across gendered worlds—become evident in Naxalite women's discussions in subsequent chapters.

Chapter 3 considers the ways in which revolutionary femininity was lived in the everyday underground life of the movement, drawing on women's narratives to underscore the politics of their marginalization from key political tasks. My discussion in this chapter also identifies the violence of everyday underground life that was gendered but not always sexualized, and that continues to be buried beneath a mythic narrative of fugitive life. I end the chapter by exploring women's responses to the political use of violence, drawing attention to how changed political and ethical commitments in the present shape their understanding of this contentious part of their collective past. Chapter 4 turns to narratives of love, marriage, and sexuality—themes that have found little or no attention in Left historiography—that continue to probe cultural constructions of revolutionary masculinity, heroic femininity, and those of revolutionary romance. While the analysis of this chapter explores the production of subjectivities through popular narratives, it also begins to unravel the way in which the achievement of subjective composure is premised upon the ability to deny, silence, or abject discomforting aspects of the past, especially around sexuality.

Chapter 5 returns to the memory of the underground and the shelter to engage with women's testimonies of sexual and domestic violence experienced in these spaces, and the politics of current remembrance in a wider context of naming *and* silencing such forms of violence. Besides mapping the continuities between acts of injury at the micro level to an originary political violence (including those between marriage and sexual abuse), I detail the manner in which the party responded, or not, to sexual offences. Women's (and men's) negotiations of 'good' and 'bad' violence, explored in the second part of the chapter, are revelatory of their conflicting identifications with forms of heroic identity, idealized masculinity, and class, which entail, in some cases, a *dis*identification with the violence of their past. In bringing out the full costs and consequences of composing masculine cultural imageries through a repudiation of the feminine, this chapter makes an argument that is central to the book. Chapter 6 considers both the public and the personal memorialization of political violence. This visibility does not, however, guarantee the recognition or alleviation of individual suffering. The chapter explores to what extent public forms of commemoration and personal testimony create or preclude the possibility of individual mourning, an important step towards healing in the afterlife of violence.

Finally, the central elements of these arguments are summarized and drawn together in the concluding chapter in a bid to relate the book's main approaches and findings to broader theoretical issues in the study of radical politics from a feminist perspective. This is especially timely given the current political climate in which the loss of the parliamentary Left in West Bengal is being mourned in a deeply melancholic fashion. In drawing out the implications of such mourning—evident in feminist investments in the moral worth of radical politics—the chapter ends by arguing for the need to move beyond melancholic mourning to reinvest in life. This requires, as the analysis of the book throughout suggests, a closer consideration of the psychic life of radical political movements.

1

Mapping the Movement, Situating the Study

There are various ways to approach the history and meaning of Naxalbari: as a study of urban discontent and student revolts linked to a global narrative of New Left radicalism and student protest in the 1960s (Dirlik 1998); as constituting a major break from the politics of Nehruvian socialism and that of mainstream Indian communist parties through a pro-poor peasant agrarian revolution (Nigam 2007; and Ray and Katzenstein 2005);[1] as an important predecessor to the rise and radicalization of 'new social movements' through the 1970s and the 1980s in India (Omvedt 1993); as consolidating, at least in the context of West Bengal, the dominance of the parliamentary Left that governed the state for thirty-four unbroken years; and, finally, as the first of the radical Left in independent India to employ violence as a principle political tool (Ray 1998). The Naxalbari *andolan* is the origin of what is varyingly termed the Indian 'far left' or the 'ultra left' comprising of various Marxist–Leninist and Maoist groups that are currently leading armed struggles of the rural poor against the Indian state.

The bulk of the existent academic scholarship, which is formidable and will not be rehearsed here, maps the cause and impact of the movement in a history of sectarian Indian communism (Damas 1991; Dasgupta 1975; Franda 1971; Sengupta 1983; and Singh 1995). Some are specifically concerned with the question of violence (Ray 1998 and Basu 2000). The most insightful studies focus on contextual details including socio-cultural particularities of the movement and its distinct categories of participants (Banerjee 1984; Duyker 1987; and Ray 1998; for a recent appraisal, see Sinha Roy 2011). Gender is absent in this historiography even as a few studies have noted the participation of peasant women

(Roy 1995; and Sen 1985). There has been a recent emergence of (feminist) interest in the gendered dynamics of the movement, as I go on to detail. Outside these political histories, lies a vast and rich body of literary work (in Bangla) that can be loosely termed as 'Naxal *sahitya*' or Naxal literature, produced by leading literary personalities and activists, men and women. This genre that Donner (2009: 330), in a recent piece on Naxalite middle-class masculinities, rightly calls 'a mixture of fiction and "testimony"' includes novels, poetry, short memoirs, essays (in Kolkata's '*Little Magazines*'; see Nag 1997), and even plays and films. Some of these alternative forms of historiography, which the book draws on throughout, have begun to interrogate the gender and sexual politics of the movement. Mapping the manner in which class and gender are entangled and embedded in the life of the movement, besides opening a window into female subjectivity, the value of these sources cannot be underestimated.

The Event

In academic historiography, the origin of the Naxalbari movement is rooted in a singular, iconic episode from which it and the scores of militant struggles that have come to assume major roles on India's political scene take their name. In May 1967, after months of clashes with local landowners, a violent confrontation broke out between armed peasants, mainly tribal, agitating over landownership, and the police in the Naxalbari area of northern West Bengal, bordering Nepal and Bangladesh (then, East Pakistan). The death of a police inspector led to a police firing the next day that left, in what some called a deliberate 'revenge killing', six women, one man, and two children dead (Banerjee 1984). That such state brutality had been unleashed under a newly elected coalition government, including the Communist Party of India (Marxist) or the CPI(M), did not go amiss by public or press, least of all by those party workers who had coordinated the struggle over several months. What followed was the gradual consolidation of dissidents of the CPI(M), the original revolutionary party that had turned 'revisionist' by prioritizing parliamentary participation, and various revolutionary groups from different parts of the country. They coalesced to form the All-India Coordination Committee of Communist Revolutionaries in 1967, and eventually, in 1969, a third communist party and the first of many Maoist parties, the Communist Party of India (Marxist–Leninist), the CPI(ML) (Ray 1998: 83). The latter was thus propelled into existence by the uprising at Naxalbari that had tried and failed to bring about change two years ago. Composed of those local leaders who the CPI(M) had consequently expelled, it was also a product of the factionalism that characterizes the history of Indian communism (Franda 1971). The CPI(M) is itself born out of this history, in 1964, out of a split of the centrist and left factions from the Communist Party of India (CPI), originally founded in 1921 (Mallick 1994: 12). The left wing was further divided between the radicals and the Maoists, who eventually formed the CPI(ML). While the latter promised a radical break from the history of communist politics, it reiterated the dominant idioms and typologies of the established Bengali Left (see Dasgupta 2003, 2005; Franda 1971; Mallick 1994; and Sarkar 1983) that struck a deep chord amongst the people, especially the middle-class intelligentsia and youth. It also drew upon a long history of peasant mobilizations in Bengal and in other Indian states organized by communists (at least since the 1930s), of which the event at Naxalbari itself was a product against its popular construal as a spontaneous uprising.

Part of an older generation of Bengali communists who had been involved in the Tebhaga sharecroppers struggle that took place in undivided Bengal in 1946–7, Charu Mazumdar grew into prominence with Naxalbari, emerging as its undisputed king, over and above other more long-standing peasant mobilizers like Kanu Sanyal. Mazumdar's belief that the peasants had fought for political power rather than simply for land, marked for him, the uniqueness of the Naxalbari episode from previous communist-led struggles (Ray 1998). Naxalbari served as an indicator that the time was 'ripe' for revolution, that the potential for resistance was everywhere, and that the global defeat of imperialism and revisionism was imminent. Revolution itself was interpreted as a guerrilla struggle conceived in terms of the Maoist model rather than an 'economistic' one (Ray 1998: 160), and to which the rural peasantry, as opposed to the urban proletariat, was key. Encouraged by the backing of the Chinese Communist Party who proclaimed an eruption of 'spring thunder' all over India, Mazumdar and his party members concretized their programme of waging a 'people's war' against the Indian state through the mass mobilization of landless peasants and workers. It was soon replaced by the political line of *khatam* or the annihilation of class enemies; a move that is generally considered to have cost the movement its wide support base besides ascribing to it the notoriety for which it is famous. Mazumdar's detailed views on forming a conspiratorial guerrilla unit—that evoked the Chinese Red Guards *and* Bengal's anti-colonial 'terrorist' tradition[2]—to carry out annihilations of village landlords were published in the party's English mouthpiece, *Liberation*, in February 1970, popularized as the 'murder manual'. It advised 'petty bourgeois' activists to instigate the annihilation campaign in the countryside through conducting propaganda amongst the rural peasantry, subsequent to which the peasants were expected to take the lead. Armed with a copy of Mao's *Red Book*, young, educated, city-bred (mainly male) students left homes in order to 'integrate' with the peasantry. Leaders of the movement (like Ashim Chatterjee) also emerged from the ranks of students, marking the emergence of a new generation of Left activists.

Armed struggles had already sprung up in different parts of the country: most noticeable in Srikakulam in Andhra Pradesh; Mushahari in Bihar; and Palia in Lakhimpur district in Uttar Pradesh, besides Debra–Gopiballavpur in West Bengal (Singh 1995: 33). From the 1970s, there was a gradual enlargement of the scope of the movement to include urban acts of terror to the extent that it was eventually the city of Kolkata that emerged as the unlikely locus of revolutionary activity.[3] For Ray (1998), it is this paradox of the movement that has been least captured and understood, that is, how a political party committed to agrarian revolution came to be involved in large-scale urban terrorism. Male and female students emerged as a wide base for urban 'terrorist' activities, first gaining prominence in an indigenous cultural revolution which included the decapitating of statues and the desecration of educational institutions, and marked, for several scholars, a significant break with the middle-class if not elite heritage of leftist politics in Bengal (Seth 1997, 2004). Naxalbari politics had, however, made significant inroads into the university scene even before the formal launch of the party, including Presidency College, the premier college of Kolkata (Ray 1998: 155)[4].

From the middle of 1970 to the middle of 1971, Naxalite violence, which was at its all-time peak, rapidly transformed the cityscape. Indeed, it is the city that is the privileged point of departure in the literary, cinematic, and popular memory of the movement. Satyajit Ray's camera in *Pratidwandi* (The Adversary, 1970) pans across city walls that scream 'Power grows from the barrel of a gun'; Presidency College erupts with slogans of 'down with this colonial education'; and the metropolis pulsates with what Arendt calls '[the] old combination of violence, life and creativity' (Arendt 1990: 74). Inter-party violence dominated the urban war which also included the annihilation of 'class enemies' and large-scale snatching of arms (Banerjee 1984). Small guerrilla units of men (some as young as 13 years) indiscriminately killed traffic policemen and local schoolteachers as representatives of the state, including, it is alleged, the Vice Chancellor of Jadavpur University (Ray 1998). According to Singh (1995: 75), the total number of people killed between March 1970 and June 1971 in Kolkata was 139, out of which twenty-eight were policemen. Businessmen, moneylenders, and slum landlords constituted only 12 per cent as against 40 per cent of 'class enemies' in rural areas.

The 'red terror' unleashed by the Naxalites was met with a brutal state offensive. The organized state violence that was launched with the aid of preventive detention and anti-terrorist legislation, counter-insurgency measures, and centrally enforced police and para-military forces marked the most violent period in the history of independent West Bengal (see Banerjee 1984: 244–5). The legendary repression of the Naxalites and their sympathizers—through torture, unlawful detention and imprisonment without trial, indiscriminate jail killings, and infamous 'encounters', a euphemism for the daylight murders of young activists by the police—attracted the attention of global human rights organizations, such as Amnesty International, and international left-wing intellectuals who campaigned on their behalf. The Cossipore–Baranagar massacre of August 1971—in which more than 150 young men, activists but also sympathizers, were killed in a rampage carried out by Congress supporters—remains one such iconic moment of this counteroffensive. Charu Mazumdar's death in police custody in 1972 is usually seen as marking the end of a phase given that the andolan was, by then, breathing its last, partly ascribable to the factionalism that had plagued it since its infancy. Fractured Naxalite groups continued to operate in various parts of the country until a state of emergency was declared by the Government of India under Indira Gandhi in 1975, only to be lifted in 1977. The Congress-led state repression was simply extended in this period when all civil liberties were curtailed and several political activists imprisoned without charge.

The *bandimukti* andolan or the movement to free political prisoners in 1977, an important chapter in the state's civil rights struggle, brought

Naxalite groups and civil liberties organizations together, with urban middle-class women forming a considerable part of this initiative (see Chatterji 2000). The mid-1970s were, in general, a watershed in Indian politics, and witnessed the beginning of new social movements and autonomous grassroots organizations led by adivasis, women, Dalits, and peasants. The CPI(M)-led Left Front government finally released all political prisoners upon its election in May 1977. A landmark in the history of democratically elected Left parties, the CPI(M) remained continuously in power till May 2011 when it lost, in an equally historic defeat, the state assembly elections for the first time. The rise of the CPI(M) has been attributed to the events around Naxalbari, 'either as a necessary effect of militant policies, or a reaction to the suppression of civil rights during the 1970s' (Donner 2004a: 2). Its recent death has also been attributed to the state repression and parliamentary Left betrayal that came to immortalize the original event at Naxalbari.

The Legacy

Although West Bengal seemingly relinquished its attraction to 'people's war', subsequent years saw the consolidation of Naxalite politics in other parts of the country in what is often referred to as the second phase of India's 'far left' movement (Menon and Nigam 2007: 119; see also, Banerjee 2009). The post-Emergency period saw the development of two dominant currents: the emergence, from the remnants of the original CPI(ML), of 'above ground' Naxalite groups such as CPI(ML)-Liberation who favoured parliamentary participation; and the persistence of others with the 'line' of armed struggle. These latter groups developed in radically different ways from the original movement, becoming more militarized and embedded in class, caste, and recently, adivasi struggles in states like Andhra Pradesh and Bihar under the auspices of the People's War Group (PWG) in the former, and the Maoist Communist Centre (MCC) in the latter (Banerjee 2006; Bhatia 2006; Harriss 2011; Shah 2006, 2011; and Singh 1995).

The 1990s and the subsequent decade mark the third and current phase of the movement in which the two of the major Naxalite groups, namely, the PWG and the MCC, consolidated in September 2004 into a singular party, the Community Party of India (Maoist). The Maoists—a term that lays claim to a wider South Asian development stemming from the powerful Maoist insurgency in Nepal (Menon and Nigam 2007: 123)[5]—entirely reject parliamentary participation for the sake of armed struggle on behalf of the rural poor and tribals who are bearing the brunt of India's economic liberalization policies since the 1990s. The fact that the parliamentary Left (that is, the CPI(M)-led Left Front) has not only abdicated 'the space of mass struggle' (Menon and Nigam 2007: 123) but has also recently emerged as a supporter of industrialization and privatization at all cost has contributed to this development (see also, Bag 2011). Declared by the Indian Prime Minister to be the gravest internal security threat faced by the country, the Maoists today control a long 'red corridor' stretching from the Nepali border, across the plains of Bihar, and through the east coast of India down as far as northern Tamil Nadu (Harriss 2011: 310). Counter-insurgency operations launched by the Indian state (such as 'Operation Green Hunt') have led to mass killings and evictions of civilians in epicentres of the conflict like the state of Chhattisgarh (Shah and Pettigrew 2009: 246; see also Shah 2011)[6]. Naxalite and Maoist groups have, for their part, increased their indulgence in 'arbitrary' acts of violence; acts that have displaced the earlier emphasis on mass mobilization and escalated the spiralling of violence and conflict with the state. Contestations over their indiscriminate use of violence have become intense in recent times, with one collective statement acknowledging that 'by and large, the civil liberties and democratic rights movement has fought shy of condemning Maoist violence' (Nigam *et al.* 2008).[7]

In West Bengal, Maoist resurgence has been noted in the tribal belt of Bankura, Midnapore, and Purulia, which borders Maoist-dominated areas of neighbouring state, Jharkhand. As elsewhere in the country, the Maoist infiltration into this area reflects the socioeconomic failures of the Indian state, particularly the limited and inadequate land reforms of the Left Front government, generally considered a marker of its success (Banerjee 2002, 2006). Maoist leaders described the adivasi uprising against police brutalities in Lalgarh in West Midnapore in November 2008 as a 'second Naxalbari', although some saw the Maoists co-opting a people's struggle (Sarkar and Sarkar 2009). Brutal state repression of peasant mobilizations against the creation of industrial projects and Special Economic Zones (SEZs) on agricultural land in Nandigram and Singur in West Bengal in early 2007 (see Menon and Nigam 2007) was further reminiscent of the Naxalbari episode. These recent events and the middle-class metropolitan solidarity shown towards them—most tellingly, in the spontaneous silent demonstration of over 1,00,000 people against the Nandigram killings—also hark back to an earlier Kolkata; a Kolkata of India's Naxalbari which was 'vibrant with political passion and engagement' (Sarkar 2007). Amongst middle-class Bengalis, at least, 'Naxalbari' constitutes a metaphor for the original impetus towards social justice, on the one hand, while constituting, on the other, a locus of nostalgia and tragic romanticism. Deeply embedded within the imagery of the city, Naxalbari continues to be one of Kolkata's dominant legends.

The Bhadralok Naxalite

The Naxalbari agitation occurred at the tail end of the 1960s, by which time the country was 'caught in a dual crisis of economic stagnation and political instability' in what has been called a crisis of deinstitutionalization (Kudva 2005: 241). The Nehruvian interventionist state had failed to deliver the growth and development that it had promised two decades ago, and by the early 1970s, poverty and inequalities rose sharply (Ray and Katzenstein 2005). Post-independence West Bengal, particularly its capital city of Kolkata, suffered the effects of gradual deindustrialization and disinvestment together with an influx of Hindu refugees from East Pakistan (now Bangladesh): 'Calcutta, more so than other cities in India with the exception of Delhi, and certainly more so than rural West Bengal, was very much marked by the legacy of partition' (Donner 2011: 29). By the end of the 1960s, a whole generation of educated middle and lower middle classes found themselves without jobs as industries and businesses were forced to shut down, and food, fuel and other living costs soared. Young people and students were steadily politicized through urban protests that had begun to take place on a routine basis since the 1950s, culminating in the 1966 Food Movement in West Bengal (considered by many to be a turning point in this history), and through student strikes and campus unrest over an outmoded education system across the country (Banerjee 1984; Dasgupta 1975; and Dasgupta 2006).

In the popular imagination of the 1960s and the 1970s—especially evident in Satyajit Ray's and Mrinal Sen's respective 'Calcutta Trilogies'—it is the India of a betrayed generation of midnight's children that takes centre stage.[8] The 1970s is characterized by the steady corruption of urban culture, the politics of survival in lower middle-class life, and a specifically male malaise produced through a crisis in modernity

(Ganguly 2000). Cinema also documents the other changes of the time, namely, women's urban employment which rose from 6 per cent to 20 per cent between 1961 and 1971 (Karlekar 1982; see also Standing 1991). The underlying conflicts faced by the new 'working woman' have been immortalized in cinematic characters like Neeta and Arati of Ritwick Ghatak's *Meghe Dhaka Tara* (The Cloud-Capped Star, 1960) and Satyajit Ray's *Mahanagar* (The Big City, 1963) respectively. Neeta and Arati were also 'refugee' women who were compelled to earn a family wage in the face of post-Partition migration and dispossession, something that was unthinkable to middle-class Bengali families whose 'respectability' relied on women's withdrawal from economic labour (Donner 2008). The Partition forced women's entry into the public domain, indirectly contributing to the changing nature of the Bengali *bhadramahila* and the transformation of the social landscape in the 1950s and the 1960s (Bagchi and Dasgupta 2003; and Kundu 2009).

The leaders of the CPI(ML) and a vast section of its cadres were of the middle-class intelligentsia from metropolitan centres, even though the andolan had a significant rural dimension. The communist movement in Bengal has generally been considered an elite one, drawing its leadership and character from the wealthier, educated sections of the middle class, which partly explains its longevity. One of the more enduring popular images of the Naxalbari movement, responsible for much of the romanticism associated with it, surrounds the participation of bhadralok students from elite colonial institutions. Sacrificing their lives of luxury and promised careers, these 'brilliant' students are represented, in popular film and literature alike, as the core aspirants of Naxalite politics.[9] Popular imageries of this sort tend to deflect from the subtle but substantial differences within the class composition of the movement and the category of the 'bhadralok' itself; one that has merited much historical and sociological attention (Broomfield 1968; Chatterjee 1998; and Mukherjee 1970).

Sarkar (1997) defines the Bengali middle class (*madhyabitta*) as that which originally located itself below the aristocracy and above the labouring classes in the nineteenth century. The bhadralok madhyabitta has thereafter come to signify a heterogeneous middle class in Bengal with culture and education as its primary social capital. Even though caste is not as salient to Bengali society as it is elsewhere in the country, it does shape the class hierarchy. The bhadralok is composed of the three upper castes, namely, Brahmin, Vaidya, and Kayastha, while the landless and poor have traditionally been 'low-caste, Muslim or both' (Bag 2011). Upper-caste status and middle-class capital is also maintained through the production of respectability in which women play a key role. Symbolic of 'the new Bengali woman', the bhadramahila first emerged as an amalgam of those Victorian ideals that were embraced by nineteenth century social reformers along with traditional Hindu feminine attributes to emphasize feminine chastity, modesty, and domesticity (Borthwick 1984: 54; see also Bannerji 1995; Engels 1996; Karlekar 1991; Sarkar 2001; and Sen 2000). Distinct from the Western woman (*memshahib*), on the one hand, and the lower-caste woman, on the other, she was educated but economically dependent, and exclusively equated with domesticity and the inner life of the home in service of an elite Indian nationalist project (see Chapter 2).

The urban Naxalites came mainly from the ranks of the lower middle-class or the *nimno madhyabitta*, a majority of whom were refugees from the Bengal Partition and relied on a salaried job (*chakri*), rather than the affluent bhadralok who were historically landowners or zamindars (Donner 2008; see also Ganguly–Scrase and Scrase 2009). The movement, as a whole, had a strongly entrenched lower middle-class character, dominated by a 'vernacular' intelligentsia that was antagonistic towards the English-speaking elite (Ray 1998: 69). As with lower middle-class Bengali life in general, the lower middle-class character of the movement has been largely ignored (see, however, Donner 2011).

The CPI(ML) also carried with it the legacy of 'refugee' identity given that several activists were amongst those who had been forced to migrate to West Bengal during Partition in 1947. The refugee population, as Manas Ray (2002) notes, has provided Left politics in West Bengal a steady stream of cadres and leaders, given their antagonism towards the Congress Party over the loss of homeland (see also, Chakrabarty 1990). Several Naxalite cadres had grown up in 'refugee colonies', listening, as Bandyopadhyay (2000: 16–17) notes in his fictionalized memoir, to stories of a lost *desh* which appeared recoverable through radical politics. But it was not only the melancholic yearning of a lost homeland that determined the move towards Naxalbari. Young men like Bandyopadhyay, like some of the women interviewed for this project, were also amongst the most deprived and depressed of the urban youth, with an 'almirah full of books' to remind them of a now lost gentile past (A. Das 2001: 69), and a government job to procure against all odds. Many interviewees cited the pain, deprivation, and poverty of refugee life as the origin of their political consciousness:

> This [politics] began from the angst of the 'refugee', from the burn of 'refugee life', the constant cries of *thakuma*, *ma*'s pain, the refugee colonies grew in front of my eyes. The pain of the refuges—all this influenced me in a big way ...This was my thinking that if you want to do something seriously; you have to do politics. (Personal interview, Kalyani, August 2003)[10]

Politics was also not unknown to these young men and women. Amongst those who were not brought up in communist families (and several were; see, for example, Banerjee 2009), there were members of the wider kin who had been part of nationalist politics, especially militant Bengali nationalism. For a majority of young Naxalites, this was their primary inheritance of Indian nationalism, popularized through the revolutionary poetry and songs of the 1940s (Chakrabarty 2004). It shaped a popular sense of the political that was deeply romantic, epitomized in cultural figures like the swadeshi terrorist ('Khudiram') and the revolutionary poet ('Sukanta'), besides inscribing for the middle classes, a commonsensical notion of what it means to be a communist.[11] That a later communist repertoire of images dovetailed with an earlier anti-colonial 'terrorist' one is not surprising, given the manner in which Bengali communism incorporated revolutionary terrorism within its ideology and (centralized) organization (Basu 1982; Dasgupta 2003; and Sinha Roy 2011). For many commentators (for example, Duyker 1987), the Naxalites are a direct heir to this history of 'terrorism' explicit in official rhetoric and in the movement's popularizing.

Gendering Left Politics

The Naxalbari movement thus belongs to a long-standing tradition of militant nationalist and leftist politics in Bengal, which has attracted bhadralok and peasant women alike to its folds. In her work on women's taking up of revolutionary terrorism in Bengal in the 1930s, Sarkar (1984 and 1987; see also Kumar 1993; Mandal 1991; Mukherjee 1999; and Thaper–Bjorkert 2006) shows how nationalist women's complicity with anti-colonial violence was accommodated within caste-based norms and ideals of female nurture, especially through the evocation of religious sacrifice, enriching rather than contradicting these hegemonies. Equality with men in religious sacrifice did not extend to equality within or outside politics, such as in domestic or family life (Sarkar, 1984, 1987; see also Mukherjee 1999). Left-led mass movements like the Tebhaga agitation might have attracted greater numbers of women than the politics of individual terror, but its leadership failed to take up the challenge that peasant women presented, particularly to 'private' issues of sexual harassment by landlords and wife-beating by their own husbands (Chattopadhyay 2001; Custers 1987; Punjabi 2002; and Sen 1985).

The contemporary women's movement in West Bengal is largely defined by a political culture or a 'hegemonic field' structured by the CPI(M) that was in government for thirty-four years (Ray 1999). Politically affiliated women's organizations, along with non-party affiliated or 'autonomous' women's groups to which some of the women interviewed belong, have to be located within a political field instituted primarily by the Bengali Left and hostile to feminism.[12] It is a 'Marxist–Leninist ideology tempered by nationalism' (56) that frames the woman's question. The Marxist framework renders issues of gender subservient to those of class, while Bengali nationalism foregrounds a chaste, sacrificial femininity through motherhood. Sarkar finds a 'profound symbiosis between the variant of Left culture [embodied by the Left Front government] and the broad cultural traditions of Bengal' (Sarkar 1991: 215). While the middle-class urban woman is essentially ascribed a 'giving and nurturing role, i.e., serving the party and the class struggle', militant and heroic roles are attributed to 'exotic and distant figures', such as tribal and peasant women (Sarkar 1991: 217). Located in this culturally inflected political field, feminist groups are numerically small in Kolkata and considered less 'radical' in nature and impact than elsewhere in the country, especially when it comes to politicizing the personal (Ray 1999). The women's wing of the CPI(M) is seen to prioritize protection from the party over the protection of individual women, epitomized in its negotiation of a major gang rape case that implicated party members in the early 1990s (Da Costa 2010; Kumari and Kidwai 1998; and Sarkar 1991).

While there has been some critical discussion on the gender politics of the parliamentary Left, there is much less research into the gender and sexual politics of contemporary Naxalite or Maoist groups. This is in spite of the fact that a growing number of women cadres have been reported (see Arundhati Roy 2010; and Vindhya 2000). The media face

PHOTOGRAPH 1: Maoist cadre, Manki (19), near the Maharashtra–Chattisgarh border. *Photograph credit* Ishan Tankha.

of the revolution is often female (see Photograph 1), serving to bolster the feminist credentials of the party besides showing that 'the woman Maoists here are every bit as fierce as their male comrades' (Pandita 2010; see also Arundhati Roy 2010).

Naxalite groups are generally considered to be more open to issues of gender (and caste) than mainstream communist parties, with some of the earliest 'autonomous' feminist groups like the Progressive Organization of Women in Hyderabad emerging, post-Emergency, 'within the broader universe of the Naxalite movement' (Nigam 2010; see also Kumar 1993). Women Naxalites, including those interviewed for this project, later turned to the women's movement in an important instance of the radical Left legacies of Indian feminism that partly explains it privileging of poor women and focus on state violence (Kumar 1993; see also John 1996; and Sinha Roy 2011). A meeting between Maoists and feminist activists in 2004 was seen as providing some cause for optimism 'on feminist politics and its impact on revolutionary movements' even as key issues remained unresolved, such as 'the relationship between masculinity and the bearing of arms' (Kannabiran *et al.* 2004: 4877).

Even so, feminists have noted a rhetorical recycling of older beliefs and values, that is, the revolution will overthrow patriarchy, a discomfort with independent expressions of women's struggle as paradigmatic of 'bourgeois feminism', and 'stereotypical and hierarchical masculinities and femininities' (Kannabiran 2010), together with a deep unease around female sexuality (Kannabiran and Kannabiran 2002; Manimala 1995; Stree 1989; and Vindhya 1990, 2000). In the recent case of the Maoist insurgency in Nepal, the initial enthusiasm with which feminists welcomed images of 'young, gun-toting guerrilla women' (Pettigrew and Shneiderman 2004) as a measure of the leadership's commitment to the 'woman's question' seems to have waned in the face of the lack of any visible advancement of women's rights by the newly formed Maoist government (Gautam *et al.* 2001; and Manchanda 2004).

From the communist-led Tebhaga and Telangana struggles in the 1940s to contemporary Maoist movements, Sinha Roy summarizes how, in radical politics in India, 'the question of sexuality is either defined in terms of promiscuity and licentiousness, which are manifestations of bourgeois decadence, or in terms of propriety, which is the virtue of activists' (Sinha Roy 2011: 166). It is also inscribed upon the female body so much so that the containment of sexuality becomes synonymous with that of the female body. Radical politics are, to this extent, entirely continuous with mainstream political movements in which, at least since the anti-colonial struggle, 'it was not women's sexual experiences that were at stake, but the elaborate codes of honour that were/are inscribed on female bodies' (John and Nair 1999: 1). If anything, as we shall see in the ensuing analysis of this book (especially Chapters 4 and 5), modalities of control are more elaborately enforced in conditions of guerrilla warfare where the suspension of normality exacerbates the need to protect the 'respectability' that women's bodies are seen to be custodians of. In the final analysis, even as radical politics propel women into the public domain and arm them with an agency that is conventionally unavailable, they seem to continue to 'contain' women through regulative patriarchal ideals 'at the very moment of their most innovative empowerment' (De Mel 2001: 212). What merits more specific attention, especially in context of Naxalbari, is the mobilization of women by a politics of violence.

Feminist Understandings of Revolutionary Violence

Political violence, especially that of the state, has been a primary point of address for feminist theorizing, critique, and organizing in post-colonial India. A self-consciously 'feminist' women's movement first emerged in the late 1970s as a response to the institutional violence of the state (Kumar 1993). In more recent times, feminists have turned to the violent underpinnings of the right-wing Hindu nationalist or Hindutva movement, viewing it as equally oppressive and deplorable as the state's exercise of violence, notwithstanding the possibility of politicization that it might offer women. There is, however and as I have detailed elsewhere (Roy 2009a), no comparable assessment or critique of revolutionary violence from a feminist perspective. This might stem from the 'sustained, if qualified, support' (John 2004: 305) that post-colonial feminism has offered Left-led struggles, even those that deploy violence to achieve their ends. As Omvedt (1993: 216) notes, the leftist inheritance of Indian feminism has had specific implications for the question of political violence. Besides the political alternative that it provided to 'paternalistic Gandhism', revolutionary violence was morally acceptable because of the appeal of the 'heroism of guerrilla warriors', starting with the Naxalites but also owing to the popularization of images of 'the woman with a gun in her arms and a baby on her back' (Omvedt 1993: 216). The combined force of these symbolic structures meant that the question of women's empowerment could be readily decoupled from that of violence in the context of these struggles.

This separation between emancipation and violence is also implicit in the feminist recovery of women's participation in revolutionary struggles. Violence, in this mode of feminist history writing, is identified in the leadership practices of these movements ('the party') that thwarted the possibility of emancipation, that revolutionary upheaval—that 'magic time' (Kannabiran and Lalitha 1989; Sinha Roy 2011)—held for women revolutionaries. Works like these, including evaluations of contemporary Naxalite and Maoist movements, remain limited to clearly identifiable 'women's issues' but do not extend to broader concerns of political violence and its implications for feminist ethical aspirations and ends. Most crucially, they fail to emphasize how the regulation of sexuality—thought to be key to redressing gender hierarchies in contemporary Maoist struggles—is not separable from a wider politics of legitimizing violence and militarizing identities and everyday life. Bhatia remains a lone voice in this debate when she asserts of contemporary Naxalite movements that the 'violent nature of the movement has contributed to this (patriarchy) since patriarchy and violence have much in common and tend to reinforce each other' (Bhatia 2006: 3180). There is also a tendency to view sexual violence as the dark underside of progressive politics, its perverted form rather than a product of militarized political cultures. Rape *within* revolutionary cultures is thus allocated to the realm of exceptionalism, even as rape is considered a routine part of oppression at the hands of state. In recent feminist analysis of radical politics, including Naxalbari (Sinha Roy 2011), sexual violence within such movements does not assume centrality even as it does in published recollections of women activists.

An underlying belief in the moral worth of revolutionary resistance seems to have generated an evasion of the question of violence and militarism, and their underlying patriarchal assumptions, even as feminists have debated issues such as sexuality, the politics of housework, and female political representation in the context of Left political cultures (see Kannabiran and Kannabiran 2002). It has thus become possible for feminists to engage the contemporary 'far left' on these issues, and even declare such politics as the most radical in the country (Kannabiran and Kannabiran 2002), without addressing the extent to which this radicalism might be implicated in (and reproductive of) the very structures of power and violence that feminists are attempting to dismantle.

Philippe Bourgois' (2004) ethnography of post-war El Salvador challenges, head-on, the liberal romanticization of guerrilla warfare, demonstrating how political repression and resistance against it transform into forms of symbolic and everyday aggression such as internal killings and gender oppression. Together with Scheper–Hughes (2004) he proposes a violence continuum that shapes the contours of everyday life as well as the more visible expressions of genocide (see also, Banerjee *et al.* 2004; Kelly 2000; and Moser 2001). Equally, in the context of post-war El Salvador, Silber (2004) maps the intertwined and gendered spaces of violence that are not neatly separable from one another, and that come to be inscribed upon women's bodies and subjectivities. In exploring how rural women's narratives of everyday life 'contain violence, in masked or veiled ways' (Silber 2004: 573), she raises a question that has particular resonance for this study: how certain types of violence are rendered invisible and do not 'count' in post-war El Salvador. As these works show, the concept of a continuum is especially productive for an analysis of situations of conflict in which 'spectacular' political violence tends to deflect 'unspectacular' forms, contributing to the social invisibility and normalization of the latter. It also makes it impossible to separate the question of gender/sexual politics from the logic of insurrectionary struggle by linking patriarchal and class-based ideologies to those of righteous, revolutionary violence. My usage of a violence continuum in the pages that follow also includes the epistemic classification of violence in a particular society; its ways of mourning some and silencing others.

Interviewing Naxalite Women

I began my field research in Kolkata in June 2003 and remained there till the end of January 2004, and returned for a further three months in the summer of 2004. In the Introduction to this book, I have noted how the project on which it is based shifted from being an oral 'her-story' of the Naxalite movement to a wider analysis of gender and violence in relation to its cultural memory. This shift led to an expansion of the field of research to include other sites of memory, especially literary and popular representations of the movement. Violence also emerged as a key theme in personal narratives, and I used later interviews to probe personal experiences of violence not limited to those of imprisonment and torture.

Another shift in the project was my decision to focus exclusively on the urban madhyabitta experience rather than both urban and rural aspects of the movement. As my understanding of the movement deepened, I began to see how distinctly textured its urban phase was as with the experience of its participants, middle-class activists. Indeed, Donner (2011) makes a persuasive case as to why the urban dynamics of Naxalbari activism need to be studied against the construal of urban middle-class activism as inauthentic. And for the movement's most sophisticated commentator, Rabindra Ray, that the Naxalites were urban and middle-class and 'fought in the cause of a class other than their own' (4) is what imparts to this phase of Indian Maoism its distinctiveness. My decision to focus on urban middle-class women was also linked to the representational economies of the movement starting with its privileging of the village, reminiscent of the way in which rural utopias have functioned in nationalist and leftist rhetoric (see, for example, Custers 1987; Roy 1995; and Sen 1985). While those I met in field typically presented rural women as the true inheritors of the movement's legacy, the activism of middle-class women was reduced to their romantic investments in activist men, and even attributed to fashion.

It is generally assumed, however, that it is these metropolitan middle-class women who have been the chief beneficiaries of historical and popular attention; that the mythical image of brilliant students from elite Kolkata colleges somehow includes them. Thus, even as Sinha Roy (2011: 73–6) has recently underscored the historical oversight of women's participation in Naxalbari which pertains to *both* metropolitan middle-class women and non-metropolitan ones, she argues that the prominence of the city of Kolkata in popular and historical memory has meant the double marginalization of the latter as 'rural/small-town based' and as 'women'. Yet, her own work shows the instability—and not merely the diversity, as she says—of the category of 'metropolitan women' which includes women from rural and small towns across the class spectrum. Sinha Roy's work further shows, against her claim of the privileging of the metropolis and by extension, of metropolitan women, the erasure of 'woman' (a blanket and undifferentiated category) from dominant male memory. The concomitant idealization and trivialization of women along the lines of class and an urban–rural divide is also revealing of deeper patriarchal meanings, particularly of the manner in which patriarchies operate through a splitting of the female subject into a series of binary oppositions. Indian feminists have contributed to such a split by affording an epistemic privilege to women of poor, oppressed classes, thereby obscuring their own middle-class status (John 1996). The leftist *and* feminist privileging of rural women as authentic political subjects also fails to examine the gendered and classed contradictions of political identities and cultures for women; contradictions that cannot be addressed through the mere inclusion of rural women's voices.

Between June 2003 and the summer of 2004, I interviewed a total of twenty ex-Naxalite women and sixteen men, all of whom were Hindu. A majority of the women can be identified as lower middle-class, several of whom were refugees from the Partition. Even this classification, as with that of 'metropolitan women', does not do justice to the diversity of lifestyles and personal biographies represented in this sample. Although the majority are currently resident in the city of Kolkata, many of the women came from neighbouring *mofussil* small towns and districts of West Bengal, like Birbhum, Bardhaman, and Bankura, from middle class and lower middle-class professional, refugee, and landowning families. Marital and family histories are more difficult to plot since many were, at the time of the interview, in a second marriage, having been married for the first time during the movement. All appeared to have children, some of whom I was introduced to in the course of the interview which tended to take place at their residences. A majority are educated (reflective of the spread of education in middle-class women, post-independence) and employed in part-time and full-time professional work such as teaching, academia, journalism, and developmental work.

What is important to emphasize is that several women are or have been involved, to some degree or the other, with a people's movement in Kolkata, such as the civil rights movement and significantly, the autonomous women's movement. Three of the women are members of a now 'above-the-ground' CPI(ML) political party. Women like Minakshi Sen and Joya Mitra, who have penned two important prison memoirs of Naxalbari and are established Bengali writers, were identified, especially by male activists, as 'Naxalite celebrities'. It is not surprising that out of the sum total of women across the rural–urban divide who joined the struggle, it is these visible and well-known 'political women' who have been the easiest to identify and locate. Only two of the women, one who identified as full-time homemaker and one as a teacher, said that they had entirely withdrawn from politics. Three other women had withdrawn from any active political involvement but kept alive their ideological commitment to issues of social justice through non-governmental organization (NGO) work or academic research. Given their relative isolation from active politics and withdrawal into professional lives (largely for financial reasons), these women fall outside of the recognizable clique of 'political' women in Kolkata. Other than that, it was hard, though perhaps understandable, to interview or even find former women activists who have recanted their participation and withdrawn into the conventional middle class. This significant ethnographic gap—that I hope future researchers will fulfil—cautions against the generalizability of some of the data presented and analysed in this book.

A lifetime of political involvement has also meant, for most, extreme material insecurity, especially in the case where both partners are politically active or 'full-timers', as interviewees would put it. Having given up higher education at the time of the movement with few chances of going back, these women have remained, as one remarked, always at the margin without any proper paid work. It is also the women who seemed to support their full-time activist husbands with part-time or full-time employment in a model common to political, especially communist, families in Bengal where the husband does *rajniti* and the wife chakri.[13] Some of these families live in fairly impoverished conditions, largely ascribable to political choices to do with lifestyle and career. For one particular family with a teenage son, this meant having to reside close to the political 'base', an industrial area on the southern fringe of Kolkata. As has been noted of other oral histories of political activists (Hamilton 2007; Passerini 1992; and Punjabi 2002), such personal circumstances inform the interviews as much as the experience of the past. The respondents, Rukmini and Bulbul, are the only exceptions who can be identified as members of the English-speaking elite in Kolkata. Their children, who are my peers, have studied at elite institutions both in India and abroad. Their interviews were conducted almost entirely in English. All other interviews were conducted in Bengali, which intermingled, to various degrees, with the English language of which a majority of interviewees had a working grasp.

Although I tried to limit my focus to full-time women cadres, their distinction from the category of 'sympathizers' was not always clear, and I have chosen not to differentiate women in these terms. It is, of course, that middle-class women have entered the popular imagination of the movement as sympathizers (see Chapter 3). An interviewee's mother who was seventy-one-years old at the time of the interview is an interesting instance of the blurring of the categories of 'activist' and 'sympathizer', given that she, like her elder son and younger daughter, left home and went 'underground'. She did not, however, leave for the sake of the party but owing to a major marital dispute. One could say that her act of personal rebellion was facilitated by the chaotic political conditions of the time. It also shows the extent to which the movement was structured through wider kinship and familial patterns. She was immediately taken in and 'sheltered' as 'x's mother' or as *mashima* (aunt). Likewise, she says that she only let her daughter go 'underground' because a young man whom she trusted and whom her daughter was infatuated with had promised to take care of her, even though they were not married. The configuring of unconventional political action in familial terms has been a dominant modality of bringing middle-class Bengali women into the political fold (Basu 1992; Da Costa 2010; and Sarkar 1984).

Gaining access was far less of a problem than I had imagined and within my first two weeks of being in Kolkata, I had a neat list of ten odd names of women who I could possibly interview. No one refused to speak to me except Molina, the only woman to be given the death penalty for murder in West Bengal (detailed in Chapter 5). After a preliminary meeting with her and two other women, it was made known to me that she was not very keen on being individually interviewed. I went into the field believing that there would be very few who would be willing to talk to me. But I think, in general, women wanted to talk. What varied is the extent to which they were willing to go; some said the bare minimum, others as seasoned speakers said what was necessary, and still others spoke over several meetings that lasted for months. Some expressed discomfort with the open-endedness and indefinite structure of a life story interview, even insisting on a written questionnaire. Kalyani was agreeable to meet only if I had specific questions to ask since she was not interested in telling me 'a story'. Direct questions are far less threatening to the extent that interviewees can take recourse to generalizations that are more often than not disconnected from their actual lives (Hollway and Jefferson 2000). Clearly the transition from a generalized, collective narrative to a more personal, even painful story is not easy for most individuals to make. As the interviews progressed, the main task of my memory work method became to facilitate this shift.

Although I focus primarily on women's movement stories in this book, I also interviewed men, both cadres and leaders. While it is almost a truism that men, especially communist men, choose to inhabit a public discourse that excludes the private (see Passerini 1987), this is possibly less of a rule than imagined. Like women, some men spoke of partners and relationships, families (especially their mothers), and the para with its community of peers, while others did not. Ashim Chatterjee and Santosh Rana, both renowned political figures associated with Naxalbari and current left-wing parties, said little of their personal lives, and nothing of their ex-wives who had participated in the movement. This was in sharp contrast to cadres whose stories often saw a more brutal disclosure of the self. I also interviewed older communist women, long-standing members of women's groups (some with Maoist leanings), present-day Naxalites, and political and civil rights activists such as those with the Association for Protection of Democratic Rights (APDR) that played a major role in the release of political prisoners.

Research Relations

In going to Kolkata, the site of my research, I returned to a city that I was born in but one that I have never really known. My relationship to it is still very much as that of an outsider's since I have spent very little *lived* time there; my school and university life being spent in other parts of India. In local terms, I am identified as *probashi* or as a Bengali who lives outside of West Bengal. My education in private English-medium schools in Bombay (Mumbai) and Delhi respectively meant that I was never taught to read or write in my mother tongue, a training one usually acquires at school. Like most of my peers who are products of post-colonial institutions, I was raised with a 'sanctioned ignorance' (John 1996) of my mother tongue; hardly a source of inferiority than one that naturalizes the privilege of being upper middle-class in urban India. English continues to be a major form of cultural capital in contemporary India, and a significant criterion for class mobility. Even in West Bengal with its strong 'vernacular' intelligentsia, the Bengali language has been unable to compete with the hegemony of English.

Throughout the research process, I was overtly conscious that my 'outsider' status coupled with my current location in the West would hinder access and credibility. I was, at times, faced with a barrage of questions which were more to do with my family background (what my father does to where I studied) than with the nature of the research project. For me, these bouts of interrogation constituted a 'test' that would establish my credibility in the field. Of course, these feelings of anxiety and powerlessness had less to do with those I met than to do with structural forms of middle-class guilt that had, no doubt, shaped middle-class Naxalite subjectivity in the 1970s.

My outsider status was mitigated, however, by the many similarities that I shared with the women I interviewed by virtue of our gender, our common political aspirations for change, and our shared cultural identities as Bengali/Indian women. Almost all the women I interviewed were, at the time of the interview, of the age group of my mother, that is, early to mid-fifties, with a few who were older. The women's perceptions of me as a *choto meye* ('little girl'), placed within the age group of their own children, facilitated a sense of comfort in the interview situation. Certain 'women's issues' were framed through shared gendered experiences of romance, sexuality, and sexism, but also in political terms, given that a significant proportion of women interviewees were involved in feminist activism. Not all women were invested in feminist discourses; some, in fact, entirely rejected them. Even so, reconstructions and interpretations of the past were shaped through an awareness of changing gender roles, which the interviewer as a 'younger' woman no doubt represented. In the absence of an explicitly feminist discourse in the 1970s, women could not politicize their feelings of inferiority or even adequately express them, as one suggested:

> ... Of course the women's issue was never clear here. We also articulated it in spurts of anger and frustration ('why can't I do this? I definitely will do it!'). I think all of us went through this phase. At one level I thought wow, you know, this is a place where I can get respect, but it went that much and not further. (Personal interview, Rukmini, October 2003)

Urban middle-class activists like Rukmini later found feminism that, in turn, nourished feminist interpretations of the past, explicit in the English title of Krishna Bandyopadhyay's translated memoir, 'Naxalbari Politics: A Feminist Narrative' (Bandyopadhyay 2008). Ajitha, an activist from *Kerala's Naxalbari* (the English title of her memoir; Ajitha 2008), maps her move from a male-dominated Left movement that entirely ignored gender to autonomous women's liberation movements in the 1980s. Naxalite women's turn towards feminism is a significant instance not merely of the leftist inheritance of women's movements in this part of the world but also of its Maoist heritage. The feminist responses that we encounter in subsequent chapters echo these distinct paths through which Indian feminism has travelled.

Whether interviewees explicitly aligned themselves with feminist politics or not (and several did), the recognition that it provides to their speech rendered those stories 'sayable' that might have been unspeakable in other contexts. Thus, Ajita and my common appeal to feminist discourses enabled her to 'come out' with a story of an abusive relationship while she was in the andolan (discussed in Chapter 5). The fact that Ajita abruptly stopped speaking of her first marriage when her adult children entered the room, resuming her story only when the door had been safely shut, implies that what she disclosed to me could not be readily articulated elsewhere. Other women punctuated their stories with the disclaimer, 'what I'm telling you now I haven't told anyone else', indicative of the difficulty of drawing on a culturally available but still marginalized story of surviving (sexual) violence.

Trauma, Cvetkovich says in her queer ethnography, 'poses limits and challenges for oral history, forcing consideration of how the interview process itself may be traumatically invasive or marked by forms of self-censorship and the work of the unconscious' (Cvetkovich 2003: 167). While the practice of oral history enables, she rightly notes, a focus on the affective (including the traumatic) that might be otherwise considered private or inappropriate, it also raises a host of challenges. The manner in which women chose to negotiate past experiences of sexual trauma, even through denial, presented me with particular challenges. As the contentions around the issue of sexual violence gained more prominence and I realized how fraught it was in the shared memory of the movement, I worried whether the interview situation might have (mis)led women into over-identifying with and privileging the issue of sexual violence. The disparate ways in which women have responded to questions of abuse, some strongly refuting the possibility of sexual violence as explored in Chapter 5, lends legitimacy to such a criticism.

Given that the politics of memory is a core concern of this project, the dissonances between memories of sexual violence is a central point of interrogation and one that is not reducible to questions of credibility or 'truth'. Portelli insists that 'oral sources are credible too but with a different credibility ... The diversity of oral history consists in the fact that "wrong" statements are still psychologically "true" and this truth may be equally as important as factually reliable accounts' (Portelli 1998: 68). The question as to whether the interviewer might have 'misled' the interviewee into a preferred response assumes that there exists a 'true' response from which the latter was directed away from, and arguably makes more sense in an approach to memory that is concerned with its factuality than its production and politics. I would also reject the claim that research subjects must share or substantiate our analysis in the name of lending credibility. As Skeggs (1995, cited in Redman 1999) argues, the fact that research subjects may not articulate the same meanings or interpretations as the researcher does not invalidate research. The standpoint of the research subject will be as 'situated' and partial as that of the researcher's. Notwithstanding these challenges to which no easy solution can be posed, oral history can do justice to the complexity of women's affective responses besides capturing, in Cvetkovich's words , 'political history as affective history, a history that captures activism's felt and even traumatic dimensions' (2003: 167).

While all female respondents are here anonymized, the politics behind the need to remain anonymous are significant for what they tell us about women's positioning in this history. When issues of anonymity were raised, some said that there was no need for the name, while others felt that I could include their names since they had nothing significant to say. With others, their present affiliations to political parties determined the choice of anonymity. Women's feelings of vulnerability with regard to their families and children also structured their need for anonymity. The entire dictum of unconditional anonymity raises larger questions as to whether researchers should always assume that their research subjects would prefer anonymity or whether anonymity can constitute a form of symbolic violence towards those who are struggling to speak and be heard. Latika and Saumen Guha, for instance, always insist on not being named in any form of publication or media, given their association with a fairly significant legal case (detailed in Chapter 6) to which they wish to draw attention. Since I refer to work published by the couple which provides full details of the case, including naming all those involved, anonymity would also be futile.

Personal narratives obtained through interviews are considered in the chapters that follow, alongside official and popular representations of the movement available in a range of archival, documentary, auto/biographical, cinematic, poetic, and literary sources. Women's published autobiographies (Bandyopadhyay 2001; Mitra 1994; Sanyal 2001) were key to the initial identification of research themes, besides providing crucial insights into their subjective experiences of the past. Notwithstanding the structural differences between the two sources that merit distinct analytical strategies (Passerini 1992), autobiographies and oral testimonies are placed in conjunction with one another in subsequent chapters, and the analysis of particular themes moves between more structured, chronological events as recounted in the autobiographies and free-flowing memories obtained from interviews. Oral and written personal narratives are also used, as they were in the field, to support one another. I used the published memoirs that foreground experiences of sexism, domestic violence, and sexual violence to open up a discussion on these issues with interviewees who did not bring it up themselves. Following the relational aspect of memory that this book privileges, women's autobiographies, like popular representations of the movement, are not explored independently; significant childhood stories of gender-based discrimination in the family, which begin with the autobiographies, thus await further exploration. Relating these 'sites of memory' to the oral testimonies and to each other enabled, however, a full analysis of the cultural repertoires at play in the memorialization of the movement. It is to this repertoire—especially to its gendered nature—that I turn in the next chapter.

2

Gendering the Revolution

Official and Popular Imaginary

The normative figure of politics, especially of war, is masculine (Puwar 2004: 6). Drawing on political theorists like Carole Pateman, Puwar (2004: 15–16) notes how the universal political subject is imagined as a disembodied agent owing to the primacy placed on reason. Feminists have shown how this disembodied subject that is effectively male appears in a 'gender-free guise'. Consequently, sexual difference and embodiment constrain women's ability to occupy such a putatively 'neutral' space. For Puwar, the arrival of women's (and black) bodies into spaces not traditionally reserved for them does at least two things. It renders women's bodies highly visible and it also makes evident that the political/public space is a normatively male one: 'These new bodies highlight the constitutive boundaries of who can pass as the universal human, and hence who can be the ideal figure of leadership' (Puwar 2004: 8).

Women enter the nation on specific terms and in fulfilling particular functions. Men, Puwar says, are metonymically linked to the nation while women serve a metaphoric function embodying and extolling the nation's virtues. Military imaginaries are equally laced with sexual and maternal imagery, even as women might be absent from the actual work of militarism and war (Elshtain 1995). Women bodies are highly visible in other ways, whether as 'beautiful souls' (Elshtain 1995) to be protected by the violent actions of men or as militant or nurturing 'patriotic mothers' who inspire and produce militarized masculinity (De Alwis 1998b; De Mel 2001; Haq 2007; and Sjoberg and Gentry 2007).

In Indian (Hindu) nationalism, the models of politicized femininity that historically recur are those of the chaste wife, heroic mother, and celibate warrior (Basu and Banerjee 2006: 479). All three rest on the control of women's sexuality as per 'ideals of heteronormative chastity' (Basu and Banerjee 2006: 479). Produced as a correlate to a refashioned colonial masculinity, chaste womanhood was located in and symbolic of a spiritually superior 'inner world' of the nation: 'A woman's body remained heterosexual and chaste, as it embodied national honor' (Basu and Banerjee 2006: 479). Any deviation from this norm—in female sexuality—not only brought dishonour but was also perceived as a threat to militarized Hindu manhood. When women are able to claim more non-traditional and politically active, even 'terrorist' roles, they have done so by erasing all visible markers of embodiment. The female 'citizen warriors' of the contemporary Hindu nationalist movement (Banerjee 2003: 174) and the 'masculinised virgin warriors' of the Sri Lankan Liberation Tigers of Tamil Eelam (LTTE) (De Alwis 2002: 4; see also De Mel 2001; and Parashar 2009) are two ready examples of women's transgression of the body for the sake of political agency. At the same time, however, women are 'overdetermined by the materiality of their bodies' (Puwar 2004: 16), especially through their association with sexuality. In the context of 'terrorist' organizations, feminist have noted and critiqued the tendency to locate women's political participation in their sexual attachments to male activists (Hamilton 2007; Passerini 1992; and Zwerman 1992).

Although it is women who need to give up marks of femininity in a masculinized world of revolution and war, masculinity remains underexplored in the context of resistant struggles in the 'Third World' (see, however, Dasgupta 2003 on Bengali communism; and Donner 2009; and Sinha Roy 2011 on Naxalbari). Besides maintaining the fiction of separate spheres, this lack belies the concurrent if not constitutive nature of masculinity and femininity, as feminist histories of nationalist identity have made obvious (Banerjee 2003; Chakravarti 1998; and Sinha 1995). Two recent approaches to South Asian masculinities bear directly on readings of Naxalite masculinity. The first concerns colonial masculinity focused primarily on the Bengali middle-class male's 'quest for manhood' in the face of its perceived loss under colonial rule (Basu and Banerjee 2006). As noted in a number of studies, the colonial power routinely belittled the Bengali *babu* or clerk for his weakness and effeminacy as opposed to the manliness of the British and the Indian martial races (Chowdhury 1998; Sinha 1995). Consequently, 'the search for manliness and the supposed assertion of virility through revolutionary violence ... became a critical component of elite nationalist resistance to colonial rule' (Basu and Banerjee 2006: 477). Renunciation and celibacy, traditionally valued ideals for upper-caste Hindu men (John and Nair 1998), were part of this Hindu Bengali nationalist model that fused the militant manliness of the 'Kshatriya' with the spiritual strength of the 'renouncer' (Chowdhury 1998; Mankekar 1999; Monti 2004; and Nandy 1998).[1] Given full expression by Vivekananda (and in Bankim Chandra's political sannyasi[2]), the 'warrior monk' (Basu and Banerjee 2006) can be seen not merely in the self-understanding of elite Hindu Bengali nationalists but also in the Bengali communist movement, the subject of which is the 'communist saint', as Ray (1998: 145) puts it.

This brings me to the second, related set of reflections that bears upon understandings of Naxalite masculinity, which pertains to the opposition between the renouncer and the householder in South Asian masculinities. The move from the householder to the militant renouncer was part of the Indian nationalist project where 'renunciation indicate[d] the necessary path to resistance against colonial oppression' (Chopra *et al.* 2004: 18; see also Monti 2004). While Donner (2009, pace Chopra *et al.* 2004) is right to argue that the standard polarization between the 'renouncer' and the 'householder' does not adequately capture the 'lived' experience of middle-class male Naxalites, the stereotypical figure of a masculine hero who is ostensibly free from all familial or worldly ties structures popular and official constructions of communist, including Naxalite masculinity. Dasgupta (2003) reads fictional accounts and memoirs of the process of 'becoming a communist' in Bengal in the 1930s as starting with the middle-class male's desertion of domestic life. The splitting of militant masculinity from feminized domesticity is, of course, key to military heroism. Male soldiering entails a flight from the private and the domestic equated with the feminine: 'the masculinity of war is what it is precisely by leaving the feminine behind. It consists in the capacity to rise above what femaleness symbolically represents: attachment to private concerns, to "mere life"' (Lloyd 1987, cited in Hamilton 2007: 87; see also Enloe 1983). The public realm has historically been constructed through the exclusion of the feminine and that which it symbolizes, such as nature, the body, and affectivity (Puwar 2004). This exclusion of women and femininity was not a marginal or accidental feature of the constitution of the public sphere but constitutive of its formation. Essentialized conceptions of masculinity and femininity together with demarcations of the private and public have thus served to render women in the political realm as 'matter out of place' (Puwar 2004: 11).

This chapter considers figurations of masculinity and femininity in a range of sources to theorize the Naxalite version of revolution as a thoroughly gendered construct that made particular demands on men and women. Imaginings of violent class struggle relied on specific mobilizations of masculinity and femininity that were not distinct from national, class, and caste categories. 'Revolution', in turn, refashioned these categories, producing preferred versions from a historically resonant repertoire of gendered and classed images. While Charu Mazumdar's apocalyptic vision of revolution, constituting the sum of official discourse, produces the icon of the male middle-class revolutionary, its subjective dimensions and private dramas are explored in the fiction and film inspired by the movement. The private, affective, and feminine are also afforded a visibility here that is not available in the party's archive. My use of heterogeneous sources in this chapter is not for instrumental reasons alone. The interrelation of official, literary, mediatic, and auto/biographical representations that blurs, moreover, the distinction between 'fact' and 'fiction', 'real' and 'imaginary', offers rich textual possibilities. These together constitute an interpretive repertoire of 'becoming a Naxalite' that informs the work of memory across public and private realms.

'Becoming a Naxalite'

In Dawson's (1994) *Soldier Heroes*, the imagining of war stages a particular model of manliness, one that is associated with a masculine world of risk and adventure divorced from the domestic and the feminine. As opposed to women, war offers men a form of identity from which they can draw pleasure and that promises to negotiate the contradictions of lived experience. The revolutionary in CPI (ML) discourse constitutes a similarly potent and pleasurable form of (male) identification that restores subjectivity in hegemonic masculine values of valour, virtue, and patriotism. 'Revolution' itself has all the triumphalist and romantic elements of war stories and soldiers' tales (see Dawson 1994; and Steedman 1988). In common with New Left radicalism elsewhere (Varon 2004: 235) and a particularly Bengali brand of revolutionary Marxism (Dasgupta 2003), Charu Mazumdar's message was overwhelmingly one of enthusiasm for the cause, contempt for the enemy, and confidence in eventual victory.[3] His optimism led him to declare the 1970s as the 'Decade of Liberation', in which the People's Liberation Army would march across the nation and a new People's Democratic India would be consolidated. From 1970 when the counteroffensive by the state began and the movement suffered losses in life, Mazumdar's exaggerated optimism resounded even more clearly, leading one historian to remark that 'from his writings and utterances in 1969–71, it appears that Mazumdar was suffering from a delusion—a delusion of power' (Banerjee 1984: 356). A story of romantic revolution could not afford to include unsettling images of betrayal, death, and loss, or even its own murderous violence. Through identification with the figure of the revolutionary martyr, the imagining of revolution undercuts any feelings of anxiety or fear; it offers excitement 'without being confronted with an overpowering sense of insecurity and danger that accompanies such forms of excitement in reality' (Dawson 1994: 54).

It is in Mazumdar's writings, published in the underground press, that a concern with the refashioning of masculinity is explicit, especially in his call for a 'new man'. For Arendt (1970), what is distinctive (and damaging) of New Left thinkers like Sartre is their claim that man creates himself not through the work of thought or labour but through that of violence. Indeed, as I detail next, the emergence of the Naxalite new man hinges upon the execution of revolutionary violence in a class struggle that is equated with a 'battle of annihilation'. Party rhetoric declared that 'class struggle, i.e., this battle of annihilation, can solve all the problems facing us and lead the struggle to a higher stage, create conditions for the emergence of a new type of man, the man of the Mao Tsetung era who fears neither hardship nor death' (Kumar Ghosh 1993: 20).[4]

It is ultimately martyrdom that 'births' the new man in common with the palingenetic logic that informs fascism and some forms of communism (Griffin 1993).[5] A martyrological consciousness was so deeply embedded within this community of middle-class activists that several kept photographs handy for the newspaper report that would follow their 'martyrdom'.[6] Sacrifice, in party polemic, is not simply the death of the physical body; it is the sacrifice of individual subjectivity. In the repeated evocation of *attotyag* (self-denial or self-abnegation) in party literature, sacrifice moves beyond the pale of political activism to the politics of everyday life. A dominant slogan of the time, 'change yourself, change the world', necessitates a complete abdication of self-interest and individual will for the sake of the revolutionary cause. The need to repudiate personal desire and self-interest, construed as weakness of will or as betrayal of patriotic duty, is a strong theme of Naxalbari discourse, official and popular. In Bhattacharya's memoir, *Shottorer Dinguli* (The Days of the Seventies, 2000), a middle-class *mahila* comrade relinquishes her long-standing relationship due to political differences: 'All around me so many comrades are being martyred, and I am prioritizing my self-interest' (Bhattacharya 2000: 73–4). Personal happiness in love had to be sacrificed at the altar of revolutionary good (see Chapter 4). Narratives of middle-class activists are equally marked by aspirations towards something 'greater' or 'higher' than conventional life and the felt need to move beyond self-interest, rationalized as being lowly.

The sacrifice of everyday life and individual selfhood is best captured in the communist practice of 'declassing' that establishes the subject of this rhetoric in a history of elitist Bengali communism. A personal–political project of 'becoming declassed' goes back to the early days of communist politics in Bengal. 'Declassing' in bhadralok Marxist discourse, Dasgupta (2003: 164) tells us, refers to two interconnected levels: at the level of political praxis, it refers to the problem of overcoming the ideological distance between the madhyabitta activist and the masses. At the same time, it refers to the personal, ethical, and moral transformation that 'being a communist' entailed for the middle-class activist. 'Becoming declassed', in Naxalbari politics, meant, as repeatedly emphasized by Mazumdar in his addresses to the youth, integration with the peasantry through an adoption of their ways of life. The body as the site of the inscription of madhyabitta values had to undergo a ritual of change: 'clothes, manner of speech, dress, manners, and the like became the counters in the game of declassification and "integration"' (Ray 1998: 164). The idea of 'declassing' thus encapsulates a personal crusade of transforming middle-class subjectivity as part of political practice, determining not simply how one should act but what one should be.

While 'declassing' is ostensibly about class, it calls upon available rhetorics of gender and sexuality for its articulation. It begins, as it had for previous madhyabitta communists (Dasgupta 2003), with the abandonment of material privileges and domestic life—a move that marks the idealized disembodied communist subject as male. A father's lament for his dead Naxalite son published in the radical weekly, *Frontier* (15 August 1970), deploys dominant tropes around renunciation and the singular pursuit of *bhakti* or devotion to explain the revolutionary's sacrifice. That the latter drew on an already existing repertoire of religious renunciation for political purposes, best represented in the Bengal context by Swami Vivekananda (see Chowdhury 1998), partly explains the movement's wider acceptance and popularity:[7] 'He gave up his home for his revolutionary effort to remove the suffering of the oppressed, just as one renounces the world for the pursuit of God. Revolution was his singular concern. He had no time to spare, not even a moment, for anything other than this preoccupation. We are worldly selfish creatures' (*Frontier* 1970: 15).

Banjeree (2009), in his reminiscences of 'being a Naxalite', underscores the discrepancy between the lack of responsibility in personal life and the commitment to an abstract political ideal that characterized middle-class participation as distinct from the rural peasantry. In fact, kinship bonds and obligations as opposed to ideological affiliations structured political participation amongst adivasi groups, as an earlier study on Naxalbari showed (Duyker 1987; see also Dasgupta 2006). In creative literatures, including male memoirs, it is also clear that the repositioning of masculinity from householder to political renouncer had to be borne silently by mothers and wives.

While violence is, as I go on to show, legitimized through a politics of virility, the Naxalite 'new man' is regendered and desexualized in more implicit ways. Both within and outside of party texts, the move towards a heroic self-definition is a move towards a historically and culturally resonant model of political manhood in which sexuality is salient. In Mahasweta Devi's celebrated *Hajar Churashir Ma* (Mother of 1084, discussed later), the Naxalite protagonist, Brati, is a model of moral manliness that emerges in opposition to the elder brother, a coward, and the father, a womanizer. The hypermasculinity of the latter is also associated with an immoral sexuality in ways that confirm middle-class fears and ambivalences towards sexuality *and* the strong strand of moral puritanism that informs Bengal communism. Kalpana Joshi Dutta (1979) speaks of celibacy and abstinence as being the 'iron rule' that prevailed in the revolutionary terrorist culture of the 1930s (of which she was a part before becoming a communist), which carried over to Bengali communist parties. Taking from these multiple sources of masculinity, Sinha Roy (2011: 68) notes, how the communist and Naxalite ideal of masculinity came to include sexual abstinence and purity, indirectly marking female sexuality as a temptation if not a threat. The development of a 'benevolent but austere masculinity' (Sinha Roy 2011: 68), which included polite benevolence towards women, was one way of overcoming the ideological distance between the middle-class communist and the subaltern. 'Declassing', such a reading suggests, was explicitly bound up with the refashioning of masculinity through sexual self-control. In the chapters that follow, the struggle over sexuality is established as part of the struggle to be a new man, implicating the manner in which sexual desire and violence were negotiated in the movement and in its cultural memory.

'Becoming a Naxalite' elicited distinct modalities of gendering from women and, less obviously, from men. While ostensibly about class transformation, it included a distancing of the middle-class male self from everyday feminized concerns of 'mere life' and the control of sexuality in ways that evoke older models of political manhood that fuse militancy with spiritual strength (in celibacy and renunciation). For women who represented the gendered embodiment that the male activist was meant to transgress, 'becoming a Naxalite' entailed a more explicit regendering. The regulation of sexuality, exclusively associated with women, was central to this process—evident in the representations of women as chaste warrior, wife, and mother in what follows. Such images of femininity were not only a 'structural component' (Chakravarti 1998: 265) of protective Naxalite masculinity but also of a vision of violent revolution in ways that we see in this and other chapters.

Violence, Virility, and Hegemonic Masculinity

> With every click, my confidence increased, until I began to feel that with this weapon in my hand, there was nothing I couldn't do.[8]

Violence is what ultimately makes a new man; for Sartre (1967, cited in Arendt 1970: 106), 'irrepressible violence ... is man recreating himself'. A new man, a different man, of higher quality is born through the exercise of violence. As the young, despondent, male protagonist of Mukhopadhyay's novel *Brishtir Ghran* (Waiting for Rain, 1985), quoted above, learnt, violence enabled a regaining of confidence, quickly and 'magically'. The protagonist's embrace of violence in this novel that is set against the backdrop of Naxalbari has little to do with political motivations and ends and all to do with psychic struggles brought on by the specific sociopolitical conditions of the 1970s Kolkata. The acquisition of a gun restores virility in the castrated Bengali self, undoing fears of emasculation and impotence that were heightened in the ruthless climate in which the lower middle-class Bengali male found himself at the time.

The pleasures and power to be wrought even in the mere possibility of violence, let alone its execution, are noticeable in party literature where the annihilation of the enemy, self-sacrifice, and a militarized masculinity are all interlocked in Mazumdar's envisioning of a cycle of violence.

> To go close to the enemy it is necessary to conquer all thought of the self. And this can be achieved only by the blood of martyrs. That inspires and creates new men out of the fighters, fills them with class hatred and makes them go close to the enemy and snatch his rifle with bare hands. (Kumar Ghosh 1993: 24)

The martyr's blood births the 'new man' who, in turn, wages a battle of annihilation (and sacrifices himself) in order to avenge the martyrs of the revolution.[9] Martyrdom, in Mazumdar's formulation, is thus a form of retributive justice that is closely tied to a politics of validating violence as a whole. In an act of naming, martyrdom transforms violence into revolutionary 'action', legitimate and moral. This act is part of what Ray calls 'the Naxalite reversal of values', an 'appeal to the highest moral principles to justify, vindicate and positively advocate what is usually considered the grossest and coarsest immorality' (Ray 1998: xiii; see also Lecomte-Tilouine 2009). What makes violence altogether irresistible is the violence of the other, which is beyond the bounds of justification, and must be, out of necessity, avenged and defeated. This is the fundamental discursive strategy that the hero employs to justify his acts of violence, split-off from those of the anti-hero's, reviled as contemptuous, unjust, and criminal. In contrast, the violence of the revolutionary is a source of positive projections—of heroic, sacrificial action, of a means to a just and egalitarian future. This enables, Dawson (1994: 37) says, employing a Kleinian analysis to discourses of nationalism, a coding of 'our' atrocities as righteous and divinely sanctioned whilst 'theirs' are named *as* atrocities alone (see Kakar 1992, 1996, for a similar reading of communal violence in India). The hero can even take pleasure in his act of righteous violence since its framing frees him from feelings of guilt or remorse, more than evident in the economy of pleasure and desire that underlies Mazumdar's 'murder manual'.

While the enemy is demonized as the repository of aggressive and evil qualities, he is also characterized through those of fear and cowardice, evident in repeated usages of the Sanskrit term, *kapurush*, referencing the failure of manliness (Nandy 1998). Oppositions between the revisionists and revolutionaries are also established through the politics of masculinity. The revisionists are derided for 'emasculating' the communist movement (Kumar Ghosh 1993; see also Mazumdar 2001) just as Gandhian satyagraha is said to have rendered the anti-colonial struggle 'impotent' (Kumar Ghosh 1993: 83). Much of Bengali (and Marathi) antagonism towards Gandhian non-violence stemmed from the fear that it was effeminizing and emasculating a Hindu India. Gandhi's sexuality is explicitly in question in Mazumdar's slander: 'This traitor whose life was hypocrisy abounding, even whose lechery and sexual depravity passed off as brahmacharya, perished in the flames he and his reactionary and revisionist accomplices had kindled ... naturally, the reactionary children and the revisionist bastards whom this man fathered are gripped with alarm ...' (Kumar Ghosh 1993: 108).

Mazumdar's words are also suggestive of Gandhi's symbolic castration to the extent that he 'fathers' children who are ultimately 'bastards'. Not surprisingly, the father of the nation is construed as the father of revisionism, the very embodiment of *kapurusata*. The fight against emasculation becomes constitutive of national identity, and Mazumdar implores every 'Indian' to fulfil his 'pure' duty to fight those who are kapurush. In the final instance, cowards are not authentic Indians; *purusatva*, the essence of masculinity is the essence of Indianness. The rifle-snatching campaign is another instance of the restoration of virility through violence. 'Snatch[ing] away a rifle from the police or the military' depletes the latter of its virility just as it reinstates 'pride' and 'honour' (*izzat*) in the peasant (Kumar Ghosh 1993: 112). The rifle, a supreme phallic symbol, becomes definitive of power and powerlessness, of virility and castration.

The idealized figure of the Naxalite revolutionary is, it should be clear by now, essentially a male one that is put into the service of a righteous, revolutionary 'good' violence as against the 'bad' violence of the state. Such a normative political identity is also constituted in class–caste terms even as the category of caste suffers the same invisibility that does gender in party literature. The silencing of caste or its collapsing under class is typical of Indian communist parties (on the communist Left in Kerala, see Menon 2006). In thinking of themselves as 'atheist' and secular, Omvedt (1995: 40–1) suggests that (elite) communists of pre-independence India relegated their caste identities—much like gender—to the 'private' domain and out of public scrutiny. She also remarks how the 'new left intelligentsia' avoided the recognition of caste and stressed a mechanical class framework that sought to override traditional identities rather than reinterpret them …' (Omvedt 1995: 40–1). It is only now in Naxalite struggles, in Andhra and Bihar, that caste has become central to a critique of the movement (Nigam 2007).

That the Naxalites belonged to an essentially elitist Bengali communist tradition is not only evidenced in the middle-class nature of the movement's participants but in the wider cultural repertoires of representing the revolution and its subjects. This included the representation of the peasant, a key icon of Naxalbari. Indeed, the greatest martyrs of the movement were the women adivasis that the state fired upon at Naxalbari when the 'spring thunder' first broke. Historians of Indian nationalism (Chatterjee 1993a; Sarkar 2001) have observed a representational continuity between peasants and women, both ready subjects of patriotism. Both were equated with motherhood in nationalist literature through their relationship with nature and nurture, signalling a realm of emotional affectivity for the disembodied male hero. As in nationalist writings, the subaltern, male and female, is deified as an ideal and already-constituted political subject in Naxalbari literature. The peasant's subjection to suffering, deprivation, and state oppression is a source for her/his idealization as the supreme validating principle of class struggle. The subaltern is a hero because he is a victim. The Naxalite romanticization of the peasantry echoes that of other New Left groups at the time for whom the subaltern classes had an instinctual disposition to revolutionary violence (see Varon 2004). Peasants and workers are further placed within a discourse of paternalist protection in ways that confirm nationalist perceptions of subaltern masculinity as infantile and feminized. Dasgupta (2006: 1924) and Sinha Roy (2011) rightly emphasize the 'vanguardist' role assumed by the bhadralok male leadership who were meant to pass on their political knowledge and consciousness to the peasantry, positioned in the role of the receiver and not the agent (see also Bandyopadhyay 2000; and Banerjee 2009).

When not conceived of as in need of conscientizing or protection from the vanguard, the male peasant is a repository of middle-class perceptions of subaltern aggression. He is presented through an almost animal-like aggression in which the body is the primary tool or instrument of political agency. While the middle-class leader relies on rifles and pistols in the guerrilla war, the peasant 'fights' with his 'bare arms'; 'with [their] nails,

[they] rip open the heart of anybody who dares to oppose [them]' (Kumar Ghosh 1993: 290).[10] Such a characterization of bhadralok and subaltern political labour is in complete conformity with the social divisions of Hindu Bengali culture. For men of the bhadralok class and higher castes, hegemonic masculinity is defined through its association with intellectual labour and concomitant distance from menial labour, the preserve of the *chotolok*, the 'serving' or lower caste–class that works with its hands. Through its association with such body work, the subaltern subject embodies a less valued masculinity than the bhadralok, who defines himself not through physical strength but through Brahmin intellectual potency. However, the subaltern is not always emasculated given his representation through the use of brute force and aggression. The subaltern is, as Ray (2000) observes of Bengali manliness more generally, sometimes more than a man and often less. In Naxalite rhetoric, the male peasant is similarly represented as being closer to the body in some instances while his deification rests, in others, on a distancing from the body. Such a move is explicit in the party's failure to implicate male peasants for sexual violence towards middle-class women activists, as shown in Chapter 5.

In the discussion thus far, as well as in the figurations of femininity to which I now turn, we begin to see how certain bodies and subjects served to legitimate if not produce hegemonic political identity. Both the woman and the subaltern were 'useful' to the construction of an unmarked yet normative male bhadralok Naxalite identity and to the validation of its violent politics. Such bodies and subjects were thus made to matter in the political domain (where they were largely 'matter out of place') even as they mattered very specifically. As Gedalof (1999) has persuasively shown, the manner in which 'woman' is made central to the composure of identities and communities is key to women's subordination. In what follows, we see that the symbolic utility of 'woman' to the vision and life of violent revolution flattens their complexities as subject–agents whilst reproducing class-based patriarchal power relations.

Of Mothers and Militants: Empowering and Subjecting Women

Gedalof's (1999) Foucauldian emphasis on the productive capacity of power for feminist theorizing of identity practices has important implications for understanding how 'woman' is central to the logic and actualization of violence and war as against studies that emphasize what these 'do to' women. We have already seen how ethical distinctions between good and bad violence and its subjects and objects were secured through (middle-class, Hindu) presumptions of masculinity. Femininity was equally mobilized to restore masculine agency in violence if not to legitimate violence itself. There is, today, a vast body of feminist scholarship that considers the mobilization of femininity in ideologies of political violence even as women have been excluded from its practice: be they nationalist political projects (Chatterjee 1989; Jacoby 1999; Sarkar 2001; and Yuval–Davis and Anthias 1989); war and wider practices of militarization (Chenoy 1998; and Enloe 1989); discourses of humanitarian intervention (Young 2003, 2007); right-wing nationalisms (Bacchetta 2004; and Banerjee 2003); ethnonationalist struggles (De Alwis 1998a; De Mel 2001; Haq 2007; and Tambiah 2005); and anti-colonial liberation struggles (see, most recently, White 2007). In these varying forms and expressions of (mainly nationalist) struggles, what Scott has called 'the legitimising function of gender' (Scott 1986: 1070) is evident, especially in the militarization of masculinity.

The category of 'woman' as it intersected with that of subalternity and sexuality was key to the repertoire of rationalizing the 'good' violence of the Naxalite and producing its heroic (male) subject. The sexual victimization of peasant women at the hands of the state and the 'ruling classes' was a major justification for armed struggle, discursively configured as a battle for honour or *izzater lorai*. Mazumdar (2001: 107) himself underscored the need to raise subaltern consciousness in order to shift class struggle from economic determinism to a battle for honour. Women were central to this project given the cultural and middle-class construction of izzat or honour as located in the female body that sanctions, in turn, violent masculine protection and a limited degree of female agency.[11] It is the body of the subaltern woman that is equated, par excellence, in party discourse with 'rapability' (Marcus 1992) and the potential loss of the izzat of the entire community. The deployment of rape as a form of class oppression suffered primarily by subaltern women has important implications for the party's response to forms of sexual violence that were not sanctioned by class privilege, as will be explored in Chapter 5. The language of izzat also validates subaltern female militancy. Mazumdar applauds a landless peasant woman for 'snatching away a rifle from a CRP [Central Reserve Police] man after hacking him to death' and expresses amazement at how peasant women 'valiantly resisted the police and landlords with indigenous chilli powder and even with bare arms' (Kumar Ghosh 1993: 112). Sinha Roy (2011) shows that this instrumental utility of subaltern women's activism did not preclude its construal in male memoir as being primarily of a supportive nature.

Middle-class women also acted as ready causes of revolution, whether as an enslaved mother/land that needed liberation or as a warrior mother that aided the struggle against the 'bad' violence of the state. Lloyd writes that 'socially constructed motherhood, no less than socially constructed masculinity, is at the service of an ideal of citizenship that finds its fullest expression in war' (Lloyd 1987, cited in Hamilton 2007: 101). The evocation of motherland or *matribhumi* finds mention in the writings of Charu Mazumdar, and the image of an enslaved mother is not altogether absent from the official rhetoric. In party literature and male memoirs, mothers are represented through images of nurturance, love, glorious courage, and untold sacrifice.[12]

As in the anti-colonial movement, the burden of awakening and inspiring their sons to battle and even death falls on a collective of Bengali mothers or a *mayer* jati (Sarkar 2001: 258). In a series of published letters from a jailed Naxalite to his mother, we find a son repeatedly urging his mother to dry her tears and bless, enthuse, and inspire the sons of the revolution: 'Like you, thousands and thousands of mothers are wiping the tears from their eyes and awakening enthusiasm in their sons. These words will perhaps not be written in big letters in the pages of books. But these tears, this sacrifice, this inspiration will itself fill the pages of history' (Dasadhikari 1998: 110).[13] This inspirational task falls on the shoulders of mothers by virtue of their complete equation with the principle of self-sacrificing love. The cultural roots of this equation are obvious given that Bengali mothers have traditionally stood for an undying spirit of sacrifice for the family (Bagchi 1990). Indeed, the male revolutionary is narratively imbued, in Naxalbari literature, with maternal love, the highest and purest form of love (see Sarkar 2001).

As shown in a number of studies (Bagchi 1990, 2000; Chowdhury 1998; Das and Sen Chaudhuri 2007; Sarkar 2001; and Sen 1993), elite Hindu Bengali nationalism mobilized the contradictory qualities of enslavement and militancy—of 'abject victimhood and triumphant strength' (Sarkar 2001: 253)—that the Hindu mother goddess or the *debi* is said to embody for the patriotic cause. She was, on the one hand, a figure of enslavement (under colonial rule) and, on the other, an image of power, strength, and destruction associated with the principle of female strength or *Shakti* in Hindu religious symbolism. Shakti, the hidden strength and violence endemic to female nature (Sarkar 1984), has historically been called upon to explain women's violence in exceptional moments, as Sinha Roy (2011) notes of both left-wing and right-wing politics in India.

Not surprisingly, Naxalbari discourse draws on the contradictory qualities of power and powerlessness that are inherent to the 'heterogeneity' of the mother figure (Das and Sen Chaudhuri 2007). An armed Nirmala or a martyred Ahalya[14] finds mention in Naxalite poetry, while activist writings draw upon the mother–warrior coupling that is epitomized in Laxmibai, the Queen of Jhansi, or, as Loomba (1991, cited in Sunder Rajan 1993: 135) puts it, 'the honourary man who is one of the models for Indian womanhood'. In his memoir, prominent middle-class activist Ajijul Haque seems to explicitly evoke the image of Laxmibai as plunging into battle with a child on her back in envisioning his wife raging against the police:

> A woman saddled with two children steps into the battleground with the pure intention of saving the lives of two children. I don't need to know who she is. She is a gladiator. Completely unarmed. The enemy wants to rip her apart with a four-headed spear. Society, economy, government and tradition—all combine to wound her. Her spilled guts bloody the ground. She fights in that bloodied ground ...! We need not know who she is. All I know is that she is a woman. Fighting the demons (*danab*). Struggle has found life in the form of a woman. She is no individual. Her name is struggle. (Haque 1991: 35)

The warrior mother is here the very embodiment of violent struggle. Haque hints at another dimension of this culturally resilient iconography around the warrior mother, which is its reliance on the transcendence of womanliness itself. Indeed, Laxmibai is able to claim warrior status by striping away womanly weakness, as Loomba (in Sunder Rajan 1993) notes, and by 'erasing all visible markers of her sexuality' as Basu and Banerjee (2006: 481) show. Woman-as-struggle is here similarly founded upon the obliteration of the individual woman ('she is no individual'), transformed into disembodied female strength. The female subject is split such that her militant public role rests not simply on anonymity but on the erasure of the embodied, gendered, and sexualized subject–agent. Her private self is equated with supreme sacrifice, principally of her husband, for the revolution. Haque's memoir makes evident that such was the minimal demand of the revolution on wives and mothers.

True to their lineage, the Bengali Maoists were less comfortable with a militant mother than a domesticated and nurturing one, 'the presiding deity of Bengali kitchens and sickbeds' (Sarkar 2001: 257). Both Bagchi (1990) and Sarkar (1987, 2001) find an eventual domestication of feminine power in the Bengali nationalist transformation of militancy into a domesticated, gentle femininity. They also suggest that the mother-as-nation implied a passive and not an activist role for women besides sanctioning their subjugation in a number of deeply exploitative social practices. Male auto/biographies of the Naxalite period are replete with stories of women giving up food and bed for the *biplabi*, demonstrating a (male) yearning for feminine softness at a time of war. In a piece of semi-fictionalized writing by a male activist, the wives of prominent Naxalite leaders are lauded for sacrificing their lives of comfort for the uncertainty of revolutionary existence. These women, described as modest and submissive (*binoi*), are said to 'help' the party by doing 'something or the other'. One of the women is described thus: 'Rome *boudi* went away laughing. She wore a red yellow sari. Her back was covered with open hair—a red dot on her forehead. A mother-like behaviour (*bhab*). Deepak felt like sitting under her feet' (Dasadhikari 1998: 83).

This image of women as wives and mothers is also in aid of their desexualization. In the writings of nineteenth century Hindu Bengali religious leader, Ramakrishna, women's innate sexuality was presented as a threat to the path of the male renouncer (see also Chapter 4). The 'woman of flesh and blood, woman in the immediacy of everyday life, with a fearsome sexuality', to use Chatterjee's (1993b: 54) description, had to be transformed into the comforting, non-threatening mother figure, 'erased of sexuality' (see also Sarkar 1997). Chatterjee (1993b: 60) argues that the former feminine figuration had little to do with 'women in actuality'; it signified, instead, the social and political subordination of the Bengali bhadralok under colonial rule. The latter figure of woman as chaste and pure mother and wife, devoted to her husband and children, emerged as the perfect complement to the effeminate or 'frail hero' of colonial Bengal (Chowdhury 1998). As with the warrior mother previously encountered, the motherliness exalted in this historical moment rested on the transgression of the individual, ordinary mother to embody the very principle of 'inner' spiritual strength in the face of 'outer' subservience.

As we see later in this chapter and also in Chapter 4, women's bodies are equally split between threatening and non-threatening femininities in the creative output of Naxalbari, associated with a specific set of significations. Suffice it to say for now that the activist woman is invariably presented as asexual comrade, or the good wife, or *shahadharmini* (one who shares the husband's dharma; Chowdhury 1998: 75; see also Punjabi 2002 in relation to Tebhaga). An oppositional relationship between middle-class and subaltern femininity is also established on the grounds of sexuality. As Basu (2001) explains and as I detail in Chapter 4, sexual modesty is a sacrosanct marker of respectability for the Bengali bhadramahila. Active sexual desire is associated with elite, Westernized women, on the one hand, and low-caste women, on the other. While middle-class female activists are attributed qualities of modesty and sacrifice, adivasi women are routinely described as *jongi* or militant in auto/biographical texts. In another semi-fictionalized work, a middle-class male Naxalite describes his love interest, an adivasi girl, as the 'female panther' of the village, whose 'speed' and 'attack' is immediately contrasted with the political failure of certain middle-class women activists (Dasadhikari 1998). Common middle-class assumptions of tribal society and tribal women as being sexually permissive are not absent from these literary representations even as such perceptions have historically contributed to the sexual exploitation of subaltern women.

As in the colonial context, Naxalbari politics was infused with middle-class ideologies of 'pure' womanhood epitomized in a nurturing, sacrificial, and desexed motherhood. As transgressive of ordinary womanliness associated with the body and the banalities of the everyday, motherhood represented the truly renunciatory revolutionary principle for the madhyabitta male. Together with motherhood, feminine sexual vulnerability consolidated images of violent retributive revolution in a protective communist masculinity. Gender (and even sexuality) was thus not 'absent' in the cultural imaginary of the movement in any straightforward sense; it signified particular power relations that might not have always had to do with women or women's lives (Scott 1986). Given, however, the very specific significatory status of women in revolutionary discourse, the agency of individual middle-class women activists were circumscribed in several ways. Subsequent chapters draw out the tensions between the experiences of 'real' wives and mothers and the expectations embodied in specific significations of 'woman' as sacrificial, heroic, and disembodied.

'Your' Revolution and 'Mine' in Popular Culture

Nations, we know, are frequently etched upon the bodies of women associated, above all, with the private domestic sphere. The perceived loss of masculinity in the public sphere under colonial rule led elite Indian men to 'asser[t] their masculinity in the "inner world," or the domestic sphere' (Basu and Banerjee 2006: 482). In the patriarchal nationalism (what some historians have called the 'new patriarchy'; Chatterjee 1989, 1993; Sarkar 2001; and Walsh 2004; see also Majumdar 2009; and Sen 2000) of nineteenth century Bengal, the inner domain of home came to represent the singularity of the nation, secured through the presence of women, the 'embodiment of cultural difference' (Niranjana 2007: 212). The 'new woman' of the nationalist project (primarily a bhadramahila; see Chapter 1) came to stand for the nation itself, associated with the home, domesticity, and spiritual (that is, feminine) virtues, to be preserved from an 'outer' material, modernizing male world. Women in post-colonial India continue to bear the 'burden of maintaining the distinctiveness of Indian culture' (Niranjana 2007: 212) in ways that men (and 'Western' women) do not. Hierarchies of gender and sexuality were simultaneously mobilized and contained within these spatial reconfigurations that determined the very nature of the public and private, inner and outer domains, and the home and the world.

In militarized discourses, whether in aid of the nation or of revolutionary renewal, the division between the public and the private along the lines of gender is inscribed with greater force. Hamilton suggests that 'the military represents the opposition between the private and public both at its most false and extreme' (Hamilton 2007: 87). Militarized organizations like the Basque Homeland and Freedom (ETA) and the Irish Republican Army (IRA) were conceived of as being disassociated from home and family life even though heterosexual coupling and childbearing invariably occurred. The stringent ideological divide between the two spheres is further complicated by the fact that it is women's invisible labour in the private domain that is critical to sustaining the activity of male soldiering and the practice of warfare (Hamilton 2007; see also Enloe

1989, 2004). While privileging masculinity, the everyday practice of war and militarization is deeply dependent on women's acquiescence and on presumptions and mobilizations of femininity, as already noted.

Women's complex location within the public and the private along with their symbolic function as preservers of cultural identity raises relevant questions in the context of the popular imagination of Naxalbari, especially in filmic and fictional representations. Both novels and films (although I only focus on two representative novels of the movement in this discussion) are valuable sources for documenting changes in gender relations with women characters embodying wider sociocultural changes if not crises in post-colonial urban middle-class India. In considering 1960s popular Bengali fiction, Ghosh underscores what is a common theme of some of the popular texts I consider: the manner in which women are ambiguously presented, 'though modernised and educated, they retain their traditional roles and conventional gender relationships are valorised' (D. Ghosh 2001: 951). Ghosh writes that these roles were seemingly under threat in the 1950s and the 1960s Kolkata given the increasing break-up of joint families, women's contribution to waged work (including new practices and identities around consumption), and the rising cost of urban living.

It thus proved imperative to retell the story of the nation wherein women and the feminine have clearly ascribed roles and functions which ensures, in turn, social harmony and order. Women who stray from normative feminine goals in becoming too educated and liberated (synonymous with being 'Westernized') spell social havoc, in a long literary and popular tradition of demonizing what Sarkar (1991: 217) calls the 'non-mother', the flipside of the nurturing and sacrificial mother–woman. It is, above all, the autonomous woman who 'aspires to a life beyond mothering' who bears the hostility and the distrust afforded to the non-mother (Sarkar 1991: 217). Epitomized in the young urban career woman, she represents the dangers of modernization itself, especially through a repudiation of the 'spiritual role' that women were meant to fulfil for the new nation (D. Ghosh 2001). Novels like Devi's (2001) *Hajar Churashir Ma* (discussed next) and Sunil Gangopadhyay's *Pratidwandi* (The Adversary, 1969, English trans. 2005) which was made into a major film by Satyajit Ray represent women in similar terms: as the conduit through which a miasmatic urban culture is brought into the heart of the middle-class bari but also as the agents of the restoration of order in the private sphere (Ganguly 2000).

Amongst the rich crop of 'Naxalbari literature', Devi's *Hajar Churashir Ma* has been critically acclaimed and popularly received.[15] Written in 1973 (and first published in 1974), this moving portrayal of a middle-class mother's journey into the life of her dead Naxalite son has been translated into several languages, repeatedly dramaticized and televized, besides being made into a major Hindi feature film. The beloved son, Brati Chatterjee, reduced to a corpse bearing a number '1084' is a powerful metonym of state repression but also, as his mother Sujata, the novel's protagonist, discovers, of a debased middle-class epitomized by the bourgeois family and its dysfunctional members. When Sujata leaves home to discover Brati's life outside of it and the characters that peopled it, including his Naxalite girlfriend, Nandini, she is forever estranged from her class and its corrupt bourgeois morality. At the end of the novel, Sujata brings the revolutionary cause into the heart of the domestic sphere in her singular act of patriarchal defiance; an act that powerfully weds the personal and the political in the revolutionary imaginary. While Sujata rallies against expected norms of wifely devotion and submission to familial authority, she is also the main agent for the preservation of inherited moral values in the face of their bastardization. In this manner, she continues her son's struggle who, as it says in the introduction to the English translation, was 'at one level ... reacting against the immorality of this lifestyle that celebrated and cultivated survival at any cost' (Bandyopadhyay 2001[1997]: xv). 'Immorality' is represented in terms of patriarchal power and authority but also in terms of a lax sexual morality and rampant consumerism, symbolized by the other members of the Chatterjee household, especially the two daughters, Neepa and Tuli. Political activist Nandini is, in contrast, resolutely righteous even after debilitating police torture that has cost her an eye. Her love for Brati is represented as a de-eroticized form of *bhalobasha*, pure as their revolutionary commitment.

Ray's cinematic version of *Pratidwandi* (The Adversary, 1970) similarly maps the decay in public and private spheres, in wider middle-class society and within the middle-class home, symbolized, to a large extent, by the character and choices of the protagonist's, Siddhartha's sister, Sutapa (see Photograph 2). Educated with a good job, beautiful, confident, and glamorous, she epitomizes (much like Neepa and Tuli) the degradation of middle-class mores in the face of an increasingly ruthless materialist culture. Her deviance is balanced by the presence of Keya, the girlfriend, who operates, like Devi's 'ma', as the agent who

PHOTOGRAPH 2: Siddharth and Sutapa in *Pratidwandi* (1971). *Photograph courtesy* Sandip Ray.

restores 'normalcy'. Ganguly remarks in his reading of the film that in being everything that Sutapa is not, that is, 'asexual, nonaggressive, nonmaterialistic, and above all, nonthreatening', Keya 'fits the prototype of the respectable middle-class woman with whom [the protagonist] can feel "safe"' (Ganguly 2000: 131). A chief characteristic of such oppositional femininity (and masculinity as represented by the father in *Hajar Churashir Ma*) is an immoral and destructive sexuality that indulges in adultery, sexual licentiousness, and alcoholism under the pretext of bhadralok respectability. Sutapa is linked to a prostitute in her brother's subconscious just as Neepa is called a 'nympho' and Tuli is party to her father's adultery, glorifying him as 'a model of the virile man' (Devi 2001[1997]: 98). While women like Neepa, Tuli, and Sutapa herald social doom, it is also women, especially mothers, who restore normalcy, harmony, and order in a male world. Devi's mother's struggle against the immorality of the madhyabitta family is also in aid of preserving some of its traditional values, especially that of sexual propriety. Motherhood is a ground for restoring stability even as it challenges dominant norms of femininity and patriarchy within the family.

A stronger and more complex characterization of femininity can be found in Majumdar's *Kalbela* (The Omnious Hour, 1983).[16] The novel's male protagonist, Animesh, combines in him the fierce youthful idealism of the authentic revolutionary subject but not without a touch of fragility in the face of political betrayal, state terror, and eventually, in his own manliness. It is his lover, Madhabilata, who emerges as the story's super(wo)man, leaving her natal home behind to start earning and living independently, suffering police torture for the sake of her lover, and eventually bearing (and raising) a child out of wedlock. Madhabilata single-handedly bears the burden of domestic abandonment and the lack of security that the male revolutionary commitment entails. The novel is a powerful representation of a femininity that incorporates rebellion, independence, autonomy, and even sexual desire. Right through the novel, however, it is clear that the preferred novelistic trope is that of maternal sacrifice rather than that of feminist agency. Madhabilata stands unflinchingly by her revolutionary lover, at the cost of domestic (and legal) security and supreme societal abandonment. Her one-woman rebellion is, strictly speaking, for the sake of love; it is hardly one that is born out of some feminist impulse towards emancipation.

In novels like *Kalbela* and *Hajar Churashir Ma*, the rebellion against inherited middle-class values of home and family is made an integral part of the revolutionary cause, thus suturing the home and the world in a departure from the historical impulse to keep them separate. However and as crucially demonstrated in *Kalbela*, the literary imaginary reinscribes the private sphere as normatively feminine *even as it* reconfigures it as a space for female resistance. Thus, women battle against the hegemonic norms of gender and marriage but they do so resolutely within the circumscribed space of the private and *not* in the public. This is illustrated by the painful fact that throughout the novel, Madhabilata is not only politically inactive but is completely removed from the public world of politics, coded as masculine and divorced from the domestic and feminine. The gendering of revolutionary discourse is beautifully captured in these lines, voiced by Madhabilata in midst an argument with Animesh: 'Given that I am not preaching to you about your revolution, you leave me to think of mine'.

Similar narrative strategies are employed in the films *Padatik* (The Foot Soldier, 1973, directed by Mrinal Sen) and *Dooratwa* (The Distance, 1978, directed by Buddhadeb Dasgupta) that explore politicized left-leaning masculinity in the backdrop of Naxalbari. In both, as in *Kalbela*, the female rebellion against gender norms and middle-class values within the private sphere takes place alongside a masculine struggle in the politicized public realm. *Padatik* documents these parallel but distinct rebellions in the lives of a Naxalite activist who is on the run and the woman who shelters him; an unconventional upper middle-class woman who has left her husband and lives alone. Although their lives momentarily converge, the spheres of rebellion—separated and policed by a conventional public–private division—remain distinct. In *Dooratwa*, Anjali marries Mandar, a former revolutionary, to provide an identity for the illegitimate child she is carrying, and also because she believes he is 'different'. Unable to accept her premarital affair, Mandar rejects her. The film ends, however, with the possibility of a convergence between public and private spheres. Mandar's revolutionary masculinity is chastised for his failure to recognize the embeddedness of Anjali's struggle in the larger revolutionary cause, thus interweaving private and public worlds.

Novels and films like these are chronicles of the gendered repertoires of power and resistance, of 'your' revolution and 'my' revolution that are split across the public–private divide. Sujata and Brati and Animesh and Madhabilata travel parallel paths, waging battle in their culturally ordained spaces that never seem to converge. The revolutionary remains a guest, to use Nigam's (2007) coinage in relation to the filmic version of *Kalbela*, to everyday private and politically ambiguous spaces. This despite the fact that it is the women who don the masculine mantle of 'householder', bear children out of wedlock, have premarital sex, and live on their own. While fiction of this sort enables a more active, politicized role for women than official constructions of motherhood do, it does so cautiously as not to disrupt the stability of a masculine world of revolutionary action as distinct from the concerns and dramas of the private. These worlds blur in Naxalite women's (and men's) narratives that show how the movement itself came to be configured in familial, kinship, and community terms against ideological boundaries between home and the world, policed by the bodies of women.

Media Images of 'Terrorist' Women: The Mary Tyler Affair

While historiography has entirely failed to capture the gendered dynamics of urban political action, mainstream media appears to have done a better job. Leading English dailies like *The Statesman* regularly reported the arrest of 'extremists' that, at times, included a woman and even a 'girl leader'. Women, rarely named, were arrested in their capacity as couriers but also for hording arms and ammunitions, and, at other times, for 'hacking' someone to death. Media representations of young women indulging in acts of political violence fit pervasive stereotypes of the female terrorist as extraordinarily powerful and fierce (Zwerman 1992), as 'grotesque aberrations of femininity' (Mohan 1998: 69), even monstrous (Sjoberg and Gentry 2007). In unpacking the mediatic representation of Germany's Red Army Faction women, Melzer argues that 'while terrorism as a political strategy is considered deviant to begin with, the discussion of women within that practice is systematically gendered and sexualized in ways that of men is not' (Melzer 2009: 52). While mostly misogynist and sexist, mainstream media coverage is still an important site for analysis given its representation (and indeed construction) of wider cultural anxieties around the figure of the armed female terrorist or women's political participation more generally.

As with media reportage of anti-state radical movements worldwide (Hasso 2005; Melzer 2009; Naaman 2007; and Zwerman 1992), media coverage of urban Naxalite 'terrorism' focused on the more sensational aspects of these events which the presence of women only accentuated. Images of female Naxalites permeated public speculation but also informed state perceptions of female criminality, contributing, no doubt, to the 'special' status afforded to Naxalite women in the penal system (such as keeping women political prisoners in isolation or under maximum security). The sensationalism around Naxalite women was especially pronounced in the case of Mary Tyler, a 26-year-old British woman who became embroiled in Naxalbari politics and the only female activist to receive such enormous publicity.[17] It was her arrest in May 1970 together with fifty other activists belonging to the Man, Money, Gun group, including another woman, Kalpana Bose, in connection with the famous Jaduguda Naxalite Conspiracy case that grabbed the entire nation's attention (see Singh 1995). What marked her as by far the media's favourite Naxalite had as much to do with her gender as it did with her status as a foreigner. The sensationalism of the story that included her alleged romantic liaison with a Bengali man, a Naxalite, made for a terrific potboiler. She was painted by the press as having 'secret plans of her own' that marked her as different and potentially more dangerous from other 'extremists' (in her own prison memoir, she says how she was branded a Chinese spy by Indian officials).

Dressed in male attire with short-cropped hair at the time of her arrest, Mary Tyler fulfilled a fantastical image of the white woman as the 'female terrorist', masculine and sexually virile. A home-grown rebel, Kalpana Bose was, on the other hand, located within the normative bounds of Indian womanhood even as her political identity threatened to disrupt these. Newspapers reported that she was wearing a 'red sari' at the time of her arrest, and was known as 'Kalpana*di*' within the group. While the image of Mary Tyler seemed to be imbued with 'extraordinary levels of fantasy' (Zwerman 1992: 134), Kalpana was constructed within familial terms (as 'di', short for 'didi' or elder sister), a move that mitigated the social and sexual threat that her status as a political radical might have presented. A similar move can be identified in some later newspaper reportage on Mary Tyler in prison that enthusiastically documented her 'Indianization', including her transformation into a 'Hindu housewife'. One journalist noted, 'When I saw her [in prison] she was draped in a pale blue sari over a white blouse and even spotted a red dot on her forehead. Her hair was long and held together neatly in two plaits. In fact were she not a blonde she would have resembled a Hindu housewife' (Naqvi 1973). No longer in the realm of fantasy, Mary Tyler is now firmly located within the bounds of Hindu womanhood as dutiful housewife. She is domesticated and imbued with culturally appropriate markers of feminine identity. She voices the same political aspirations as she did at the time of her arrest but political agency no longer conflicts with the demands of normative feminine identity; the threat it posed is thus considerably contained. Importantly, it is under the auspices of the paternalist state that she is transformed from female outlaw to 'Hindu housewife'.

The trope of domesticating the white female radical is stronger in Mitra's (1993) fictionalized account of Mary Tyler in his novel, *Manabputri*.[18] A young English woman, Katherine, comes to Kolkata in search of Dipayon who is embroiled in radical Left politics. She ends up marrying him and becoming involved herself, soon to be arrested. Why this novel, although not the most representative of Naxalbari fiction, is interesting is because of its rare depiction of a female Naxalite as the novel's protagonist. The characters are constructed through the recycling of a number of well-known clichés. Dipayon is a model of virtuous manliness—calm, restrained, fearless, and unmovable in his love for the people and in his commitment to revolutionary change. His mother, Aarti, is a sea of love and comfort, emblematic of Indian womanhood. Katherine continuously turns to this ideal man for inspiration and strength while trying to mould herself in his image. A devoted wife, she scarcely ever questions his judgements, and is content to follow his lead. *Lajja* or shame is a word that is often used to describe her feelings towards him and towards herself. At the same time, she is resolute, headstrong, and embodies an appropriate degree of politicized femininity. Mere emotions such as love will not deter her from standing by the side of India's poor. Early on in the novel, Katherine muses to herself:

> While she had come to serve the masses, her soul moistened with affection (*mamta*) for Dipayon. Instead of thinking of an agenda for the benefit (*upkaar*) of the poor saddened masses of India, she is thinking of Dipayon ... This injustice! Utter injustice! She was ashamed. This sort of feminine mentality did not suit her education, her taste. (Mitra 1993: 62)

Love that is not oriented towards a social good is no longer love but a source of shame and an act of injustice, as I detail in Chapter 4. It is also revelatory of feminine weakness. The expression of love in Katherine is, in fact, entirely feminized, a quality that needs to be transgressed for the sake of authentic political agency manifest in selfless devotion to the people. The representation of love as feminine weakness conforms to the demands of a heroic femininity that is rooted in a transgression of feminized attributes and emotions (and 'womanliness' itself, as previously seen) in order to embrace masculine potency. Yet, perhaps unsurprisingly, and much like the 'real' Mary Tyler, Katherine also embodies middle-class virtues of shame, sexual modesty, and husband devotion, sacrosanct markers of bhadramahila identity. In the case of both media and literary representations, patriarchy's resilience to define women within its terms are obvious in the extension of the prescriptive codes of Bengali womanhood to all women, including, in this case, a non-Indian.

The discussion in this chapter shows how masculinity and femininity played a part in imagining the revolution just as 'revolution' produced particular versions of masculinity and femininity thereby making distinct demands upon men and women. The unmarked revolutionary martyr here emerges as the staging of a normative (middle) classed and masculine identity that is split across gendered worlds. For the middle-class male, 'becoming a Naxalite' was an embodied process. It materialized through an appropriation of middle-class markers of gender and sexuality, in the repudiation of feminized domesticity, and in sacrificing and being sacrificed. The middle-class male activist is not, however, associated with the body in ways that women and peasants seem to be in the cultural imaginary of the movement. His body remains unmarked by gender, sexuality, and class–caste, by virtue of which it can, like the white body, take up the 'unmarked normative locale' (Puwar 2004: 58). In contrast, women are marked and highly visible by virtue of the gender and sexual difference that they embody; in the movement's archive, they are exclusively associated with (hetero)sexuality, chastity, domesticity, and motherhood, all of which seem innate and natural to women as opposed to men. Women's bodies are also firmly located in the 'inner' realm which is produced, in fiction and film, as analogous to and exclusive from the 'outer' political realm. This impulse to shepherd women into the patriarchal fold of marriage, motherhood, and domesticity has been understood by feminists as countering the threat that such politicized, even 'deviant', femininities pose to the social order, especially in their appropriation of violence. Yet women's bodies, whether sexually vulnerable and/or masculinized, were also productive of Naxalite violence. Gender and class intersections were particularly 'useful' since the legitimation of violence relied on (Hindu Bengali) middle-class repertoires of izzat, Shakti, and renunciation. I turned to Gedalof's (1999) Foucauldian insights to emphasize that particular groups of female embodied persons were mobilized by and for the purposes of violent class struggle in specific ways.

These figurations of masculinity and femininity composed, in turn, the perceptions and identities of those middle-class women activists who entered the revolutionary domain 'not as reproducers of male activists, but as activists themselves', as Hamilton (2007: 105) remarks of the gendered politics of the Basque movement. Their bodies mattered politically but in very specific ways, and in ways that they could not always successfully perform. As we see in the chapters that follow, middle-class women activists had to occupy discursive stereotypes of glorified motherhood just as they had to perform actual roles as wives and widows, providing nurture and support for middle-class male revolutionaries. Their sexed bodies were in need of regulation and control (Chapter 4) just as their gendered bodies had to be shed or 'declassed' in order to inhabit the space of the revolutionary subject (Chapter 3). On their part, women activists strived for equality and agency. They struggled to inhabit an idealized (male) revolutionary subjectivity, which entailed a transgression of the everyday and the affective, and a denial of sexual difference. They struggled not to be 'othered' on its basis, to escape, in other words, the sheer political presence of their bodies and what they represented. The discussion in the ensuing chapters makes clear the tensions between women's embodiment and the demands of a disembodied political identity that served even more to render them in the political domain as 'matter out of place'.

3

Everyday Life in the Underground

> ... When that smell comes to me, I feel like I'm away. The moment I close my eyes I feel that I've gone there—to another life, a previous birth; it feels like a dream. Now it seems like a 'cinema' to me, which one can re-wind and see. (Personal interview, Supriya, October 2003)[1]

Supriya's recollection of her time spent in hiding in the 'underground' expresses beautifully the cinematic and dream-like quality that Passerini (1992) has detected in the memories of the 1968 Italian students' movements. They reveal, she argues, certain aspects of the terrorist phenomenon, such as the illusion of a free and adventurous life—of an everyday life that is intense and spectacular, on the fringes of the law, or outside it. Such a conception of everyday life is in sharp opposition to the qualities usually associated with the everyday, that of mundane routine, habitualness, and the ordinary or the taken-for-granted (Lefebvre 1971). On the contrary, these memories seemingly fulfil the criteria of a 'heroic life', one that seeks to transcend the everyday for the sake of a higher cause (Featherstone 1992: 160). As noted in Chapter 2, the revolutionary leaves behind the sphere of the everyday and the ordinary, that of women and domesticity in particular (Dawson 1994; and Featherstone 1992), in order to fulfil a historic task in an 'extraordinary' situation. In the political upheaval that characterized the 1960s (and certainly predating it), women, too, left the sphere of the private and the everyday to lead fugitive lives and participate in the highly male culture of the New Left. They led exalted lives of courage and adventure while still performing the everyday labour of care and feminized domesticity. The banal vulnerabilities of daily life constituted the unseen, often unspoken, backgrounds of such a 'heroic life'.

While Chapter 2 discussed the figuring of femininity in tropes of heroic, sacrificial, and even transgressive femininity, here I outline the ways in which revolutionary femininity was performed and lived in the everyday underground life of the movement. By privileging the category of the everyday, this chapter explores the 'seen but unnoticed' (Featherstone 1992: 159) and rarely theorized aspects of political life. The everyday assumes particular relevance in a feminist perspective not simply because it is an overwhelmingly feminized domain where gendered hierarchies are silently reproduced (Felski 1999–2000; and Smith 1988), but also because of its repudiation from the world and work of revolutionary action (and that of militarization and war). The discussion in Chapter 2 noted the exclusion of the feminine and the domestic as 'a constitutive, not a marginal or accidental feature' (Puwar 2004: 15) of military spaces and identities. But it also noted how femininity was simultaneously privileged in party discourse through a culturally resonant (middle-class) repertoire of sacrificial motherhood, disembodied feminine power, and dis/honour. Urban middle-class women activists had to delicately balance the burden of such representations in everyday underground life, which was not always welcoming towards them or sensitive to gender differences. Their reconstructions of political activism and identities at the time of the movement take place within a set of reified ideas around politicized femininity in a predominantly masculine context.

My discussion in this chapter also begins to identify the violence of everyday life and lived, intimate spaces, which was gendered but not always sexualized. This violence was informed by the exceptional political situation of the time but also made possible by the diffuse forms of vulnerability contained in everyday life (that renders the everyday as other than the site of the ordinary, as Das and Kleinman 2000 emphasize). I turn, in the final part of this chapter, to the 'extraordinary' violence of political terror, which is more readily acknowledged than some of the other forms of violence described in this chapter. The manner in which political violence was rationalized and routinized at the time of the movement makes it a part of rather than a disruption of the everyday, as is generally assumed.

'You Make the Tea and I'll Make the Revolution': Gender, Class, and Political Labour

Middle class women were involved in the andolan at a number of levels and in different ways. They were affiliated as friends, family members, wives, and lovers—often encompassed in the inadequate category of 'political sympathisers' (Passerini 1992: 188)—some of whom later became full-time cadres themselves. In a pattern discernible from other radical organizations (Hamilton 2007), young male and female activists were recruited through networks of family and friends. A majority of the women interviewed had a sibling, usually an older brother, who was already involved in Naxal politics. A majority also formed heterosexual relationships once a part of the movement with some having children in its course. The few whose stories of politicization begin before Naxalbari came into 'Marxist–Leninist (ML) politics' through their involvement in student politics (in the leftist student organization, the Student Federation) and early radical formations like the Man, Money, Gun group. Those who joined the CPI(ML) at a later stage moved quickly to splinter groups, if not incarceration, in the face of the party's rapid disintegration. These temporal markers are important as the movement's assumption, from 1970, of an entirely conspiratorial (*gopon* or hidden) character structured, as I go onto show, the nature and scope of middle-class women's participation, in particular.

Women's narratives often express excitement at the new possibilities for political participation that the CPI(ML) offered in its early days. Politicization meant the possibility of doing a '*bhalo*' or even a '*boro kaaj*', something good, something great for the sake of the nation or a once loved, now lost desh (see Chapter 1). But it also meant the ability to establish and articulate an independent identity, traditionally denied to bhadralok women for whom respectability entails the rejection of public let alone political life. In their interviews (as in women's published memoirs; see Bandyopadhyay 2001; and Sanyal 2001), several women drew a relation between their political aspirations and the patriarchal culture at home, suggesting that they saw in the movement, the possibility of a new, liberatory gender order, outside the stranglehold of patriarchal society epitomized by the middle-class family (see also Kannabiran and Lalitha 1989 on women's participation in Telangana). In her essay on Naxalite women, which includes interviews with former activists like her, Kalpana Sen identifies the progressiveness of the Naxalites with respect to gender as a central motivating factor for the women who joined; more women, she says, came into this andolan than any other because they saw in it 'the opportunity to breathe in the air of liberation' (Kalpana Sen 2001: 166). One can speculate that these women also saw the possibility of an alternative lifestyle with like-minded people in the movement, and that the party appeared to them (as with Chinese communist women; see Gilmartin 1995) more as a subculture than as a political institution.

Once in the party (for which no formal membership was required), middle-class women activists, like their male comrades, were organizationally divided into those who did 'technical' jobs and those who did organizational work at a higher political echelon. Female cadres were mostly employed to do 'tech kaaj' such as courier work that included the transportation of papers, arms, and information. Few did organizational work, recruiting individuals to the party, campaigning, and forming squads. Fewer women were on local committees, and none were in senior positions of leadership. To be sure, women did participate in semi-terrorist forms of 'action' such as providing logistical support to large-scale robberies, stealing arms, desecrating public institutions, disrupting classes and examinations, and throwing bombs. As the logic of annihilation deepened and state repression grew, women were also involved in the creation of squads for the murder of 'class enemies', and participated in armed jailbreaks.

Although responses to the question of political activity differ, several women articulate, *contra* Kalpana Sen (2001), a gendered critique of the party and of male ideologues who confined them to subsidiary, supportive roles and marginalized them from key political activity. Interviewees assert that they were 'dumped' with politically subordinate technical jobs, besides having to perform the everyday drudgery work of domesticity.[2] Women activists equally fought for recognition as 'comrade' rather than as *ma*, the predominant Bengali form of address towards all women, irrespective of age or status, and one that the Bengali Left has propagated (Kumari and Kidwai 1998; and Ray 1999). Political activity was thereby 'recast' as a familial one, as Sarkar (1991: 217) notes of Left Front government in West Bengal, even as political life was conceived as a radical break and distancing from conventional family life. The possibility of politicizing family life, including sexuality, motherhood, and childrearing, was minimal given their construal as private, non-political concerns. The inability to articulate 'women's issues' constituted, for Gopa who left her family including a small child for the village in 1968, an important measure of the extent to which the party was gender blind. Recalling the private sense of injustice that Rukmini spoke of (in Chapter 1), Gopa says that there was no public discussion on women's issues so much so that women rarely spoke to other women given that they did not want to be perceived as being 'different' (Personal interview, June 2003). Puwar argues that women tend to repress gender differences in organizations that deny 'the gendered nature of the "individual" upon which it is modelled' (Puwar 2004: 133). The need to do so is all the more pressing in the field of politics where the normative political subject is a disembodied one, and where women are politically marginalized in being reduced to their bodies. Even when women manage to enter the political domain, they are meant to perform stereotypical gendered—and classed—scripts.

Rukmini draws attention to these dynamics when she notes that the 'dominant thinking' within the party was that women could not carry out *songothon* kaaj (organizational work):

> ... I remember having great fights especially with one chap who was there; I used to have fights with him always. There was a very condescending attitude he particularly had, and by him I don't want to generalize but he also reflected a dominant position in the party and in the organization, [a] very condescending attitude towards women, and that too don't forget, I came from a very bourgeois background ... there was less of a condescending attitude towards the men ... It was very ironical. I tell my friends, nobody took me seriously until I got arrested! (Personal interview, Rukmini, October 2003)[3]

Rukmini became embroiled in radical Left politics through friends (including her first husband) whilst at university in Kolkata while Bulbul, another upper middle-class woman, was involved in the andolan together with her brother. He found ready acceptance in the party while Bulbul remained 'extremely isolated' right from the beginning because, she says, of her upper middle-class status and of the way she looked ('Westernized'). Given that the movement as a whole had a strongly lower middle-class character, she found very little acceptance among the women as well. Bulbul's *tek naam* (technical name or activist pseudonym) was 'memshahib' reminiscent of the nineteenth century stereotype of the *mem* who was the butt of much popular satire and farce (Chatterjee 1989; and Sarkar 2001). When Rukmini says that she was only taken 'seriously' once she was arrested (an experience that is recounted in Chapter 6), she draws attention to a public memory that commemorates women only as victims of state repression, emphasizing heroic if not sacrificial femininity, and erasing, in turn, all other modes of subjectivity. Imprisonment (and torture) was central to female agency given that women had, at their disposal, fewer modes of political subjectivity than men.

Recognition in the political sphere was also governed by women's marital status. As wives or even widows of prominent male Naxalites, women were afforded positions of privilege in the movement but these came with certain costs. At least three of the married women of the sample spoke of their struggle to conduct political work in the face of their 'political' husband's lack of support or open hostility. Lata, whose story I detail in what follows, was particularly vocal with her partner that she had come into Naxal politics 'to fight not to cook for [him]' and that she was 'doing organizational work here not in terms of [his] wife or as a girl'(Personal interview, July 2003). In her memoir, Krishna Bandyopadhyay (2001: 94) draws attention to the politics of recognition afforded to women as widows of male martyrs. Like Rukmini, Krishna too found her way into the movement through friends along with her then partner, Dronacharya Ghosh or Dron, who was killed in a clash with jail security forces in 1972. She writes: 'At that time my work was to inspire other comrades as the widow of a martyr. Dron's death seemed to bring me a different kind of "respect" within the Party. And it created an imposition on me to maintain him as the only adored man in my life. Nobody could accept my second relationship' (Bandyopadhyay 2001: 94).

As Ramphele (1997) shows in the context of South Africa, the widow's body becomes a metaphor of suffering and sacrifice. Bandyopadhyay's second relationship was not recognized because of the narrative of the widow's sacrifice, the ultimate familial sacrifice in the cause of the revolution. Like her, other women found it hard to win 'approval' for future relationships. The irony is that within the radical redefinition of marriage in the movement that I discuss in the next chapter, the labels of 'wife' and 'widow' were largely rendered redundant. Yet, women were made to perform symbolic (and actual) roles that served to restore middle-class codes and expectations of womanhood in 'unconventional, non-traditional feminine activity' (Sarkar 1991: 217). Women activists resisted their reification in this manner but resistance could also take the form of denying the gendered self altogether, evident in Lata's statement given earlier and in Gopa's before her.

While femininity tends to be normative even in the revolutionary domain, courier work—the predominant form of political labour that women perform in 'terrorist' organizations (Cunningham 2003)—mobilizes such a normative feminine identity as a political resource. Naxalite women deliberately carried their children with them while transporting arms or to infiltrate police-patrolled areas. The female body was a particularly useful tool for beguiling the police. Lata provides one such scenario:

> We heard 'halt halt' from the back. There was a lorry full of CRP [Central Reserve Police] men with guns yelling 'halt' from behind. I got off [the rickshaw] and ran into that house (my daughter had been there earlier). I opened my hair, wore *sindoor*, in a few seconds. The incident was in the morning. I went downstairs and started to wash dishes. The police came ... They went up to the roof to search. One policeman even came and spoke to me [laughs]. Then they left ... Why would they pick on me amongst the other *bau*? If I was wearing a sari and sitting on the bed then they might have asked who's this? (Personal interview, July 2003)

In Lata's case, the femininity that she performs is not only domesticated but also classed in particular ways. She roots the success of her hoodwink in a domesticated, 'lower' middle-class femininity that materializes in hard work as opposed to idle leisure, a luxury that elite women have traditionally enjoyed. Here, as before, we see that the femininity that bhadralok women were expected to perform within the political domain was of a specific kind. It forms a continuum with the idealized bhadramahila described in Chapter 2 as different from the elite and/or Westernized woman who was the locus of significant social anxieties in nineteenth century Bengal (see Sarkar 2001). For upper middle-class women like Rukmini and Bulbul (referred to earlier), 'declassing' would have had to take place in terms of these specific registers of gendering.

In 'subversive performances' (Butler 1990) of courier work, women parodied those icons of middle-class femininity (and motherhood) that the movement itself propagated. The use of gender and class by women does not, however, have the same pay-offs as it does for men, as Skeggs (2004) has shown in a different context. Middle-class male activists could freely employ class (and gender) characteristics in the political ritual of 'becoming declassed' without becoming symbolically fixed or read as subaltern. As wives, widows, couriers, and organizers, middle-class women embodied, on the other hand, fixed points of identification that could not be 'used' as a political resource (Skeggs 2004). In what follows, we see how the intersection of sexual difference with class contributed to their marginalization from crucial revolutionary tasks.

Going Underground

With Charu Mazumdar's call to go to the villages, the city lost its privileged position. '*Gram, gram aar gram*', writes male activist, Raghab Bandyopadhyay (2000: 17), in his *Journal Shottor* (*Journal Seventies*); Kolkata becomes a 'myth' or exists simply as 'a thought'. The middle-class activist is filled with anticipation and desire for the gram he has never seen, whose 'tradition, behaviour, dream, nightmares [he] knows nothing of' (Bandyopadhyay 2000: 17). This was the phase of guerrilla warfare in the countryside, of clandestine activity in the formation of a 'guerrilla unit', of living and becoming 'one' with the peasants. The party had gone underground. From early 1970 (given also the severity of the state response), an 'underground' existence became mandatory forcing activists into a series of displacements.

Like their male counterparts, women activists from Kolkata and the mofussil left the sphere of the habitual and the ordinary as a first step into radical politics. Apart from a small number of anti-colonial 'terrorist' women,[4] this was the first time that young, married and unmarried, middle-class women entirely left the confines of the domestic sphere and the regulatory control of the family to freely move across the rural and urban landscape. The significance of this step—often viewed as a measure of the party's progressive nature—should not be underestimated given that the option of leaving one's parental home existed for very few middle-class unmarried Bengali women at the time (and even today). Once in hiding, which entailed a complete break with natal and conjugal homes and even, for some, the leaving behind of small children, women assumed alternative identities and led new lives. Resonating the experiences of female Red Guards in China (see Honig and Hershatter 1988), these years spent 'underground' away from home irrevocably changed, as most women strongly emphasize, their lives and sense of themselves.

Mobility and freedom were not unproblematic for urban middle-class women. Kalpana Sen emphasizes how the transformation of the party from an open to a hidden one focused solely on gram *biplab* had certain gendered consequences:

> As long as the *Naxalponthi andolan* was open and legal and had a character of its own in the urban context, women did not face many problems. When the Party decided that the city would be captured from the village, and that the village had to be made a base, the village

> had to be freed, and this was the sole reason for forming guerilla outfits, it was at this point that women fell behind men. If it was difficult for men to find a shelter from which to organise, then for women, it was an insurmountable barrier. (Sen 2001: 162)

The party was seemingly not very keen on women's participation in the political campaign in the countryside. Charu Mazumdar himself wrote that squads should not be made up only of women 'because women need a place to stay at least for the night' (Mazumdar 2001: 101). Some of the men (and women) I interviewed evoked biological differences between the sexes to explain women's marginalization from the gram. Questions of security, appearance, and even the lack of toilet facilities to fulfil women's 'natural' needs were the problems they cited. While these explanations are ostensibly about gender with the sexed body construed as a liability for genuine political participation, they are also about class. According to Sinha Roy (2011: 121), 'going underground' was more informal for peasant women who did not have to leave homes and localities. We also know from discussions in previous chapters that leftist and radical imagination has been more comfortable with expressions of agency from peasant and tribal women. It is this significant intersection of gender and class that not only legitimizes women's exclusion from the political domain but also marks the latter as masculine. The evocation of sexual difference in these explanations is also reminiscent of Scott's definition of gender as signifying power relations; as legitimizing and constructing social relations 'that may include sex, but is not directly determined by sex or directly determining of sexuality' (Scott 1986: 1057).

Bhadralok women's marginalization from the rural domain needs to be situated within a larger ambiguity that structured their entry into the party. Some went so far as to suggest that the party made no explicit effort to recruit women, and was less than enthusiastic about accepting women 'full-timers' who had left home: 'It's natural for men to join but there was no realization amongst the leaders that extra effort is required to bring in women. Also, even when women did come out, there was little "full acceptability" from the party' (Personal interview, Ajita, August 2003). From 1972, the party, it seems, began to actively discourage women from leaving home since they could not be 'accommodated' in the face of severe state repression. The lack of shelters, thanks to massive police raids, was a large part of the explanation. Women like Supriya who had gone through an arduous process of soul-searching before making the decision to enter radical Left politics were suddenly told that there was no space for them in the underground. Others were asked to go back to their natal homes when state repression accelerated. The absurdity of this position lies in the party's limited understanding of the reality of middle-class women's lives, which were invariably caught between irresolvable familial tensions and the individual desire for sociopolitical change. They could hardly leave and return to their families at will.[5]

The limitations posed on middle-class women's mobility within the political domain are also significant for what they tell us about the organization of space within the movement. Political space was divided into zones of safety and zones of danger. Women were excluded from certain spaces on grounds of 'security' attributable, no doubt, to the perceived sexual vulnerability of the female body. As potential victims of a 'rapist state', the party could draw women within its protective, paternalistic care, which manifested itself in a gendered division of political space and in restrictions placed on women's mobility. It also manifested in, as I show in what follows and in Chapter 5, the inability to perceive the possibility of violence in safe spaces and outside limited categories of 'victims' and 'aggressors'.

Everyday Violence in the Underground

Everyday life in the underground, whether in rural or urban areas, is memorialized as being outside the realm of normalcy, as being 'another life'. It constituted a space where conventional norms were broken or turned upside down. Thus, hunger was cultivated and food, or rather the lack of it, became key to a daily ritual of political initiation. The body (clothes, posture, speech) as the custodian of madhyabitta values had to be continually 'declassed' through daily gestures like the relinquishing of soap or a wristwatch. Indeed, life as a political outlaw with its attendant risks and thrills transformed the everyday into the 'extraordinary'. Women like Gopa, Malini, and Krishna Bandyopadhyay who joined the movement from the start, through student politics, spoke of the 'songothon kaaj' they undertook in Purulia district in West Bengal and in adivasi areas in neighbouring Bihar. For the vast majority of women who were not part of the rural struggle, 'integration' with the working classes in urban industrial belts in the outskirts of the metropolises and in districts elsewhere provided an opportunity for political presence.

In Rukmini's memory of being 'underground' as a factory worker, it is her relationship with other women workers that is foregrounded:

> I was working in a *bustee* for a few months ... I was working in a leather factory, you know, they produce those Shantineketan bags. That was a hilarious experience I had, but it was very nice, very nice ... I said I had run away from Assam because there were problems for Bengalis and all that; tried to 'declassify' myself by wearing a simple sari, no make-up, but still, you stand out like a sore thumb! Our middle-class upbringing, our posture everything shows, however much you 'declass' ... They used to call me Aparna with a lot of respect—I was the Aparna*di* of that factory. I would earn forty-five rupees a month for working from morning to night ... I was very close to them ... on a personal level ... then I realized that you don't have to just talk to them about ML politics, politics is something beyond the party, about so many things, about change, about progress ... To them it was a different world opening up ... so we had developed a very good rapport. (Personal interview, Rukmini, October 2003)

'Becoming declassed' demands, in this instance, specific modes of regendering such as the absence of make-up and the wearing of a simple sari. Whilst shedding these markers of bhadramahila identity, Rukmini emphasizes the inscription of class on gendered bodily deportment (what Bourdieu calls 'hexis') such that class can still be read off the body, 'however much you "declass"'. She emphasizes the affective ties that were engendered in declassing, between herself and the women workers, in ways that extended definitions of the political. The exceptionality of underground life made manifest, at least for the middle-class activist, the everydayness of working-class women's lives, which was not an explicit area of politicization for the party.

But if the underground was composed through bonds of camaraderie and friendship that crossed conventional class boundaries (as in the case of prison, explored in Chapter 6), it was also constituted in the shadow of violence or what Jeganathan (2002), in the context of the Sri Lankan ethnic conflict, calls the anticipation of violence to come. The 'underground', Raghab Bandyopadhyay (2000: 35) writes, was a 'nowhere' or an 'invisible world' within which a 'fairytale about death' had been created. This collective fantasy broke only at the time of arrest when a different 'no where' engulfed the revolutionaries (A. Das 2001: 70). For women, everyday life in the underground was impregnated with the potential for violence from multiple sources and not solely from the state.

The forms of gendered vulnerability (and sexual violence that I consider in Chapter 5) that they faced suggest how hard it was, at least for women, to transcend the cruel banalities of the everyday as per the demands of revolutionary identity.

Take, for instance, Lata who came into the movement from Behala in eastern Kolkata, and whose 'movement story' begins much earlier with student politics in that area followed by a stint with the Man, Money, Gun (MMG) group and seven months incarceration. Lata and her siblings, who also joined the CPI(ML), come from a long, familial history of left-wing politics. Whilst underground, Lata worked in a factory at Dum Dum in north Kolkata from seven in the morning to seven at night for two rupees a day. For her, it was a good opportunity to meet the workers and to create a squad. Lata would leave her daughter, still a child (she was arrested while eight months pregnant), at a political shelter in south Kolkata where she stayed. Invariably, she would come home to find that her child had been unfed almost all day. So she began to buy a quarter piece of bread, which she would mix with some water and feed the child, reserving the burnt part for herself. Party comrades accused her of prioritizing her daughter (a complaint she had to repeatedly hear) and of suspecting them of not feeding her. Lata was subsequently able to fix up another shelter where she could leave her daughter and visit her occasionally. When I asked how she could have possibly left her only child with strangers, she replied, 'my work is bigger' (Personal interview, Lata, August 2003). She was eventually fired from the factory job given that she had resisted the manager's advances. Seven women workers had already been impregnated there.

The multi-sided character of violence is obvious from Lata's experience as a factory worker, a political activist, *and* a mother. Her narrative moves incessantly from one shelter to another, from middle-class families who almost threw her out to the homes of local anti-socials who threatened her. Lata's husband was in prison for most of this period. By the time he was released, they had already separated. What perhaps constitutes the leitmotif of Lata's story is her estrangement from her natal home and her in-laws. Much of her movement story can be read as an attempt to acquire for herself and her child a modicum of security in the face of the complete failure of her kinship network to do so. However politicized, the lower middle-class family had very little sympathy or resources to offer to a daughter who had been abandoned by her husband and her in-laws, the true custodians of her person.

Together with the family, the experience of betrayal at the hands of the party assumes a predominant role in her story. Begetting a child was a crime, Lata told me, since the movement was not supposed to be a place to set up a household. While, as I show in the Chapter 4, romantic liaisons and marital practices flourished in the course of the movement, the consequences of conjugality such as the begetting of children were largely ignored. Women like Lata who married for the sake of political expediency and ended up having children received no support from the party.[6] On the contrary, male party ideologues continuously proclaimed her maternal feelings to be 'counter-revolutionary'. The insensitivity of male party members with respect to motherhood was mentioned by other women, including an incident wherein a new nursing mother was branded as being 'lazy, selfish and madhyabitta' by male comrades (Personal interview, Gopa, June 2003). What Gopa today names 'exploitation by another comrade' was, at the time, trivialized as a personal problem that lay, as with women's bodies as a whole, outside of the political realm. The normative utility of motherhood in party discourse (explored in Chapter 2) did not extend to 'real' mothers of 'flesh and blood'. On the contrary, and as noted of other Left-led movements (Kannabiran and Lalitha 1989), the transcendence of motherhood in the sacrifice of a child is considered the ultimate sacrifice for the patriotic cause (see also Sunder Rajan 1999). Histories glorifying Naxalbari are replete with images of women who left their children or even lost them to the revolution as exemplary of truly heroic femininity (for example, Kalpana Sen 2001).[7]

Interestingly, it is the discourse of heroic femininity that subordinates motherhood to the goals of the revolution that governs Lata's self-perception. In saying that 'my work is bigger', Lata makes it clear that she, like militant women elsewhere (see De Mel 2001), has rejected the conventional world of maternal identities and embraced a language of militancy that takes precedence over all 'natural', 'maternal', or 'familial' ties. In negotiating perhaps what is the most contentious part of her past, motherhood, Lata 'composes' the self through a transgressive, sacrificial femininity that was made available by the movement's discursive repertoire. While she voices her sense of betrayal towards the party, she does not question a model of political identity that demands the transgression of the individual and the everyday in (maternal) sacrifice. Lata's 'taking-up' of such cultural constructions of heroic, sacrificial femininity introduces, however, an element of choice into her narrative. It transforms her decision to leave her child into an agential act, and not one that was predetermined by her very limited survival options as a single mother who was also a political outlaw.

Interpersonal Violence in the Shelter

Pivotal to the memory of the underground is the place occupied by the political shelter. While in the city or the gram, activists were 'sheltered' by peasants, labourers, or by middle-class households who were either sympathizers or families of political activists themselves. Outside the masculinized 'battle zone', the shelter was conceived of as a place of sanctuary, trust, and renewal, often guarded by older female members of the household. The politicization of the domestic space or the bari was effected through its use as a political shelter, which recreated, in turn, the character of the movement within the ties of family, kinship, and locality. The bari was transformed into a commune that hosted anything between ten to twelve men a day, and is often described through the metaphor of the family. Bandyopadhyay (2000) speaks of the commune as a 'communist family', and one that increased the prestige of the lower middle-class household in the locality, and by extension, the status of its members. This was particularly true of women, especially mothers, who became objects of affection and respect beyond the bounds of the immediate family. Male narratives speak of the risks that mothers, aunts, and grandmothers of the household bore unflinchingly, and the quality of their sacrifice. The shelter together with the family (and even the para; see Donner 2011) and the party were thus 'separate but highly dependent, spheres of activity', as Hamilton (2007: 99) notes of the family in the radical Basque nationalist movement.

Notwithstanding this interdependency, the shelter was configured as a space of refuge from the battle waging 'outside', a familial space associated with safety, domesticity, and feminine nurture. It was this metaphor of the family that constituted the shelter as a private 'non-political' space, protected from encroachments from the outside world. The shelter thus emerged as a zone of safety, especially for middle-class women whose very entry into the political domain often hinged, as previously seen, on the availability of shelters. At the same time, however, the bari was politicized in its transformation into a shelter, especially as the 'urban battle' seeped more and more into the households of ordinary residents. Against its association with safety and security, in women's narratives, by contrast, it is this space that emerges in its dailiness as a site of vulnerability and terror (see also Chapter 5).

As with Lata, everyday life in the underground is punctuated in Supriya's case with endless calamities and a coming to terms with the potential violence contained in them. From a lower middle-class family in Bardhaman, Supriya felt propelled to join the andolan on her older brother's arrest and torture, ambivalent of its politics until that point. In her memoir (Sanyal 2001), the state recedes as the sole source of violence even though Supriya joined at a time when its presence was most felt (at the end of 1972). There is the concomitant fear of bodily harm by local goons and moneylenders, resentment by women workers, hostility by female members of political shelters, and the everyday drudgery of voluntary poverty and uprootedness. Sexual violence structures, as I detail in Chapter 5, almost the entirety of her experience in political shelters.

Supriya contrasts her experience of being sheltered in middle-class homes with working-class families. While she was treated with respect and affection in the latter, there were times when she was simply abandoned by her 'sister–workers' in the face of threatening goons and moneylenders. On at least two separate occasions, she was left stranded in the middle of the night in areas well known for assaults and robberies. In middle-class homes, in contrast, the women of the household treated her as a free, full-time domestic servant. At other times, she was accused of having an affair with the patriarch of the house. In one particular middle-class family, such a situation took an extreme turn when the wife actually threw her out in the early hours of the morning. Female hostility towards Naxalite women is common to other stories of underground life. Another interviewee recalled with laughter how a woman threw her out of the house by her hair for trying to politicize her elder brother: 'They [the family] thought that if the *dada* goes [to the movement] then they would starve to death. It was a middle-class family ...' (Personal interview, Roma, August 2003). Fear of losing the sole breadwinner of the family was a common cause for such violent outbursts. These women seemed to underscore, in this manner, their resistance to a 'class struggle' that was grounded in their abandonment.[8]

Relations between women, especially between the woman activist and the women of the household, assume significance in other ways. In the last shelter that Supriya writes of, the mother of the household sets down certain conditions for her, and not the two other male activists, to follow in order to continue living there:

> 'First, she [Supriya] cannot leave for anywhere on the spur of the moment. If she has a programme or wishes to stay away even for a night she has to inform me beforehand. Second she has to enroll herself in a college, although I have come to know that she studied science once, I don't think it's feasible anymore. She has to study Humanities ....' I don't remember what else *mashima* [aunty] said except for these that left a deep impact on my mind. Her monologue disturbed me greatly. One year has passed and now the issue of respecting the discipline of the household is raised? Am I still an under-age girl? (Sanyal 2001: 30)

At this juncture when the movement was fast disintegrating, the 'political shelter' is reinstated as the household, and women are meant to resume their former roles as daughters and wives that politicization had only temporarily disrupted. While, for male activists, the shelter was a refuge from 'outside' terror in which they enjoyed the nurturance of women, for women, it invariably functioned as a domestic space that enforced regulatory control through the authority of the family. Their security, in turn, hinged upon a submission to the middle-class values of normative femininity.

While Supriya's narrative bears testimony to the forms of interpersonal aggression that women were vulnerable to within the shelter, it also idealizes this space. In the account of her time spent in two colliery bustees, Supriya denies the harsh aspects of underground life and posits a degree of heroic stoicism with respect to the everyday:

> ... I visited Kalipahari [colliery] for the second time. It was the summer of 1973. An extended family offered me shelter ... I lived there in a room which was supposed to be haunted. Thus no stranger ever approached it. There was a tattered mattress and bric-a-brac strewn all over ... In order that he [the moneylender] has no inkling of my presence I was forbidden to move around while living in that room ... While living there, I never once saw daylight, never stopped outside the house even for my basic needs. I would suffocate in the room. At times, one of the wives would enter with a tray of food ... Under the patriarch's strict supervision the women of the family would draw water from the well for my bath. I would bathe at night under their watchful eyes. I had long hair and would spread it, fan like, on the pillow to dry. Rats would tug at my hair at night. I was always terrified of roaches and rats but I had no option. *The entire family took such wonderful care of me that I never felt the least discomfort.* (Sanyal 2001: 25; emphasis added)

Supriya's written text confirms to a discourse that frames other movement stories as well—one that mythicizes the underground and idealizes the shelter. It is, not surprisingly, the working-class household that is the repository of idealized values. Her experience, here recounted, is also testament to her successful 'integration' into the subaltern world and transformation into a Naxalite. The positive affect produced by this narrative negates its many troubling dimensions which echo in other women's narratives: the restrictions placed on women's mobility and, as previously noted by Supriya herself, the complete surrender of autonomy and independence to members of the shelter; the traumas of voluntary poverty; and the transference of the burden of care to the poor and vulnerable (critically mentioned by other interviewees; see Bandyopadhyay 2001). These everyday traumas of 'becoming one' with the subaltern are countered with revolutionary resilience and stoicism in ways that resonate with Lata's evocation of a heroic femininity to counter the vulnerabilities of single motherhood.

Idealization of this sort is not exclusive to those who were sheltered. Kalpana Sen, whose published article I have previously referred to, became embroiled in the movement together with six of her eight siblings. Her main function was that of a courier. But it is the transformation of her own lower middle-class bari in Kolkata through its use as a shelter that dominates her memory of the movement:

> My house had a certain picture. My *baba* was an engineer, *dada* was studying and so on ... but suddenly the house became different. We didn't eat at home but food was cooked for ten–twelve people a day. At the end, *ma* started to sell things to support so many people eating in the house. One kettle was always on the stove. [You didn't have a problem with this?] No, I liked it very much because ... I would tell *ma* that this has to be done. *Ma* had understood as well ... *ma* was very happy. There's a long history of my house. (Personal interview, Kalpana, October 2003)

'Ma' in Kalpana's narrative continues the long tradition of mothers who fought unwilling husbands to shelter fugitive revolutionaries at the risk of their own safety and at the cost of the household. These women epitomize the sacrifice of the entire household and the community for the sake of a higher, worthier cause. Romanticization of this sort lends to a forgetting of the darker aspects of this history, such as the draining of the family's resources, the threat that male comrades often posed to younger female members of the household, and the infinite police raids that havocked the bari, leaving it desolate and its women members eventually alone (see Bandyopadhyay 2000). In an interview of her mother, Rajlakhi Debi, published in an article by Kalpana Sen (2001), the former says how she sold utensils and jewellery to provide for the six to ten people who would take shelter in her home everyday. Eventually, the house was raided, and two of her younger children were arrested. Her husband who was not directly involved in the movement was arrested, tortured, and died soon after. At the end of the interview, Rajlakhi Debi says that she feels proud that her husband died a martyr. Here, the language of the movement, particularly that of a self-sacrificial and patriotic motherhood, works in powerful ways to conceal past trauma, especially the violent loss of a loved one.

The (Im)Morality of *Khatam*

While the 'little' violences of underground life described thus far have rarely been acknowledged, political violence is readily so even as its meaning might be disputed. Amongst the community of middle-class activists here interviewed, there is a basic recognition that what took place in their collective past was, indeed, violence. It was not 'misguided idealism' or 'infantile adventurism' as labelled by the mainstream media, or as in the movement's general history, symptomatic of New Left excess or of the misgivings of an inexperienced leadership. Very few studies (like Ray 1998) have taken seriously the fetishization of Naxalite terror. In the movement's afterlife, violence has become moot to critical mappings of contemporary Maoist politics giving rise to renewed discussions on the efficacy of non/violence, and the tension between, Banjeree (2009) writes (in his reflections on Naxalite violence) 'the moral basis of revolutionary ideology and the practical compulsions of revolutionary action'.

In this final section, I consider the relationship that the women interviewed have with this more contentious part of their collective past. To a majority, the violence of the 1970s is no longer ethically defensible while to a small minority, it is politically incoherent, a 'strategic error' if you want. Underlying these narratives is the larger question of what makes violence just. Is it the end, or the means, or the motivations; the cause or the character of violence? Chatterjee (2001: 18–19) speaks of two strategies that have been employed to bring reason and order to the facts of violence in 'modern political life': an ethics of violence; and an economy of violence. Both strategies were employed in party rhetoric at the time of the movement, as indicated in Chapter 2. The exercise of violence was justified through the evoking of universal categories ('justice'), and for the sake of a transcendent cause ('revolution') located in a fictitious world-beyond (a 'red society'). It was also placed outside the domain of ethics, within a carefully deployed economy of forces and effects where it was measured against the violence of the state. Within such an economy, revolutionary violence was a defensible act to counter the state's monopoly of violence.

In at least some of the narratives considered here, women question the party's impetus to bestow rationality and moral purpose on political violence. In so doing, they refuse to accept the parameters of either ethics or economy in talking about Naxalite violence. The latter was certainly the predominant mode in which violence was legitimized at the time of the movement. Khatam, for Mary Tyler, for instance, amounts simply to a misguided political strategy. I quote from an interview of her's published in 1973:

> ... Killing landlords and other class enemies is not immoral ... yes the cult of individual terrorism adopted by some of the Naxalites was a mistake—comrade Lenin has said that only at a certain decisive phase of the revolution can individual terrorism prove a turning point; otherwise we have got to gain the sympathy of the masses. (cited in Naqvi 1973)

Tyler draws a sharp distinction between violence as a locus of ethics and morality and violence as subordinated to a political end, as a means that requires judicial application and execution. Her speech employs the rhetorical strategies of the radical Left to present a consciously instrumental rationality from which questions of ethics are entirely absent. To this extent, she remains rooted in a political culture in which the use of violence was not only natural but also necessary. For Arendt (1990), the hallmark of all successful revolutions in the twentieth century has been this coupling of necessity and violence. What Tyler questions is not the necessity of violence but its strategic deployment within an economy of violence: when can individual terrorism be deployed, how much, and to what end. It is important to note that this extract is from an interview with Mary Tyler published in 1973 when state repression was at its peak with most activists already behind bars. One wonders if her response would be the same today or would it align more with the feelings of ambiguity expressed by some of the other women. For several (but not all) of them, violence was not so easily reducible to the 'grid of an economy' (Chatterjee 2001: 19). It was located, instead, in everyday life and in the constitution of subjectivity.

As in the case of militant student politics elsewhere, activists initially embraced violence as part of revolutionary culture, driven by intense loyalties to the political community outside of which the individual had practically no existence (Passerini 1992; and Varon 2004). As the annihilation campaign gained force, the choice to engage with political murder posed no real choice at all; it became, as Varon notes of Germany's Red Army Faction, 'an act of political and existential necessity' (Varon 2004: 204). Revolutionary commitment was measured by a willingness to take up arms, and violence became a metonym of revolutionary identity itself. As one member of the former Weather Underground put it, 'we were revolutionary; you had to do it' (cited in Varon 2004: 79). And as one of the women interviewed for this book said: 'If you don't dip your hands in blood, you won't be a communist', evoking Charu Mazumdar's notorious proclamation that 'he who has not dipped his hands in blood can hardly be called a communist'. Revolutionary culture allowed little room for reflection, as did the war-like conditions under which everyday life was lived out. There was no time to think, I was told more than once, as a war was on. But the individual guerrilla, as Rukmini's discussion of khatam suggests, was often torn by contradictory impulses that even the 'cause' could not always justify. As detailed in Chapter 6, she was involved in the armed 'Alipur jailbreak' to free Naxalite prisoners, including her then partner.

> At that time we thought that was the correct thing, *na*. At that time, you felt a kind of discomfort—why traffic policemen? Then we would think that they also have guns, they will use these guns to form their army ... self-justification, there's no end to it. When you want to believe in something you keep drawing lines out of it and trying to justify it. It's only later you realize that you have this discomfort and you start putting everything together but at that junction, its just there at some corner of your mind, you know, traffic policemen, what does he have do with it? Or you know, er, principal of a college, why should he be bumped off, even if he believed in some bourgeois politics? Then we'll have kill off 50% of the world. But you're not putting it together, not arguing because you're handicapped by your understanding. (Personal interview, Rukmini, October 2003)

Beneath the instrumental rationality of the collective, a quiet meditation on the ethics of violence takes place, 'at some corner of your mind'. The experience of violence occurs precisely at this level of individual conflict, where one begins to question the legitimacy of a 'line', and the ethics of political violence itself, of who should be hurt and to what end. This is where the possibility of self-justification, Rukmini says, runs dry. The self becomes fractured in its engagement with violence, unable to justify its need and yet committed to its execution.

> You shut yourself and think this is what is expected, this is a right thing, and yet I saw how shaken my friends were, and for days they could not sleep. And today looking back, it only made them more human. They were not hardened criminals. Whatever bravado they showed or spoke of, 'look ... got a revolver'; 'my god can't sleep at night, I still remember that face, that man screaming, shouting ...' Parrallely [*sic*] this kind of talk would continue ... And yet they thought they were doing a right thing because the Party's rule ... liberation by 1975, so you need arms for the army, so you're inspired and you think you're doing something very glorious. (Personal interview, Rukmini, October 2003)

The revolutionaries that Rukmini's memory privileges were hardly the cold calculating combatants that they were meant to be. At one level, these were young men who were being initiated into manhood through the use of political violence. They tried to reconcile what their newly acquired masculine identity demanded of them with individual aspirations for grandeur but also with deeper ethical conflicts. Such private torments speak of a discontinuity that lies at the heart of New Left radicalism, as pointed out by Arendt (1990) amongst others (De Beauvoir 1976; and Passerini 1992), between its ethical inspiration and its darker side, the public glorification of violence and death.9 Activists could not always reconcile their contradictory selves, fractured and at war with one another, in the face of violence. Personal memories of Naxalbari continue to be torn by these private moments of regret and guilt. Forgetting is sometimes the only aid. In a published interview, Krishna Roy, who was expelled from the party for criticizing the 'line', speaks not of the triumphalism of political violence but of its pain:

> The memory of clandestine party life does not attract me now. My daughter often asks me to tell stories of that time. But I get stuck in speaking. There is nothing to tell except being chased by the police, death, self-sacrifice ... I want to forget that I was ever a believer of a

> political line that advocated the murder of human beings. (cited in Sen 2001: 172)

Other women share Rukmini and Krishna's retroactive rejection of the use of political violence. Women's current political identities and commitments shape memory to a large extent here. Those active in women's groups tend to adopt a socialist feminist language of rights and needs that is far removed from a politics that stems from the 'barrel of a gun', and, though not stated, the obvious excesses of far left violence today. Yet women, even feminist women, continue to be sympathetic and committed to the need for armed struggle. A long-standing member of an autonomous left-leaning women's group in Kolkata, Maya drew on established leftist idioms of revolutionary heroism and self-sacrifice to validate the need for violence. Her conversation with me strove to explain all forms of violence committed by the party as a response to the injustices of the state. Violence was also justified due to structural reasons like poverty. Finally, it was vindicated on the basis of personal loss and injury, especially the police torture that both she and her husband suffered that I detail in Chapter 6. A feminist critique of revolutionary violence is here subsumed to the power of radical Left discourse perhaps given the inability of the former to bring meaning to personal injury and trauma. At the same time, Maya voices another key contemporary feminist position which has particular resonance in Kolkata's leftist political field; one that does not posit the ideals and values of feminism as incongruent with those of the radical Left, even on the issue of violence.

I began this chapter by noting the gendered division of political labour and the gendering of political space within the movement that alert us to the politics of urban middle-class women's marginalization from core revolutionary activities and spaces. These are equally revealing of the ways in which gender functioned in the political domain to legitimize particular power relations pertaining not only to patriarchy but also to class. The specific nature of the movement, including its hidden, familial, and classed character, determined the possibility and quality of middle-class women's participation. It served to marginalize them from crucial revolutionary tasks (such as the rural campaign) just as it naturalized the association of political labour with middle-class masculinity. While the female body was discursively constructed as a 'problem' that must be overcome for political participation, women used the body and their femininity for the sake of political expediency (in courier work). Women's performance of political labour—their ways of 'becoming one' with the peasants—involved specific transformations to the gendered and classed self, narrated through tropes of sacrifice and stoicism. Yet, their efforts to shed their bhadramahila skins and occupy the space of the unmarked (male) revolutionary subject were invariably thwarted.

The work that sacrifice performs not only in the constitution of revolutionary identity (as described in Chapter 2) but also in the extension of such an identity to 'actual' persons is particularly salient in this chapter's discussion. The widow's sacrifice as with the mother's sacrifice embodies the ultimate familial sacrifice in the name of revolution. Such roles were worshipped in abstraction, in deliberate transgression of their materialization in the real bodies of women activists who resisted such images or produced alternative ones (in the widow's sexual desire, for instance). The worshipping of motherhood, in particular, seems to have rested on the transgression of 'real' mothers who were objects of disapproval and distancing in the movement's everyday life. The fact that it is this discourse that women (like Lata) chose to draw on in retelling the past suggests the degree to which tensions between heroic, disembodied femininity and the consequences of women's embodiment have not been resolved, even today.

Women's memories of underground life privilege those invisible, seemingly banal forms of gendered violence and vulnerability that structured their experience of certain 'safe' zones such as the political shelter. Their narration of everyday underground life overturns normative conceptions of these spaces as 'safe' and as free from terror. These memories are not easy to revisit. I have noted a relative domestication of the 'little' violences of everyday life in personal narratives that evoke repertoires of heroism and (maternal) self-sacrifice. Violence seems to be abjected from the collective mythicization of the underground and the shelter as a repository of freedom and adventure, key features of a heroic life that seeks to transgress the everyday and the ordinary. While 'extraordinary' political violence is more readily remembered and acknowledged, it is located, in some women's narratives, in everyday life-worlds as the site of self-creation. Women's membership to feminist cultures might explain their questioning of the usual taxonomies with respect to political violence but within limits, as I have shown. I return to several of the major themes outlined in this discussion in Chapter 5. Before doing so, I turn to narratives of love, marriage, and sexuality to continue to probe cultural and individual constructions of revolutionary masculinity, heroic femininity, and revolutionary but respectable everyday life.

4

Bhalobasha, Biye, Biplab

On the Politics of Sexual Stories

When in love
Do not become a flower
If you can,
Come as the thunder.
I'll lift its roar to my breast
And send forth the battle cry to every corner

Murari Mukhopadhyay [1]

This chapter turns to cultural idioms of revolutionary romance and personal stories of intimacy in order to explore how they were lived in the context of the movement and have come to be remembered in its aftermath. More broadly, it considers the interrelated themes of love, marriage, and sexuality in the Naxalbari movement—themes that have found little or no attention in the movement's historiography or, for that matter, in that of Indian communism. Contemporary Maoist groups are, as noted in Chapter 1 (and later in this chapter), garnering feminist attention given their deployment of conjugal life as one site of enacting their politics and propagandizing their movements.

In his mapping of 'moral protest' in North America, Jasper (1997: 187) speaks of the 'libidinal economy of a movement', referring to the erotic pleasures of protest borne out of affective attachments amongst the group and the convergence of personal love and political goals. Everyday life in Naxalbari offered unprecedented freedoms that were not only political but also sexual and erotic, starting with the close proximity of bodies. The flip side of the 'sexual draw of protest' is the problem of discipline or the manner in which erotic and affective bonds interfere with the demands of revolutionary discipline (Jasper 1997: 217–18). As with other protest movements (see, for instance, De Mel 2001), Naxalites developed modes of regulating 'libidinal desires within the ranks' (Jasper 1997: 217–18), which, in turn, produced specific forms of vulnerabilities. Regulation drew on the sexual mores of bhadralok society even as these were consciously challenged.

In placing individual narratives on love and marriage alongside poetic, literary, and cinematic representations of the same, the chapter explores a wide cultural repertoire to do with intimacy, and the relationship between stories of the self and cultural narratives, articulated, in this case, through romance and sexuality. In contrast to the official or historiographic record, women often emerge central given the feminized nature of the romance genre. In poetry, explored in the first section of the chapter, the configuring of revolution as love offers women the possibility of political agency, especially through violence. I then turn to fiction and films that, as in the case of popular culture more generally (see Basu 2001), provide a space in which norms of gender and sexuality are both subverted and reinforced. Personal stories on 'marriage', analysed in the final section, negotiate cultural and political constructions of revolutionary romance and conjugality through which sexuality, conjugal expectations, *and* their betrayal were discursively constituted.[2] They also draw upon popular images of revolutionary masculinity, heroic femininity, and love-as-comradeship to compose socially recognizable identities. While the analysis of this chapter explores the production of subjectivities through popular narratives, it also begins to unravel the way in which the achievement of subjective composure is premised upon the ability to silence or abject contentious aspects of the past, especially around sexuality.

Revolutionary Romance: The Poetic Imagination

> The true revolutionary is guided by great feelings of love
>
> Che Guevara

Violence and love have long been fellow travellers in the rhetoric of revolution. Love is very often the expressed motivation behind revolutionary violence within a utopia of a new liberatory age. A martyrological consciousness is equally centred upon the notion of love insofar as the militant sacrifices himself for the love of humanity. Part and parcel of the madhyabitta ritual of self-transformation, love had to be reconfigured beyond self-interest to respond to the political and ideological demands of the Naxalbari revolution. As noted in previous chapters and of other radical Left movements in India (Vindhya 2000), themes of sacrificing personal happiness, including love, for a transcendent cause recur in the creative output of the movement. The manner in which love enters the field of the political, outside the ordinary spheres of the familial, marital, or sexual, is not only resonant of communist imperatives of disassociating love from 'bourgeois' tendencies (see Evans 1997) but also of local idioms and traditions. In making love subordinate to the demands of the revolution, the movement's cultural imaginary evokes ideas of selfless love made popular by devotional cults in Bengal (Orsini 2006). The complete surrender of the self in the love for god as evoked in bhakti is not dissimilar, Donner (2008: 84) tells us, from the way in which a woman's devotion to her husband is idealized amongst the Bengali middle classes. Similarly, in Naxal sahitya, bhakti forms a continuum with the trope of renunciation encountered in Chapter 2, while also marking conjugal relations of wifely devotion and husband worship. The use of the word 'bhalobasha' (love) in the poem that this chapter starts with expresses a different idea of love that is today associated with 'love' in contrast to arranged marriages (Donner 2008).[3] 'Bhalobasha' is expressive of mutuality and egalitarianism that is central to such 'self-chosen' unions, as Donner calls them. While Naxalite relationships were similarly self-chosen, poetry and fiction emphasize a selfless, even devotional love in contrast to the purported self-centredness of regular romance.

Whether understood as a form of bhakti or bhalobasha, the politicization of love enables certain transgressions that are evident in the poetry inspired by the movement.[4] Like revolutionary Bengali poets before him (see Dasgupta 2005), Murari Mukhopadhyay substitutes traditional romantic motifs (the moon, flowers, stars) with an array of violent metaphors (flood, thunder, storm) that express the urgency of the political present. In his poetic rendition, love is an aggressive and violent force that is in aid of battle and destruction. Indeed, love is often the imaginative medium through which revolutionary violence is represented. This isomorphism between biplab (revolution) and bhalobasha is most clearly articulated in the following lines penned by young Naxalite, Dronacharya Ghosh, written for his partner, Krishna Bandyopadhyay:

Love and revolution, revolution and love
There is no separation between them.
Love is for revolution,
Revolution [is] for love (Dasadhikari 1998: 254)[5]

Revolution, on the one hand, determines love, thus politicizing love and dissociating it from the ordinary realm of private pleasure or sexual desire. On the other hand, love also determines revolution ('revolution is for love'); love is now the end and revolution is the means. Located within such a libidinal economy, 'class struggle' is charged with a particularly potent erotic force. In another poem, the (male) lover imbues love with revolutionary passion while also evoking a militant femininity in 'Ahalya' and 'Nirmala' (see Chapter 2).

Haven't you heard of Ahalya? ...
That is not your evening lamp
It is the light of the moshaal
You have heard wrong
It is not ululation; it is
The roar of the rifle
In Nirmala's hands (Dasadhikari 1998: 128–9)

In these lines, it is not simply a romantic imagery that is substituted by a violent revolutionary aesthetic (the roar of the rifle; the light of the *moshaal*) but also a traditional domesticated femininity that is replaced by a militant one. The evening lamp, the sounds of ululation, common images that are associated with a feminized ritualistic Hindu world, are replaced by the motifs of revolutionary violence that are bestowed upon women. In the last stanza of the poem, the (male) lover addresses the following plea to his *premika* (female lover):

Beloved, if I am not there on that day
And if the spring comes
You give tune to the sound of my rifle
Remember that I loved the song of the road (Dasadhikari 1998: 129)

The beloved is here implored to take up the dead hero's rifle when the 'spring', a metonym for the original Naxalbari uprising, arrives. On the face of it, the poetic imaginary seems to conform to a dominant trope of gendering the revolution in which a supportive, dependent femininity simply aids a hegemonic revolutionary masculinity. It also confirms the popular perception, reinforced by histories of the movement (see, for instance, Singh 1995), that middle-class women joined the andolan out of their erotic and not political or ideological attachments (refuted by interviewees who noted that women formed relationships on entering the movement). At the same time, however, radical poetry seemingly enables women to invest in a form of heroic agency precisely through love. The idiom of love interpellates the feminine as heroic and militant besides validating its association with violence. This is obvious in the last poem's plea to the female lover to take up the rifle, underscoring, as Hamilton notes of nationalist violence, 'the necessary, if indirect, participation of women in reproducing [such] violence' (Hamilton 2007: 93). Love thus offers the possibility of a feminine incorporation of political action in ways that are manifest in the case of fiction in what follows.

Love's Labour in Literature

A number of common themes have found their way into the popular fiction and films inspired by the movement, which are as telling about the politics of gender, (hetero)sexuality, class, and cultural identity in Bengali bhadralok society as they are about political constructions and transformations of love and intimacy. These include: a progressive rhetoric of love as comradeship emphasizing equality, companionship, and mutual understanding between partners; the staging of femininity, even a politicized femininity, through romance; and finally, the betrayal of love in ways that place much of the liberatory rhetoric of comradeship into question. As already indicated in Chapter 2, fiction and film often critique, within limits, patriarchal structures besides marking the dissonances between a radical rhetoric of 'class struggle' and its everyday actualization, at the hands of conservative communist men. In the literary and cinematic exploration of these themes, we thus get a glimpse of the extent to which the sexual politics of the movement had to negotiate historically and culturally prescriptive bhadralok norms pertaining to marriage and heterosexual relations. Women's silenced memories of interpersonal relations explored in this, and the following chapter equally voice these tensions.

Much like the 'true socialist love' of Maoist China (Evans 1997: 88), to love at the time of Naxalbari was to share a utopian fantasy, a vision of remaking the past and inventing a new future. In literary texts as well as in personal narratives, there is a distinction between 'political' and 'apolitical' love, and correspondingly between 'political' and 'apolitical' relationships. Relationships formed at the time of the movement between comrades constituted the ground of an appropriate 'political' relationship. For male and especially female activists, the organization of interpersonal relationships was deeply embedded in the fantasy of and desire for an alternative world, exemplified in the words of Supriya (introduced in Chapter 3): 'we (Naxalites) think that we belong to another society. We are within this society but we are imagining a society for the future' (Personal interview, July 2004).[6]

Much of Naxalbari fiction locates intimacy within an empowering and progressive discourse of love-as-companionship, captured in the revolutionary rhetoric of 'comrade'. In a range of novels such as Basu's *Antarghat* (English translation, The Enemy Within, 1983),[7] Devi's *Hajar Churashir Ma* (English translation, Mother of 1084, 1997), Majumdar's *Kalbela* (The Omnious Hour, 1983), and Mitra's *Manabputri* (1993), the relationship between the male and female protagonist is characterized by friendship and mutuality, giving meaning to a form of love-as-comradeship. The rhetoric of comrade also implies a reversal of the traditional gender hierarchy that structures heterosexual relations with some interviewees emphasizing the difference between a 'husband' and a 'comrade'. Kalpana Sen (2001) writes that the Naxalite (re)definition of interpersonal relationships signalled not only a transgression of societal norms but the breaking of gender barriers for women. Unlike conventional and chiefly arranged marriages in bhadralok society, male and female relationships are configured (in literature and personal narratives) not in terms of a top-down hierarchy but as a mutually fulfilling partnership between equals.

The egalitarian rhetoric of comrade does not, however, mitigate the literary representation of a heroic masculinity and a dependent femininity. In novels like *Antarghat* and *Manabputri*, romance is represented overwhelmingly in gendered terms, with women positioned as the receivers and men as the initiators of romance. So, for instance, in *Antarghat*, the male Naxalite tells the female protagonist, 'Do you want to die with me, Bibi?' She replies: 'If that is my destiny, then yes, I do' (1983: 46). Similarly, in *Manabputri* (discussed in Chapter 2), the revolutionary tells his new wife that even Lord Ram could not leave his wife behind and go into exile. Thus, she too will accompany him into the villages for political work. The literary imaginary reiterates, in these instances, Hindu Bengali tropes of the long-suffering, self-effacing, and sacrificial wife/lover. As with poetry, it subscribes to and reinforces the idea that women are drawn to violent and terrorist movements out of love; one that has been made popular by Morgan's (1989) 'couple terrorism' model. Beyond the erotic, tropes of companionate desire and sacrifice evoke more culturally specific idioms of devotional love and dependence in bhakti. Man and woman are united, even equal, in their singular, selfless devotion to the cause. Both dream the same dream of a better world, and Bibi (in *Antarghat*) is willing to die with Antu for the sake of biplab. Love in popular fiction, like in poetry, emphasizes union and mutuality in aid of revolution.

Love transformed into comradeship is also de-eroticized just as it is dissociated from its ordinary romantic or sexual connotations in poetry. This is at least what Bandyopadhyay (2001) suggests in narrating an anecdote in which her lover, Dron, spurns physical intimacy with her for political debate and discussion (in sharp contrast to an adivasi couple who are presented as making love). She observes how romantic Dron was, on the one hand, and loved the vision of the two of them fighting side by side, but rejected, on the other hand, individual desire for the sake of the revolution. Male Naxalites are overwhelmingly presented as stoic and unflinching that reinforces, as Vindhya observes of later Maoist groups, 'the image of a strong male militant protector [and] the necessity of subordinating personal needs to a higher, worthier cause' (Vindhya 2000: 175). Sexual desire is not simply a distraction from true revolutionary impulses but a moral weakness that Mazumdar's 'new man' must rise above. A father (cited in Chapter 2) writes of his dead Naxalite son: 'I never saw the slightest weakness in his moral character. Once at a reading of Shri Ramakrishna he heard what Shri Ramakrishna had said—sexual urge dies if the name of Hari is chanted. Back home, he began to chant "Haribol Haribol" and dance. He stopped when he saw me' (*Frontier* 1970: 15).

Here, as elsewhere, the cultural imaginary of the movement employs tropes of religious renunciation for complete devotion to political purpose. Sexual self-discipline is tied up with the project of 'becoming a Naxalite' for madhyabitta male comrades. Middle-class women (and subaltern men and women) embody, in contrast, the illicit temptation that the male subject must resist or transgress. For Ramakrishna, the major obstacle in man's bhakti to god was his attachment to women and wealth (Chatterjee 1993b; Sarkar 1997). According to Sarkar, the nineteenth century Hindu religious leader, who was very popular amongst the bhadralok, was the source of the 'splitting of womanhood into the sacred mother and the dangerous non-mother' (Sarkar 1991: 217). In Chapter 2, I located this split femininity in wider cultural representations of the 1960s and the 1970s as well as in CPI(ML) literature and auto/biographical writings that privilege a non-threatening submissive femininity over an actively sexualized one. I also noted how 'woman' come to stand in for the purity of the nation as part of a particular nationalist resolution of the 'woman's question'. Kapur (2005) shows that the nationalist association of women and the feminine with a 'pure' Indian culture, uncontaminated by Western intrusion, had important implications for the entrenchment of the nation in a normative sexuality located in the sexual purity of women.[8] When Naxalite women (like Krishna Bandyopadhyay here and 'Katherine' in Chapter 2) express sexual desire or even love, they are quick to correct themselves, given the demands of normative Bengali femininity perfectly matched with those of a renunciative revolutionary identity.

This 'profound symbiosis' between Left culture and 'the broad cultural traditions of Bengal' that I noted, via Sarkar (1991: 215) in Chapter 1, is salient in the sexual politics of left-wing radicalism as presented in film. Here, the theme is that of the betrayal of love and relationships, and consequently of a shared political vision. To the extent that a partnership between two individuals was grounded in their common political and ideological outlook, personal betrayal was, at once, a deeply political act that signified not simply a personal failure but also the failure of a vision. In older films like *Dooratwa* (1978; discussed in Chapter 2) and more recent ones like *Anu* (1998), betrayal in romance and interpersonal relationships signifies the divergence between radical Left ideals that included a commitment to gender equality and their everyday realization.

Such films constitute a strong critique of the sexual politics of the movement and its bhadralok underpinnings insofar as 'political' men are depicted as being unable to accept 'impure' women. These include women with prior sexual histories as in *Dooratwa*, and the raped woman, Anu, in the film of the same name who steadfastly awaits the return of her jailed activist partner only to be rejected by him on account of her rape. Both women violate the predominant expectation pertaining to middle-class women's sexualities, namely, premarital chastity (Puri 1999: 135).[9] The limits of a revolutionary masculinity that remained attached to entrenched middle-class patriarchal privileges make for a powerful critique of the movement, itself revealed to be a mirror image of bhadralok society in film. The party's conservatism with respect to sexuality and its implicit sexual policing, as depicted in the film *Padatik* (1973; see Chapter 2), rings true for one of my interviewees, a married woman who was accused of having an illicit affair with a married man who had sheltered her.[10] Her disbelief at the behaviour of her comrades over what started as a rumour and became a full-fledged scandal in the para stemmed from the fact that these were 'political' men and women who should have known better.

In the popular imagination of the movement, revolutionary romance emerges as a complexly refashioned genre that provides an interesting set of contradictions in relation to gender, sexuality, class, and culture. By inscribing a popular model of 'couple terrorism' into the revolutionary rhetoric of 'comrade', poetry and fiction echo conventional norms of femininity (and heterosexual morality) while opening up the possibility of reclaiming female agency through love and violence. Film, in turn, poses critical challenges to the patriarchal underpinnings of Left progressivism, particularly with respect to its sexual politics. The fictional rendition of romance incorporates, in this manner, a range of discourses from the progressive to the conservative that resonate in personal narratives of intimacy and conjugality in the movement.

Reforming Marriage

Intimate spaces of conjugal and family life have been the site of reform and radicalization by nationalists and communists alike. 'Socialist monogamy' (Evans 1992; see also Gilmartin 1995) was the ideological motivation behind the progressive redefinition of conjugality based on mutual love, free will, and consent in communist China. In the Bengali communist tradition, the (undivided) CPI of the 1940s is generally credited with a degree of progressive experimenting with interpersonal relationships, even though the private is silenced in most memoirs of the period (Lahiri 2001; and Sen 2001). Several women who joined the party between the late 1930s–early 1940s were from wealthy, conservative families, and lived in a commune run by the political activist Manikuntala Sen. The commune hosted both male and female activists and is often cited as evidence of the party's potential to break gender barriers (Ray 1999: *n*186). While the CPI is noted for its advocacy of 'love marriages' amongst comrades (Donner 2008), the CPI(M) is known to take on a parental role in arranging the marriages of women members and even presiding over issues of divorce (Ray 1999).[11]

With respect to the radical Left, sexuality, as noted at the start of this book, has only recently emerged as an area of political consideration (but not necessarily one of politicizing) given the '"sex-blindness" of orthodox Marxist analysis' (Vindhya 2000: 169) that dominated earlier Left-led movements. Women's narratives of the Telangana people's struggle (Stree Shakti Sanghatana 1989) show how a Marxist economic determinism relegated questions of marriage, sexuality, and family to the private while re-establishing, in the political domain, culturally prescriptive power differentials between men and women. Kannabiran and Lalitha (1989: 195) observe, of women's personal testimonies of the time, 'an implicit but definite pressure to marry that operated on the women' given the cultural association of femininity with sexual temptation and the threat of its consequences (pregnancies and children) to 'organisational discipline'. In the case of the Srikakulam movement, a contemporary of Naxalbari, the leadership was often caught between the ideal of comradeship and pre-existing patriarchal norms that extended disciplinary control over individual lives, especially the bodily autonomy of women (Vindhya 1990, 2000).

In contrast, the contemporary leadership of Maoist movements in South Asia seem to have taken a more deliberate stance on issues of marriage, sexuality, and reproductive rights, partly motivated by adverse publicity about licentious 'underground' behaviour and the sexual exploitation of girl comrades (Manchanda 2004: 250–1). Manchanda refers to the male leadership of the Maoist revolution in Nepal which took the issue of sexual morality very seriously, to the extent that the failure to subscribe to a party-led 'uniform disciplinary code of sexual conduct' resulted in punishment and even suspension. Pettigrew and Shneiderman (2004) have, in turn, shown how marriage was forced upon young, unmarried rural women as a way of controlling female cadres and perpetuating a male hegemony. In inscribing, with greater force, conservative codes of sexual and conjugal morality which invariably manifest in the sexual control of women, Manchanda draws out the limits of the Maoist promise in Nepal: 'The brave new social world of the revolution that Prachanda had hailed in his statement, celebrating a "cultural revolution" that had turned upside down "questions of marriage, questions of love, questions of family, questions of relations between people" has turned out to be less than a field of possibilities, and more a reproducing of traditional gender relations' (Manchanda 2004: 251).

The politicization of marriage and the conjugal couple has also been noted in recent histories of Indian nationalism with important implications for the post-colonial period. Majumdar (2009) locates the novelty of the Bengali conjugal couple in the 'new patriarchy' of the nationalist era (referred to in Chapter 2; see also Sarkar 2001). The rise of coupledom did not, however, entail dissolution of the joint family but its 'modernization' in tune with changing socioeconomic realities. The valorization of companionate love and the wife as the husband's comrade and helpmate went together with an expectation of the new bride's complete devotion to her husband and his family (Majumdar 2009: 161). Post-colonization, 'modern' conjugal ideals (in companionate or even 'love marriages') continue to balance and accommodate demands of the joint family, caste and community endogamy, and class boundaries, as Donner's (2008) ethnography of marriage, motherhood, and domesticity in contemporary middle-class Kolkata shows.

Studies of Indian nationalism are incomplete without attention to the social and political reformist efforts of the late nineteenth and early twentieth centuries that focused on the family. The 1920s anti-caste, Self-Respect movement in Tamil Nadu went further than the more recognizable forms of reforming conjugality of the nineteenth century (through the abolition of child marriage as with the Bengali Brahmo Samaj; see Majumdar 2009) in rejecting and not merely reforming caste, religious, and gender hierarchies in Tamil society (Geetha n.d.; Hodges 2005; and Sreenivas 2008). Their development of a new wedding style in what came to be known as 'self-respect marriages', with no priest or rituals, was the most public performance of this rejection. Marriage was refashioned into a 'secular, contractual relationship' centred on consent, computability, and companionship (Sreenivas 2008: 86). Individual choice was prioritized over, and even at the expense of, familial and social norms.

The radicalism of the Naxalites with respect to marriage and conjugal relations reflects these various historical trajectories of Indian nationalism and social reform, and of Bengali and Chinese communism (although the evidence here is limited to personal narratives and literary representations since there is no official archive). Free choice marriages and consensual unions were privileged over, and at times in explicit rejection of, the normativities that govern Hindu Bengali marriage ideals and practices. The 'red book marriage' is particularly resonant of 'self-respect' weddings. Interviewees referred to 'red book marriages' where individuals could declare themselves husband and wife through a mere exchange of Mao's *Red Book* in front of party members. Such an alternative marriage ceremony needed neither state nor religious or familial sanction; it appears as a spectacular rejection of these multiple sources of authority. The lack of parental involvement and consent in marriage, which constitutes a key source of social recognition in the wider kinship context, is especially striking. In common with couples who elope, some activists registered their marriage. In the novel *Manabputri*, Katherine and her Naxalite partner are married in Kolkata's Kalighat temple, another popular mode of signifying marriage without or against parental consent. More commonly though, individuals simply informed the party that they were married in order to be recognized as such. As we see later, the mere giving of individual consent sanctified marriage in these instances. Even in today's milieu where individual choice has found its way into both arranged and love marriage, 'choice' tends to be determined by and even subordinate to 'filial duty and family needs' amongst the Bengali middle classes (Donner 2008: 88).

Donner (2008) remarks that there is also little choice in *not* getting married, especially for women for whom married life is a marker of Hindu Bengali/Indian cultural identity. Indeed, it is striking how a majority of the women I interviewed got 'married' in the course of the movement indicating, perhaps, that relationships could not but end in marriage. This was as much to do with the middle-class backgrounds and expectations of marriage and monogamy amongst activists as it was with the expectations of the party's leadership. Some interviewees emphasized that there was no injunction from the party to get married (in contrast to present-day Maoists). Although it appears that norms and customs were challenged through individual choice in marital practices, the party seemingly played a significant role in the organization of interpersonal relations. As suggested in the personal narratives given next, the party became the social consciousness of the collective, substituting for parental authority and mimicking middle-class morality in the underground.

Feminist Critiques and Silences

Kalyani's short discussion emphasizes the radically altered way in which conjugality came to be understood and practised in the course of the andolan. Kalyani is one of the more prominent women Naxalites, mostly because of her present-day political activism (in both feminist and labour movements). She cites the case of an activist couple who, unlike some (but not all) Naxalites, chose not to legally register their marriage even after the end of the movement:

> Kalpana and Gautam have 'lived together'; they didn't get married. My first relationship, there was no registration or red book exchange. 'We just started' ... no problems ... You would just have to inform the party as a so-called married couple. We challenged the institution of marriage, like we challenged all other institutions. [*What about the red book marriage?*] But how is that 'binding'? There is nothing binding in it. Today if I don't want to stay—lots of men married peasant women and then left them and came away. What do you understand by marriage? When an institution 'controls' you in some way. Here there is no control. (Personal interview, Kalyani, August 2003)

While almost all male and female interviewees use the term marriage (*biye*) in the context of the movement irrespective of whether such marriages were legally recognized or not, Kalyani is one of the few who spells out a distinction between 'marriage' and 'living together'. Amongst the Bengali middle classes, as with some Naxalites, 'living together' is considered a departure from normative or 'compulsory marriedness' (Basu 2001: 186) because it signifies deviance associated with premarital sex, promiscuity, and moral degradation. Male cadres and leaders like Ashim Chatterjee, cited in Sinha Roy (2011: 118), concurred that the dominant expectation of activists was the bhadralok ideal of sexual propriety which included 'proper' interaction between unmarried adults, including sexual celibacy. Given the continuing uneasiness with which the concept of cohabitation sits with the Bengali middle classes (see Basu 2001; and Donner 2008), interpersonal relationships formed at that time are defined as conjugal ones even though individuals were very often living together. In Kalyani's discussion, however, the latter is positively associated with individual freedom and choice, while marriage is negatively understood in terms of institutional control. For long-standing 'feminist' women like her, these were the offerings of genuine empowerment in the movement. As Rukmini who is also active in contemporary feminist politics put it, referring to her own partner and other male friends in Naxalbari, 'if I saw a lot of conservatism in the party, I also saw a lot of progressiveness' (Personal interview, October 2003).

While Kalyani speaks of the progressivism of marriage practices with respect to challenging social hierarchies and parental control, she also conveys a sense of disenchantment: 'But it also happened that people have not hesitated to divorce, many left. Have at any time said I'll divorce you ... divorced just through words ... It's very difficult to see individual relationships and I don't want to dissect them. I just want to speak generally. You can't capture all the "equations" of personal life' (Kalyani, August 2003). By drawing attention to the fact that many of the alliances formed at the time (including inter-caste ones) did not last, Kalyani underscores some of the limitations of the politicization of marriage, and how it could, as observed of self-respect unions, merge into 'the realm of sexual convenience' (Geetha n.d.: 31). Her own relationship in the movement that she briefly alluded to in the above-mentioned fragment broke. Throughout the interview, she fiercely protected her privacy with regard to it: '[*Were you married then?*] No, in 1978. There was a relationship; there was no marriage. These social customs were broken. '75–76 I had a relationship. I actually don't want to say anything about that, don't want to bring in my "personal life"' (Kalyani, August 2003).

I do not know why Kalyani chose to remain silent about her first relationship or what it is that she was unwilling to reveal. Her silences allude, however, to the double-edged nature of an intimate history of Naxalbari that she (along with fiction and film) partly draws attention to; of the pleasures and freedoms associated with a radical (and not merely reformist) practice of marriage counterpoised with the betrayal and grief associated with romance, however radicalized. The politicizing of marriage in exceptional times was no guarantee against its more everyday trials and tribulations. The tendency to silence or even abject aspects of the past is also bound up with the effort to constitute oneself as a recognizable, coherent subject. Throughout her movement story, Kalyani draws upon the narrative idioms of the contemporary women's movement to 'compose' herself as a radical, left-leaning women's rights activist. Yet even the language of feminism entails, it seems, its own silences that are especially significant when they include the affective and the intimate.

Bulbul (briefly mentioned in Chapter 3) too evokes the language of feminism to put forth a formidable critique of the gender and sexual politics of the movement that she roots in the party's patriarchal culture. As with the narrative that follows, her discussion speaks of some of the anxieties that the radical reform of marriage gave rise to in opening up the possibility of wild transgressions. These anxieties also serve to suggest how a 'revolutionary' discourse of love and conjugality was very much embedded in a *bhadra* or respectable sexual morality that prescribed marriage and monogamy as the appropriate and only channels of erotic desire and fulfilment for men, but especially women. In choosing their own partners and even 'living together', intimate practices might have been revolutionary but they still had to be respectable. Concerns with the latter became even more impending in the anarchic conditions of the underground, as Bulbul explains:

> It's like you have a sort of sexual equilibrium throughout society which is accepted and so the very fact of going underground and going into this perilous situation in which you are no longer in front of the eyes of moral, middle-class society; there had to be a morality inside because otherwise, you are throwing everything overbroad. So there was a tremendous fear, I think, that there will be total chaos and anarchy, and sexuality, I think, is really the crucial balance because this is where people fly off the handle ... So in that environment which was very, very male oriented, you know, the whole party hierarchy, everything was completely patriarchal, they had to give some kind of respectability to these relationships because they were not going to stop. So they decided to do the red book marriages, but it meant nothing, which was very evident for me because I had a red book marriage. (Personal interview, Bulbul, November 2003)

In the case of most guerrilla movements, the suspension of normalcy within the underground together with its isolation from 'moral, middle-class society' threatens (bhadralok) norms of gender and sexuality (see, for instance, Hamilton 2007). But sexuality, as Bulbul seems to suggest, is not merely a threat to the discipline and 'respectability' of the revolutionary group but is imbued with wider and deep-rooted cultural anxieties. Sexual propriety is, as indicated earlier, the cornerstone of respectability not only in Bengali culture. Stemming from the suturing of authentic culture and sexuality in the making of the nation, post-colonial globalized India has been increasingly marked by public outrage on issues of sex and sexuality as a 'Western' invasion which threatens Indian culture and the nation itself (see Kapur 2005). The male narrative that I go on to explore later reproduces dominant ideas of sexual licence as alien and 'other', not just to middle-class Bengali society but also to middle-class notions of Indianness.

Marriage becomes, as Bubul suggests and as is evidenced in the context of other guerrilla struggles in South Asia (De Mel 2001; and Manchanda 2004), the only way to address and 'contain' the close proximity between young men and women in the underground. She links the political ritual of the 'red book marriage' to the production of forms of respectability and regulation in a 'perilous (sexual) situation'. Other interviewees mentioned the double-edged nature of such a sexual situation suggesting how the movement offered freedoms which were affective and erotic (and not only political) but also rendered women as sexual prey with 'marriage' often providing the only means of solace, as shown in Chapter 5.

Bulbul's account also makes explicit the relationship between the patriarchal structure of the party and the organization of gender and sexual relations within the movement. Her discussion with one of the major leaders of the time is suggestive of the way in which, for the party, the 'women's question' was ultimately subordinated to the achievement of the 'democratic revolution':

> ... The only time when I bought up this question with the people who were around me in terms of a relationship which I wanted to have, then er, it was Santosh Rana who answered me and he said listen, you know, you're far ahead of our society ... how I was different from the others and other women, and therefore I couldn't ever imagine that I could consider myself exemplary in terms of the other women, because I should consider myself a case apart. And as to the other women, they would have to wait for the democratic revolution to be achieved to achieve equal status with men, and then be able to take up the question of deciding with whom they were going to partner, with whom they were going to bed or wed, you know, er that was something which would happen at a much later phase ... (Personal interview, Bulbul, November 2003)

As with the rest of her life story, this extract presents a certain version of the self as twice removed from the rest of the community. In contrasting herself with the other women in the movement who would have to wait for the democratic revolution to 'achieve' gender equality, Bubul's narrative emphasizes self-empowerment and agency. Yet, this sense of agency relies on the passivity of other women who are represented as mere victims of patriarchy, unable to discern gender inequalities, and unquestioning of feminine identity. Bulbul's story eventually becomes one of individual triumph where the female protagonist rebels against society and wins. In such a story, questions of upper-class privilege and financial security as aiding her chosen 'feminist' way of life are relatively silenced. Both the narratives considered here rest upon certain silences and omissions for the sake of grounding narrative coherence and self-identity in ways that are similar to the final 'sexual story' that I turn to.

Respectable 'Revolutionary' Sexuality

Saumen's narrative is one of the only male discussions of 'marriage', and one that fully indicates its manifest continuities with middle-class standards of sexual propriety. Saumen was a middle-ranking activist of the Naxalbari movement whose wife, Latika, was identified as a sympathizer. His discussion begins with romance in the movement:

> With regard to girls, what often happened is that (I don't know whether a lot of boys have also exploited this) 'serious girls' would love Naxalite boys. Could be because of heroism that women were attracted to heroes, but I don't think that's always true. I think the other thing that I've seen in the case of my mother, that's probably true of young girls as well, that they would think of boys like a 'spokesman'. I think that girls would, more often than not, they would consider those men as close friends or even as 'life partners' who were very 'outspoken', doing a big job, who is a 'revolutionary'. This was a 'phenomenal development', because of which, we can see that many girls took many risks as well ... usually, what happened was that educated girls, intellectual girls, not those who were only 'careerist', she wanted to see her closest friend or her life partner as a 'revolutionary', a Naxalite. (Personal interview, Saumen, July 2003)

In common with literary representations already reviewed, Saumen's narrative represents the Naxalite subject as a specifically male one and infuses him with certain qualities. Women are, in turn, positioned in the role of sympathizers (like his own mother and his wife) who took 'risks' for their revolutionary partners. Romantic love is associated with feminine weakness and presented through the imagery of 'redemption, of salvation and rescue' (Wetherell 1995: 132), especially evident in the masculine figure of the 'spokesman'. Yet, this is not simply a dependency relationship. As in fiction, the narration of revolutionary romance complicates the cultural codes of female dependency in more interesting ways. By saying that women were not simply attracted to 'heroes', Saumen deviates from an idealized heroic masculinity to represent more lived masculinities—hardworking, serious young men. Women ('in love') are also described as being 'serious', 'educated', and 'intellectual'—qualities that serve to construct and validate a particular form of female subjectivity within an intellectual and progressive leftist 'habitus'. Such a form of female subjectivity combines traditional passivity with a seriousness of political purpose and action—loving dangerously, daringly, and in so doing, incorporates power and action. In resonance with wider cultural constructions, love in Saumen's narrative stages a femininity that sutures conventional forms of female dependency with a limited degree of agency.

Latika and Saumen did have a truly revolutionary marriage. It was neither a religious nor a registered wedding; they come from different upper-caste backgrounds (he is Kayastha, while she is Brahmin), and she is at least ten years older than him. Saumen calls their marriage 'absurd' since neither his in-laws nor Latika knew his real name at the time; they only knew him by his pet name. It is important to underscore that this story of his marriage to Latika was one that I heard more than once, and is one from which Saumen derives, I believe, a certain 'psychic comfort' (Dawson 1994) given his traumatic life during and after the movement (see Chapter 6). In the extract that follows, Saumen negotiates the recognition and composure he derives from this story with discomforting constructions of revolutionary marriage as sexual licentiousness:

> In terms of relationships, if there is any question of 'sexual freedom', they are certain 'foreign elements' or you can say 'deviations'. That's how we saw it. This was not the usual matter. Some people brought it in. What I am saying as 'liberal' is something else. A boy likes a girl; the 'variables' that usually enter into this liking were absent here. But now what is being said is being forced on the Naxalite movement, that 'live together', 'pre-marital' this and that. But even in our time, these were there but were thought of as outside elements, as 'deviations', 'liberty'. (Personal interview, Saumen, July 2003)

Latika interrupts to say that these were not a fallout of the movement, and Saumen continues:

> Absolutely. These have been made up. A lot of people have done this. You won't even see this in the literature, what today, what in the name of 'feminism' or something else, you know, various types of 'free mixing'—this didn't exist in our time. But obviously some girls and boys got the opportunity to 'freely live' and work in one area, but deviations happen; there's no point theorizing them. They are just deviations. For instance, at Bankura we saw an 'apparent' closeness between a girl and a boy. I mean a real closeness that was *acceptable* to us. So we all sat and as a gang told them 'get married'. It was just the opposite actually. *We never let anyone take liberties*. We didn't like it at all. And me or boys like myself who had come into the movement, we had a strange background. We (I'll say it freely), for instance, having a lot of 'girlfriends', working with lots of girls, [it] wasn't there in our pasts. But like *today* it's taken

> for granted that a girlfriend will always be there or for a year or two, then another—this wasn't in our pasts ... We would always think that we shouldn't get a bad name ... (emphasis added)

'Liberal' for Saumen means a rupture in the traditional discourse of (arranged) marriage where love is subordinated to other 'variables' such as economic status, social class, and caste. That middle-class men married adivasi women has been remarked upon in personal narratives and wider cultural ones but inter-caste unions like his are also notable. Even more transgressive was the marriage between a female activist from a caste Hindu family and was a Scheduled Caste man that Sinha Roy (2011) reports. In the film, *Dooratwa,* the male protagonist starts a relationship with a tribal woman that does not last, which is reflective of another dimension of such intimate relations to which I turn in Chapter 5. The subversive potential of such liberalism should not be underestimated given, as Donner (2008) shows, that changing discourses of conjugality in Bengali society have not as yet disrupted class–caste biases in marital unions.[12] As with the Self-Respect movement (see Sreenivas 2008), Naxalite liberalism did not, however, extend to a critique of the patriarchal hierarchies that govern everyday sexual moralities. Liberalism as freedom from restrictive social norms is sharply distanced, in Saumen's narrative, from a (sexual) liberalism that he associates with 'living together' and 'premarital sex'.

Saumen's discussion also evokes a more shared, collective discourse of sexual respectability prompted by commonplace anxieties of getting a 'bad name'. He says: 'And generally, as a rule, if a party boy was close to a girl then it was taken for granted that she was his wife' (Personal interview, Saumen, November 2003). Others evoked this practice of 'arranging' marriages whereby the party would approach a man and a woman assumed to be in love and 'marry' them on obtaining their consent (also noted in Sinha Roy 2011). The party's actions substituted, in this manner, for the wider familiar and kin networks that are generally involved in arranging marriages; comrades and leaders took on a parental role. In a bhadralok discourse of 'heterosexual marriage rather than other forms of sexuality or even alternative expressions of heterosexual desire' (Basu 2001: 188), relationships could not legitimately exist outside of wedlock. And while there might have been no measure of force on part of the party leadership, bhadralok expectations of sexual propriety in a situation of sexual precariousness, if not crisis, rendered the question of individual consent a tricky one, especially for women (see Chapter 5). Saumen seems sensitive to the degree to which sexual desire and vulnerability, even abuse, coexisted in everyday underground life emphasizing how cadres would not 'let anyone take liberties'. The discursive category of 'liberty' was not, however, consistent with Ashim Chatterjee affirming to Sinha Roy that 'no leniency was shown to men if they were involved in "immoral" sexual relations' (Sinha Roy 2011: 121). Kannabiran and Lalitha remark, in the context of Telangana, that 'the perspective from which one decides what is clean and what is licentious does not enter the area of debate' (Kannabiran and Lalitha 1989: 198). In a discursive domain in which sexual desire itself was aligned with licentiousness and immorality, male sensitivity and protection towards women invariably became a mode of sexual (self) discipline.

Although much of Saumen's narrative attempts to deny any kind of promiscuity in the movement, it is less than consistent. At certain times, he admits the prevalence of a certain 'sexual freedom' but only as a 'foreign element', a 'deviation', something that was not the norm, and certainly not tolerated. Here, Saumen's language works in particular ways to render sexually unacceptable behaviour something that was not intrinsic to the movement. Some of his language is abstract and elusive as the language of sexuality often is in the narratives of middle-class Indians (Puri 1999). His use of English rather than Bangla to describe a pattern of behaviour that 'didn't exist' at the time or what 'we didn't like at all' creates the possibility of rejecting certain patterns of social behaviour as alien or attributable to an external agent like 'Westernization', a common culprit of the changing codes of sexual conduct in India (Kapur 2005). In discussions on sexuality, Western culture is invariably used to 'offset Indian cultural identity' (Puri 1999: 36) with marriage marking Indianness.

Middle-aged Bengali mothers in Donner's (2008: 69–70) study contrasted 'Western' ideas of marriage with 'Indian' ones, with marriage positioned as a sacrosanct Indian institution, modern but Indian. Saumen, in fact, pointedly evokes 'feminism' to explain the existence of 'various types of free mixing' in contemporary times, voicing a common leftist suspicion towards feminism as being bourgeois or Western, and alien at any rate. He also contrasts, more than once, his past with the present where the latter symbolizes greater sexual freedoms for young people in India. Thus, having 'girlfriends' is rendered normal in the present but described as being 'strange' in the past. The intersubjective dimensions of the interview, especially Saumen's perception of me as young, upper middle-class, and potentially located within a changing discourse of sexuality in contemporary India, might have determined the particular temporal ordering of this account. The rapid changes in Kolkata's cityscape such as the sprouting of malls facilitate new forms of global consumption as well as new forms of sociality and courtship in ways that were not publicly visible even a decade ago (Donner 2008). Donner's ethnography underscores generational differences even as younger people tend to prioritize familial interest over individual desire in conjugal relations.

As with sexual violence discussed Chapter 5, the possibility of illicit sexualities can be accepted only by discursively rendering them as that which occurs *outside* the movement community. By exteriorizing such acts, narrative practices preserve a certain version of the community and the self against temporal and generational shifts. The discourse of sexual licentiousness in the party not only threatens a conception of the community as a revolutionary *and* respectable entity but also a version of the (male) self, replete with bhadralok communist virtues. In Saumen's narrative, such a version of selfhood is composed through the abjection of those discourses that threaten its coherency such as those of sexual deviances.

Through the narratives visited here, we have seen how the meaning of everyday love and intimacy was transformed and potentially radicalized in exceptional political times. Yet, this radicalism had to balance the demands of respectability suggestive of the extent to which activists remained enmeshed in the very everyday that they sought to transgress. A utopian vision of comradeship and 'companionate conjugality' (Donner 2008: 71) in Naxalbari conformed, it seems, to the received conventionality with regard to gender, sexuality, and class. It demanded adherence to historically prescriptive and normative bhadralok codes of (hetero)sexuality, especially as a way of countering the possibility of sexual transgression not only in the underground but in the very liberal redefinition of conjugality as comradeship. In the context of an earlier movement, Kannabiran and Lalitha remark how sexual policing in the name of organizational discipline is one of the ways in which 'old relationships of power and authority are not only reproduced but even reinforced' (Kannabiran and Lalitha 1989: 198). Sexual policing has become pervasive to contemporary Maoist movements in the subcontinent with particular implications for women, the objects of class-based patriarchal control.

But the stories told here are not merely ones of regulation and control. They also speak of the passionate personal attachment to protest and the forms of belonging found therein which are not reducible to crude models of 'couple terrorism'. The libidinal economy of protest movements that Jasper (1997) describes (and that I started this chapter with) suggests a much wider gambit of affective ties of love and friendship that constitute everyday life-worlds in ways we began to see in Chapter 3. For Jasper (1997), these affective if not erotic attachments explain the impetus and pleasures of protest more so than cognitive understandings do. Rather than positing these divisions, we could, along with more recent ruminations on the affective (and ethical) dimension of politics (Cvetkovich 2003; Dave 2011; and Goodwin *et al.* 2001), consider such everyday affective attachments as constituting the 'stuff' of properly political motives. The voices and silences of women encountered through oral history (and in fiction) voice feminist demands of equality in heterosexual relations as well as individual aspirations and desires for new freedoms and a new world. They challenge hegemonic scripts of marriage and of the 'non-desiring, spiritually superior Bengali female body' (Basu 2001: 191), but, more importantly, forge new normative possibilities. Naxalites' redefinition and practice of marriage offered great potential for responding to women's aspirations but entailed, as is so common to moments of political disruption, its own forms of containment in the practices of normalization and control that it enacted.

Sexual stories are also part of the composure of individual identities, implicating the manner in which individuals present themselves through 'acceptable' self-images, including that of the elite feminist–activist or the bhadralok communist. In an instance of the dependence of stories of the self on wider culturally available ones, the personal narratives reviewed in this chapter 'speak' through shared (and hegemonic) discourses of marriage and sexuality in the revolutionary domain and in wider bhadralok society. Their reliance on a specific cultural repertoire also entails the need to silence or abject those aspects of the past and even the self that do not necessarily or smoothly 'fit'. What perhaps makes 'marriage' such a contested site, and demands in turn the abjection of particular pasts, is the disparity between a revolutionary ideal and its everyday actualization in the interplay of love, fear, loss, and desire that is salient to the narratives of sexual violence discussed next.

5

Sexual Violence and the Politics of Naming

Previous chapters have shown some of the tensions between Naxalite women's investments in idealized, largely disembodied revolutionary identities and their lived affective experience of intimate spaces, interpersonal relations, and forms of everyday violence. These could and could not be voiced through available tropes of self-sacrifice, heroic stoicism, and sexual propriety—key components of a revolutionary subjectivity. Consequently, some of these narratives were marked by silences and even disavowals which brought into focus the sense of being othered, of not fully belonging, of being 'space invaders', to use Puwar's (2004) apt characterization of those (gendered, racialized) bodies that are not meant to occupy normative political spaces and subject positions even when they do. This chapter takes these insights further by turning to the lived experience of sexual violence in the movement and the politics of current remembrance.[1] It brings into view some of the major consequences of women's identifications with normative political identities that were constituted through the abjection of the feminine, through rendering women's bodies in the political domain as 'out of place' (Puwar 2004).

The first part details the kinds of threats that women activists encountered in normatively safe spaces of the underground and the shelter at the hands of their 'own', that is, comrades, sympathizers, and leaders. I place sexual violence on a continuum that captures not only the varied idioms of male sexual aggression in the underground but also relates acts of injury at the micro and interpersonal level to an originary political violence. I show the continuities between sexual desire and sexual violence insofar as the progressive redefinition of conjugality enabled, in some instances, the embeddedness of abuse in intimate relationships for middle-class *and* subaltern women. I end this part by examining the shifting constructions of rape in the party's response to sexual offences, underscoring the ways in which these discursively constituted the (im) possibility of female testimony to sexual crimes. The second part of the chapter considers the narrational strategies employed in naming sexual violence today, often in the context of the necessity of silence. These, I argue, are revelatory, on the one hand, of women's complex negotiations with forms of 'good' and 'bad' violence, and, on the other, of women's conflicting identifications with heroic identities. I conclude my examination of the politics of remembering (and forgetting) sexual violence by considering its implications on questions of masculinity and class.

The Grey Zone[2]

Whether on the streets as a courier, or in industrial belts or rural areas, or in middle-class or peasant homes taking 'shelter', the female body required constant vigilance and safe keeping in the underground. In Chapter 3, I considered underground life in some detail, underscoring the multiple forms of everyday violence that infused middle-class activist women's experiences of both 'safe' and 'unsafe' spaces. The spaces of violence, for these women, were not confined to the 'public' domain of political conflict, but included normatively safe spaces of shelter and refuge. The threat of sexual violence can be located precisely at the interface of these spaces—the 'private' space of the underground/shelter and the 'public' space of armed struggle.

The construal of certain spaces as ones of safety was also aided by the perception of what lay outside their borders as dominated by the state and consequently, as a site of danger. As the custodian of all forms of violence, the construct of the state exhausted the potential for recognizing violence and terror in Naxalbari discourse. The threat posed by the state obliterated the possibility of violence existing *outside* its boundaries, transforming the movement's space into an inherently secure zone of mutual trust. The state is also masculinized in Naxalite discourse. Women, especially subaltern women, but also middle-class women activists, were defined in terms of their rapability at the hands of the state. Some interviewees suggested that the threat of rape at the hands of the police made leaving the party an impossibility. The construct of a rapist state thus not only aided the creation of an illusion of safety but also placed structural limitations on women's mobility. It magnified the violence that existed 'out there' in the public domain while rendering invisible the violence that existed *within* the movement, at the hands of one's own community. Paradoxically, as I go on to show, the violence of the state and that of 'class oppression' was also what rendered visible acts of wounding within the movement. Ideological constructions of 'good' and 'bad' violence also mediated perceptions of violence and its subjects, even by women activists.

Sheltering Violence

Women were, at times, sheltered in all-male households or left alone with male members. The threat of assault was implicit in the homes of relative strangers, and also in those of familiar political sympathizers. In her published memoir, Supriya details three incidents in which she faced sexual threats by very different categories of aggressors within the confines of the political shelter. The first incident took place in the coal mine quarter where she was living and conducting political work:

> The terror that chases women the most is the fear of being raped. That experience happened to me here for the first time. One evening, a slightly inebriated Gobardhan tried to use force on me. He was, in our thinking, the potentially most advanced worker in that area. I quickly recovered from my shock and resisted. He left with his head lowered. Later he came and begged me to keep the matter a secret. I refused. I read out some leader's quotations to him from a book to show him how one can correct ones mistakes, how one can cultivate self-criticism. (Sanyal 2001: 17)

Supriya notes, not without some irony, how the party considered her sexual aggressor to be the 'most advanced worker' in that area. Her testimony is the occasion for a powerful overturning of the movement's cherished icon, the male subaltern. It also bears witness to some of the strategic forms of resistance and self-protection that women had developed at the time. Supriya attempts to rehabilitate her aggressor through political consciousness raising in order to make him realize his 'mistake'. The discursive construction of sexual violence as a 'mistake' mirrors its popular conception as individual weakness, completely divorced from any structural conditions to do with (gendered) relations of power. Supriya's rehabilitative attempt also resonates with the political rhetoric of self-transformation or 'becoming declassed' (discussed in Chapter 2) through the acquisition of political consciousness and a correct 'class perspective' as Krishna notes in her memoir (Bandyopadhyay 2001). The disciplinary regimes of safety and managing risk that women activists developed at the time were thus filtered through official perceptions.

If rape was at an extreme end of a sexual violence continuum, there were other less clearly definable forms of male intrusion that could only be resisted through silences and withdrawals. The second incident that Supriya recounts was in the middle-class home of a male comrade. While trying to sleep, Supriya found her male comrade's father (whom she called *meshomoshai* or uncle) touching her. What Supriya can today identify and name as a sexual threat was not so easily accomplished at the time, especially as we go on we consider the party's invalidation of female speech in testimony. The location of violence within the 'safe' space of the household together with the subjective location of her aggressor—a respected, older male member of a middle-class household (as opposed to a working-class comrade who could be politically 'rehabilitated')—made naming let alone testifying less than straightforward. Supriya is quick to point out that strategies of resistance were severely limited in the exceptional circumstances of her life in the context of an armed struggle. She writes how she could not talk about these incidents or tell anyone:

> I could not tell anyone. I thought whether it was appropriate to say something merely on suspicion. Another day when I was unwell he came to see me on that pretext. However, he did not get the opportunity to do very much more than that. Many days later another sister of ours had the same experience when taking shelter in that house. She had got up and straightaway given this *meshomoshai* a slap. She asked me why I had not been able to do that. (Sanyal 2001: 17)

This inability to tell 'all things ... to everyone' that Bandyopadhyay (2001) also emphasizes overdetermined female silencing of sexual aggression. This silencing can be related to the wider demand for secrecy within the movement. Participation in an outlawed political movement that was entirely underground meant that the need to maintain secrecy was incumbent upon all its participants, especially as state terror heightened and 'informers' infiltrated the ranks of the movement. The ability to fully participate in the political domain entailed such public secrecy, understood in Taussig's (1999: 2) terms as 'knowing what not to know'. Like their male comrades, women were expected to perform this labour of secrecy as an obligation for political agency, but this commitment also came to include an active silencing of private injury. Middle-class constructs of gender and sexuality equally demand female silencing of sexual wrongs in the name of honour or respectability. Such normative expectations made it difficult to implicate meshomoshai in a discourse of sexual aggression just as it transformed, as we see later, resistance to male force into 'consent' in marriage.

The psychological costs of actively repressing the threat of abuse were high for women. Supriya was repeatedly 'taken advantage of' by a leader, a married man with children, at various shelters in which she, this man, and another male comrade lived. Supriya had left the party and joined a factional group with a man whom she calls 'comrade S' and her close confidant, Arun (both are pseudonyms employed in her memoir). They were her 'guardians', her only refuge from a hostile world of political and personal suspicion and factionalism. As her 'guardian', this man cared for her as a 'mother' while exploiting the symbolic paradigm of motherhood in everyday acts of violation.

> What used to happen was that the whole day I would sit in the room, my head would ache and he would press my head, just like *ma*, just like *ma*—press my head, my legs and in doing this, it would become more. At some point, I thought that this is not correct, it's becoming too much. (Personal interview, Supriya, November 2003)

Comrade 'S' is positioned in her oral narrative as a nurturing figure.[3] But somewhere this image of him becomes less stable. Women's testimonies of incest often express ambivalence and confusion when touch is no longer affectionate but seems just wrong (see, for example, Kelly 1988; and Puri 1999). It is still hard to cast male protectors (fathers, brothers, 'guardians') in the role of sexual aggressors. Supriya's words powerfully resonate with these testimonies when she says that she developed a 'weakness' towards this man who cared for her; 'I couldn't dismiss him right away as being bad, that was my weakness'.

In the grey zone of the shelter, knowing your enemy from your friend was not always straightforward, especially for women. This ambiguity rendered the closest of relationships precarious and not entirely free from the possibility of betrayal. Male sexual power was achieved, in turn, through an exploitation of this very structure of fear and vulnerability in which middle-class women activists were located. 'S' persuaded Supriya that while she was asleep, her trusted friend, Arun, had actually touched her. In this manner, 'S' ensured Supriya's silencing of sexual abuse by poisoning her relationship with Arun. If sexual violence silenced women's speech, it was the body that responded and resisted.

> I saw him at about 14/15 shelters. Once the people of the house had left he came and tightly held me, but when people came, he would let me go. Now this behaviour of his, is it correct or incorrect? This would trouble me, that he didn't do this in front of others. Then I felt that there was something different in this, otherwise he would do it in front of everyone. Then I started to feel bad. I would become very 'stiff' ... I kept thinking that he shouldn't think that I'm responding to him ... They were my 'guardians', where would I go? And the others at the COC [Central Organizing Committee], they were worse; you couldn't trust them at all ... I couldn't even tell Arun, how could I tell the others? (Personal interview, Supriya, November 2003)

In becoming 'stiff', Supriya's objectified body ensured a minimal degree of resistance to male dominance. Resistance could be expressed only at this level of embodiment given the minimal resources and bargaining power that women had at their disposal. 'Where would I go?' Supriya asks, making the operation of violence within private and public worlds an intimate one. The inability to leave, the compulsion to be silent, the normative spaces of 'inside' (the shelter) and 'outside' (the COC), and finally, the illusion of trust ('they were my guardians') and its betrayal ('you couldn't trust them at all'), all contributed to the temporary psychological breakdown that Supriya says she suffered at the time. Her experience of betrayal at the hands of trusted 'guardians' who were meant to protect her was a traumatic one, more so than the routinized forms of aggression that she faced from unknown male workers or sympathizers, the risk of which could, at least to a certain degree, be managed. One way to think of these latter episodes is in Das' terms as interrupting the ordinary but still as a part of the everyday. What rendered the experience with 'S' traumatic was perhaps a 'failure of the grammar of the ordinary' (Das 2007: 7), an inability to discern those who care for us from those who wish to harm us. Supriya's psychological breakdown emerged from the fact that those who were meant to afford her protection turned against her. For someone who was never arrested at the time of the movement, the violence of Naxalbari lay not so much in the brutality of the state but in the conflation of intimacy and betrayal that took place within communities of care and protection.

The Continuum between Sexual Violence and 'Marriage'

The concomitance of love and fear, desire and violence, was often manifest in the radicalization of interpersonal relations and intimate spaces within the movement, as the discussion of the Chapter 4 began to show. Not surprisingly, the flourishing of affective and erotic attachments was in favour of men with one interviewee characterizing the movement in terms of an 'unhealthy competition' amongst male leaders and comrades for a few female comrades. Women were often left vulnerable to male advances, even abuse, from which, ironically, 'marriage' offered the only means of protection. Given that the Naxalite refashioning of marriage and conjugality drew on a predominantly bhadralok moral universe, it is not surprising that marriage, however practised, was the clearest means of protecting oneself from unwanted sexual advances and ensuring the respectability of women activists. In the experience of both middle-class and peasant women, the boundary between 'marriage' and sexual violence was not always unambiguous. Much like the affective interlocking of care and betrayal already described, 'marriage' shades into sexual abuse in what follows in ways that render sexual intimacy indiscernible from violence, and consent continuous with coercion.

In the case of Ajita who came into the andolan through student politics and other radical groups, a structure of everyday vulnerability linked her to her abuser, a unit leader, whom she says she was forced to marry and whom she later divorced. In her story, the language of sexual honour and shame confounds marriage and sexual violence.

> One boy forceably wanted me, wanted me for a long time. He was a leader. He would organize the shelters in such a way that he would get me. I knew him as our unit leader but that was all. He fixed where I would stay ... [I] went to a shelter where he was, then I fell into such a situation where, and my thinking was also that if a boy stays with a girl at the same place, then she would get a bad reputation. My thinking was wrong. (Personal interview, Ajita, August 2003)

What Ajita's narrative makes clear is that the hierarchical organization of political labour within the movement in which women activists were subordinate to male leaders was an enabling factor for sexual exploitation. This together with the division of space afforded male leaders the privilege to pursue and exploit women cadres, as in this case, where a male leader effectively controlled a female cadre's mobility. What can also be noted is the fusion of revolutionary ideals of free choice and individual consent, on the one hand, and bhadralok norms of sexual respectability, on the other, that (re)produced female vulnerability in particular ways. In Ajita's case, a relationship had developed but more importantly, an 'impression', she says, had been created. It was the burden of this 'impression' that made marriage incumbent on her, even when a relationship of choice became one of force. The party, she says, 'took it for granted and didn't try to understand the condition. I wasn't in a situation where I could speak to anyone' (Personal interview, Ajita, August 2003). While individual choice and consent were privileged in movement marriage practice, their ambivalent status, especially when it came to coercion and force, in the realm of the intimate was not considered. Feminists have noted how the category of consent, which plays an extremely important part in rape law, inevitably functions to 'transform rape into consensual sex' (Das 1996; see also Baxi 2010). In Ajita's case, the pressure to conform to middle-class norms of sexual respectability, together with the threat of sexual shaming, transformed 'force' into 'consent'.

What is also significant in Ajita's story is the continuous evocation of self-blame and self-refutation that determines her relationship to a traumatic past. Although Ajita does blame the party—'... a lot of girls' lives have been ruined because of the mishandling of the party. Some are able to come out of it, some aren't and they have to suffer through their lives'—she blames herself far more for being weak and for not being able to resist male dominance. As with Supriya, the memory of betrayal by a familiar other is narrativized through guilt and self-blame, paradigmatic of what Bourdieu (2001) calls the symbolic violence of masculine domination whereby victims not only fail to recognize the oppressive power relations within which they are implicated but actually blame themselves for its effects. This symbolic violence is further naturalized in a leftist political rhetoric in which structural limitations of patriarchy (and class) are decisively transformed and attributed as individual weakness.

Like the feminist critiques of 'marriage' previously voiced (in Chapter 4), Ajita's story plots the limitations of the radicalization of intimate life in the course of the movement:

> Initially I felt that we'd work it out. Even though I made it clear that I had no personal or mental involvement ... I thought he is our leader, but later I saw that actually the man is different, especially with regard to women. His thinking was very 'backward'. He was absolutely like a traditional man. I thought at least I am in a left-leaning, liberal thinking place and its alternative was something far worse. But then I saw that he's bad (*kharap*) from that side, very different, he's not what he was supposed to be ... so my ideas about him changed from day to day. (Personal interview, Ajita, August 2003)

Much like her, several women discovered, only too late, that their communist husbands were 'not what [they're] supposed to be'. Prominent writer and ex-activist, Joya Mitra (1994) writes scathingly of her first marriage, at the age of nineteen, to an older communist man. She writes of the disparities between communist ideals and everyday practices in the manner in which she was expected to fulfil her wifely duties, curb her political involvement, and support her child in the face of her husband's renunciation of household duties as relics of traditionalism. As in the colonial context, the new normative visions of conjugality at the time of Naxalbari were unable to overthrow male power within the family, even strengthening it in some ways. New conjugal ideals have thus been linked by historians of the colonial period to the production of 'new patriarchies' (Sreenivas 2008: 7). Naxalite women had to contend with such small and large-scale betrayals in daily life—the betrayal of trust at the hands of those who were meant to protect them, intrusions upon their being by those who they respected (even loved), and finally, the failure of a vision. Perhaps it is the depth of *these* betrayals that makes the task of naming violence so painful, even today.

The 'Official' Adjudication of Rape

Women's testimonies of sexual violence at the time of the movement were structured through the necessity and active cultivation of silence. When women did testify to sexual abuse, their testimonies were often received with disbelief, disqualified, or simply ignored by party members. Women also needed certain qualifications to be recognized as fully legitimate victims of sexual violence. As we see in what follows, the party's response to sexual violence mimetically reproduces the judicial discourse on rape in India within which only certain kinds of (moral/modest/undesirable) women can be plausible victims of rape as opposed to others (Baxi 2005, 2010; Das 1996; Kannabiran 2002; Menon 2000; and Sarkar 1991).[4] The manner in which 'rape ceases to be so in the case of certain categories of women' (Sarkar 1991: 216) has also been observed of the parliamentary Left in West Bengal. Protection from the 'CPM family' is not a given for all women, as Da Costa (2010: 129) notes of its women's wing's response to cases of rape which implicate the patriarchal party, a mirror of the patriarchal family. The CPI(M) is also seen to 'emphasise class struggle at the expense of women's interests pitting "women, in contradiction to the collective" [Gupta 2002:1749] rather than seeing women as integral markers of collectivites at various levels—family, party, or state' (Da Costa 2010: 122). Rape has come to be addressed in the Indian women's movement as a mode of signifying and sanctioning other power relations (class–caste) than simply being an expression of male sexual desire (Sunder Rajan 1993).

Class (to which caste was subsumed; see Chapter 2), for the Naxalites, was central to the recognition of gendered power and powerlessness but not in unequivocal ways. So, while the rape of peasant women by landlords or repressive state forces was politically acknowledged as a form of class oppression, that of middle-class women at the hands of lower-class/caste men was routinely denied. Violence against women came to be cognized and mediated through an axiological understanding of 'class' and 'class oppression' and as a reflection of and response to the political violence that the revolutionaries were organizing against. To this extent, the violence within the quotidian life of the movement was rendered visible and made continuous with the violence that existed 'outside', the violence of class struggle.

Gopa, who I spoke of in Chapter 3, narrated an incident that became fairly representative of the party's negotiation of sexual violence faced by middle-class women. A woman activist had repeatedly complained to the party about the intentions of a newly recruited male comrade towards her. Party members dismissed her anxieties by blaming her 'middle-class mentality'. Her accusations were, in fact, falsified on the basis of the class differentials that existed between the victim and the victimizer. She was told, according to Gopa, 'you're an officer's daughter and just because he's a worker and he's dark-looking you're accusing him'. Eventually the woman was raped. The man apparently confessed his crime to the party but blamed the 'old madhyabitta vices' that still existed in him (even as he was identified as a worker). The party let him off.

Some of the women interviewed had similar stories to tell. Monu described a lengthy process of being interrogated by members of a local committee to ascertain the validity of her claim that a worker had tried to rape her. As in a conventional rape trial, the questioning included: 'did he touch you?'; 'how did you resist him'; 'why did he let you go if he could have done something?'; and so on (Personal interview, Monu, November 2003). Bandyopadhyay (2001) narrates a similar incident in her memoir where she just about escaped being assaulted while carrying out party work.[5] In both cases, the party chose to disbelieve the women owing to the working-class status of their sexual aggressors. Constituted by the party as a disembodied deified icon, the male subaltern could not be recognized as a subject implicated in a discourse of sexual violence. Bandyopadhyay points to the politics of such acts of deification when she writes:

> After so many days I have learnt that 'class dependency' means trusting workers and peasants. I have also learnt that workers–peasants are not human beings but something else. Which is why even if a peasant keeps up a woman night after night with his indecent behaviour then one cannot talk about it. 'You are losing the class perspective, comrade'. (Bandyopadhyay 2001: 95)

Indeed, it is the injured female subject who emerges not only as a lying subject but also as a victimizer who, like the state/ruling class, oppresses the male subaltern on class lines. Such an accusation that employs the rhetoric of class politics to misrecognize gendered power and vulnerability effectively silences female testimony. When not explicitly falsified, female testimony is silenced through its trivialization; it is pitted against a properly political 'class perspective', as indicated in Bandyopadhya's above-mentioned narrative. Even in this short extract, the metyonomic usage of 'indecent' is suggestive of the complex intersections of class, caste, and gender through which violence against women is articulated in the Indian context (see Rege 1998). The gendered and sexualized scripts on which particular constructions and expectations of class, class identity, and indeed of 'becoming declassed', relied on are equally flattened in this particular Naxalite 'class perspective'. While women's sexual vulnerability was structured through the interplay of gender, class, and caste asymmetries within the movement (as in wider society), women were divided and pitted against each other on caste–class lines. The party's differential politicization of middle and working-class women's sexualities, given the demands of a reified 'class struggle', further suggests how the violence of the everyday was reduced to the exceptional political violence activists were organizing against. The experience of being harmed *within* the movement by its members was thereby conflated with the violence suffered from without. Once again, the public domain occupied by the state emerges as the sole site and source of violence.

Acts of injury within the movement are repeatedly located outside its boundaries. I am thinking here of the first incident in which the man confessed his crime but reduced it to a madhyabitta 'vice'. His deployment of such a defence is not surprising given that the party imbued social categories of class with moral worth. 'Class' is also naturalized in such a discourse; it is reduced to a biological or psychological as opposed to a normative type of behaviour. While in legal discourse men are said to act out their 'natural sexual instinct' when they rape women (Das 1996), here they fall prey to class-based vices. In the former, rape is normalized through the naturalization of male sexuality; in radical Left discourse, its normalization operates through the naturalization of class, abstracted from its intersections with other social categories and relations of power. The reduction of rape to a reified construct of class also minimizes the need to act against instances of abuse since these are constructed as something the community has inherited from an external agent. The community itself is purged of all evil which is projected onto larger madhyabitta society, observable in some of the narratives discussed next.

It is important to note the manner in which party ideologues did condemn and convict male offenders, and the politics of retribution in these instances. Krishna Bandyopadhyay narrates an incident in which a woman activist complained to the party leadership about a middle-class comrade's inappropriate behaviour towards her that deserves quoting in full:

> A meeting was called to prosecute the male comrade. Almost all the members of the leadership and few of us women gathered at a house for the meeting. Several discussions followed. It was decided at the meeting that the women would make the final decision. The woman who had suffered the harassment began. Shaking with rage and hatred, she uttered only one thing: 'The only punishment for this crime is *khatam*'. The other women got very excited; one by one they all uttered the same word, 'khatam'. I began to feel rather nervous about putting forth my own view. Although I knew that my sole refutation would not stop the 'khatam', I still had to voice it ... [She tells the gathering] 'No man has the right to disrespect any woman. If a male comrade has behaved inappropriately towards a woman comrade then he must be severely punished. But why *khatam*? We have all become intoxicated with the idea of *khatam* ... Then we will have to kill some others present here' [She asks the other men present there] 'Can all of you honestly say that you have never behaved inappropriately towards your women comrades?' ... I had said this as representative of all the women comrades since I knew that many of them had faced similar experiences. (Bandyopadhyay 2001: 97–8)

Within the qualified space instituted by the party (the 'trial'), it became ideologically consistent to punish/kill middle-class men as plausible perpetrators of sexual violence.[6] The avenging of sexual harassment with 'annihilation' is a frightening instance of the replication of the 'extraordinary' violence that the movement was organizing against, within its own structures and internal relations, such that violence became 'a banal instrumental necessity' (Bourgois 2001: 11). Internal killings within the CPI(ML), and later Maoist groups (much like those documented by Bourgois 2001 of the guerrilla culture of El Salvador), are another instance of the mimetic process by which the revolution can end up using the very same power it attempts to overthrow. I was told of two prominent cases where dissenters within the party were 'annihilated'.[7] Within the culture of the movement, the taking of life was not viewed as an excess but simply as the natural order of things. This common sense normalization of political violence at the time of Naxalbari deemed khatam as the only justice for sexual violence.

The incident narrated by Krishna Bandyopadhyay is not an isolated one. Molina Dhak, the only woman in West Bengal to be given a life sentence, murdered her rapist, a middle-class political sympathizer who had given her shelter.[8] An article on Molina published in *The Telegraph* describes the party's support for her action: 'Molina reported the incident to the Party which took great exception: firstly, a woman was humiliated; and secondly, members saw the act as a deliberate threat to their work and safety of the activists' (Dasgupta 1996).

As before, the party recognized acts of abuse committed by its own middle-class cadres and sympathizers even though it normalized the exercise of sexual violence by subaltern men. The class distinction is significant; it suggests a redistribution of class capital within radical Left politics. Unlike in juridical discourse, it is men of upper caste/middle-class groups and *not* of the lower classes who are constructed as plausible perpetrators of crimes against women in ways that are consistent with the wider ideological motivations of the Left. The act of sexualized wounding is also presented, at least in the article just quoted, through the language of humiliation (that is, gendered female) and as a threat to the security of *all* party members. Sexual violence is no longer an act that simply 'humiliates' women but affects the 'physical safety of *all* bodies' (Menon 2004: 137).

While there were certain qualified spaces within the movement in which violence against women was afforded a degree of recognition, these were also seemingly spaces of misrecognition. By making examples of a few middle-class male perpetrators, the party could relinquish its own responsibility towards its members and install a safety valve for a repressive community. Such a safety valve did little to alter or even recognize the structural determinants of patriarchy, class, or caste within (and outside) the movement. The sanctioning of khatam as a form of retributive justice carried out by or on behalf of the wounded female subject was also seen as the natural order of things. At least in the case of Molina, the party seemed to have sanctioned female militancy only when there was a confluence of individual interests with those of the larger community. By contrast, women's naming of violence as violence *towards women* tended to remain unsayable or be disqualified.

The category of sexual violence and that of the perpetrator and victim were not stable. They were varyingly constructed within the discursive field of gender and class relations in the movement. Some forms of sexual violence, such as the rape of peasant women by the state, were more easily politicized and incorporable into a reified discourse of class oppression. Others that defied such easy incorporation were suppressed and misrecognized. As with legal constructions in 'normal' times, rape was varyingly constructed as a metonym for class oppression or as an offence against the community as a whole. It was rarely recognized as an offence against 'the bodily integrity of *all* women' (Baxi 2005; emphasis added; see also Das 1996). These constructions of rape enabled, in turn, the discursive (im)possibility of women's testimony and normalized the exercise of male sexual violence.

Naming Sexual Violence

In examining the lived experience of sexual violence in the movement, I have pointed to the possibilities and limitations of women's testimony to male sexual violence at the time. These limitations were structural, linked to their everyday realities in the context of a conspiratorial underground movement, and discursive in that women activists had to negotiate official discourses and perceptions of 'good' and 'bad' violence. In the cultural memory of the revolution, the battle lines are drawn all too starkly with the righteous violence of the revolutionary falling on one side, and the illegitimate force of the state on the other. How does one recollect experiences of betrayal and violation suffered at the hands of one's comrades and *not* at those of the enemy within such a landscape of memory? Such memories are often experienced as a burden or as risky insofar as they constitute a zone of ambiguity or a Levian grey zone where the division between the protector and the persecutor begins to blur.

The testimonies of violence that I have examined (like Supriya and Ajita's) continue to be voiced in the context of a normative silence, exemplified in their emphatic need to remain anonymous. There are, of course, varied reasons for women's need for anonymity, including, as noted in Chapter 1, their feelings of vulnerability with respect to their own children when it comes to their political pasts. While the need for anonymity can thus be attributed to the demands of class, family, and respectability, or even to concerns of privacy, it is also attributable to the specificities of Kolkata's leftist political field in which many have noted the difficulty in speaking out against patriarchy and violence (Da Costa 2010; Ray 1999; and Sarkar 1991). Ray (1999) shows how both autonomous and party-affiliated women's groups in Kolkata generally link rape to wider political violence rendering it difficult to name rape as violence against women per se. The Indian women's movement is also known to be more comfortable in its focus on exceptional forms of brutality, like custodial rape, than more routine manifestations of patriarchal violence, partly ascribable to its Left inheritance (Kumar 1993).[9]

It is, then, not surprising that women interviewees spoke of the difficulties involved in publicly naming sexism and sexual harassment, especially for 'political' women who continue to be members of various left-wing political parties. Women's in(ability) to 'speak out' is also linked to the movement's legacy. Krishna Bandyopadhyay, one of the few women to have publicly condemned male sexual violence, has, for instance, been accused by her own comrades of trying to 'destroy' the movement, and that too, by other women activists. Even at the start of the English translation of her original Bangla essay, she writes: 'Several times, while composing this piece, I debated whether it would be better not to do so. With such critical reflections one always runs the risk of isolation; and who wants to be isolated?' (Bandyopadhyay 2008: 52). In her interview with me, Krishna said that she had experienced a distance with most of her fellow female comrades over the issue of sexual violence that she explicitly wanted to draw attention to in her writing. She suggested that this was partly to do with preserving a particular (positive) image of the movement which her testimony threatens. Supriya, whose published reflections are even more scathing, echoed her thoughts.

Oppositional or 'unapproved' memories held by subordinate groups that threaten the status quo are always at risk of obliteration or silencing (Edkins 2003; Motsemme 2002; and Watson 1994). Female testimony to sexism and sexual violence becomes, in the context of Naxalbari, an act of betrayal. Perceived as a threat to an imagined political community, such stories are not openly articulated even as they circulate in private, like a 'public secret' in Taussig's (1999) sense as that which is known but not publicly articulated. The need for silencing also suggests that an affective community of listeners who can bear witness to women's experiences of wounding has not come into its own, in spite of the flourishing of several alternative discourses, including feminism within and outside of the Kolkata context. The power of the latter is clearly limited given the difficulty women feel in drawing on a culturally available but still marginalized story of surviving sexual violence.

The inability to publicly name sexual violence lies, for me, at the heart of the cultural practices of remembering Naxalbari that glorify some forms of violence while eliding and normalizing the experience of others. These wider politics of remembrance implicate the individual negotiations of 'bad' violence that we now turn to. Women's (and men's) discussions of sexual violence are enveloped in layers of ambivalence and contradiction. Women often disassociate themselves from sexual victimization, downplay, disavow, and deny male sexual violence, and defend the party against accusations of complicity. Focusing on the narrative strategies deployed in (not) naming sexual violence, I am interested in what they reveal to us about the complexities of women's identifications with and investments in fantasies of heroic selfhood as well as the attendant costs of such forms of identification and composure. These costs are all the more pronounced when negotiating risky memories that have, as yet, no place in a triumphant narrative of revolution.

Conflicting Identifications

A fantasy of revolution offered Naxalite women powerful points of identification in idealized images of heroic selfhood. Becoming a revolutionary appealed to their desire for a new (gendered) order, of belonging to a counterculture, and their guilt of being middle class. It also came with the possibility of rejecting traditionally passive femininity and embracing heroic agency and other positive (masculine) qualities. Women activists internalized the symbolic structure of the movement largely through the image of the self-sacrificial martyr who rises above 'ordinary' feelings and familial ties in the pursuit of heroic ends. While it offered women powerful and 'wish-fulfilling' (Dawson 1994) subject positions, revolutionary femininity was not without its contradictions or costs. While the sacrificial (in motherhood, for instance) was emphasized in the construction of heroic subjectivity, 'real' women were expected to repudiate certain 'feminine' qualities such as love and maternal drives. Women's political participation also demanded of them a divesting of markers of gender difference and embodiment even as they struggled, as previously seen (in Chapter 3), not to be 'othered' as *meye* or girl.

Noting this dynamic in the Second World War, Summerfield (1998: 137) argues that in trying to emulate 'a male super-norm' by denying any feminine weakness, women marked themselves as different. Men also had a stake in maintaining traditional gender differences and thus 'othered' women through chivalrous treatment and even sexual exploitation. Summerfield's hypothesis is particularly relevant when we consider the potential of sexual violence to violently mark the woman activist as 'other', and heighten, as Puri notes in a more everyday context of sexual harassment, women's 'self-consciousness of embodiment' (Puri 1999: 77). The threat of sexual violence placed under considerable threat, if not disrupted, women's identifications with apparently unmarked (by gender and class–caste) disembodied political identities.

Supriya's narration of a certain incident exemplifies the complexities of these identifications. The incident involves two men who took Supriya to be a sex worker when she was on the road one night.

> At first I thought he must be a policeman in civil dress. He continued to walk alongside and the interrogation started. He asked me about myself, where I stayed, whom I had been visiting and how could I venture out in the dark in a place that was obviously of ill-repute. I made up each answer in keeping with the line of questioning ... [When the man took out a wad of notes] Shamed and insulted, I said that he was wrong about me; I needed no protection and was perfectly capable of being on my own.... Meanwhile another person reached me ... another round of interrogation ensued ... I now realized that there was no escaping from their attention today. In a fit of desperation I entered into counter arguments, fervently hoping for the bus stop to be close at hand ... The moment he clasped my hand a wave of repulsion came over me. I thought it was time to disclose my true identity. It would be much more honourable to be imprisoned by the police than to be pawed by them. *I had dreamt of being a martyr relentless in the pursuit of*

class struggle. And now, what was happening to me? (Sanyal 2001: 24–5; emphasis added)

Supriya's text gives voice to certain 'class-based concerns of sexual respectability' (Puri 1999: 98) that structure perceptions of the self and the female body. Her feelings of shame and insult are directed at the fact that she was identified as a sex worker, an identification that not only contradicts her revolutionary aspirations but also the inherited cultural codes of middle-class sexual respectability. Her account suggests (as Ajita's previously did) that the responsibility *and* respectability of the female body was very much a burden that individual women internalized and carried (Puri 1999). Significantly, the police, in Supriya's story, pose a more 'honourable' option than the two men who were harassing her, in a departure from their discursive construction as rapists in official party discourse and in other women's narratives.

Supriya's words, 'I had dreamt of being a martyr relentless in the pursuit of class struggle. And now, what was happening to me?', also reveal a certain crisis that the self is thrown into by virtue of the threat it faces. Sexual violence generates a conflict between a 'true self' that is configured in the image of a disembodied martyr and a 'false self' that is rooted in feminine embodiment and is open to invasion and objectification (Bartky 1990; see also Young 1990). Supriya is forced to confront her self as an embodied and gendered (and classed) object; she is made to feel conscious of her body and its objectification in ways that a disembodied and desexed (not to mention, 'declassed') political subject was never meant to. The threat of sexual violence thus pushed to the surface what had been abjected from the political domain, and from what political identity itself had been constituted in contradistinction.[10] It seemed to disrupt her attachment to normative revolutionary identities by (re)inscribing feminine and sexual difference, and together with it, feelings of acute vulnerability. Such feelings had little place in the mythic or organizational structure of the movement that tended 'to suppress gender rather than to incorporate it explicitly' (Puwar 2004: 133). It needs to be mentioned that the situation itself arose due to Supriya's abandonment by her fellow 'sister–workers' who refused, on being intimidated by local moneylenders, to shelter her for the night.

As with Supriya, the narratives that I now turn to exemplify the ways in which the female revolutionary seems torn between conflicting identifications; exemplified in the apparent need to minimize, elide, or deny past experiences of sexual aggression and to guard the self (and the party) from the threat these pose. Gopa, an early entrant into the movement who also married and divorced at a young age, draws attention to the problem of sexual violence at the time of the movement but resists her own victimology in sexual objectification.

> No one ever behaved badly towards me, never. When I read about other women's experiences, I think this has happened to me once or twice but in very different circumstances. A very close person has 'disturbed' me, not a stranger. It could be because I was never conscious that I am a girl and they're boys, and they're different. I didn't know if they were taking liberties from other girls but it didn't happen to me. From the beginning I was *didi*. I don't know why ... I think of those times a lot now. Like when I read Supriya's article or others writings where, time and time again, how women were 'sexually' ... or later I met two, three women myself. When I hear all this I think how come I didn't face any of this? What I think now is that perhaps I was so naïve, I was so 'insensitive' to this issue. My mind was always involved with some other work, 'plus' my marriage. I mean, 'I knew all the bitterness of these relationships'. These thoughts didn't come to my mind then, this 'consciousness' wasn't there in me which actually, is very natural for a twenty-one-year-old girl, she's with so many boys all the time but 'somehow or the other' I didn't think of it. It could also mean that because I wasn't conscious of it, neither were they ... When I came back from jail, I faced this and when it happened, I was very angry. I get very angry about these things. If someone ever even hinted at treating me like a 'girl' I would get very angry. (Personal interview, Gopa, June 2003)

The many contradictions in Gopa's narrative—the simultaneous denial and assertion of the experience of sexual aggression ('no one ever behaved badly towards me, never; I think this has happened to me once or twice ...'), the professed 'insensitivity' to the issue despite being a married woman *and* one who was in an abusive conjugal relationship at the time—suggest an investment in not seeing sexual abuse, even against her own experience. How can we understand such an investment? One way of doing so, as suggested by feminists like Kelly (1988), would be to recognize denial and contradiction as part of a coping strategy in the face of a traumatic past. Feminists have also suggested how women's acts of denying or minimizing abuse can be seen as a form of resistance to a discourse of victimology, generally understood to be profoundly disempowering. The associated risk is that of rendering violence against women invisible or even of normalizing male sexual power (Jackson 2001). Another way, in the context of the movement, would be to recognize the specific demands that revolutionary identities made upon women which entailed, in turn, a loss of alternative, competing identifications or even a *dis*identification of some sorts. By disidentification, I mean, following Butler (1993), the repeated denial or disavowal of an identification that threatens the 'composure' or coherency that one seeks. The term best signals the manner in which some Naxalite women seem to simultaneously identify *and* disidentify with or even reject the past experience of sexual victimization rather than simply silence or 'forget' such experiences as some others do. The experience of disidentification stems from 'the uneasy sense of standing under a sign to which one does and does not belong' (Butler 1993: 219), which perfectly captures women's experiences of being, in the political domain, outsiders even as they might have been insiders.

In Gopa's case, the struggle to occupy a coherent identity seems to entail a disidentification with female alterity, and along with it, the experience of sexual violence, a key signifier of gender difference. While testifying to the problem of sexual aggression, Gopa's narrative ultimately makes it rest with the individual woman and her consciousness of herself as a gendered being. In contrast, she explicitly distances herself from the experience and situation of the female body: 'it could be because I was never conscious that I am a girl and they're boys, and they're different'. In couching her relationships with male comrades in kinship terms (as 'didi'), her narrative also divests the self of any sexuality. Gopa seems to have a stake in privileging a subject who is above ('never conscious of' or 'insensitive to') gender difference and sexuality; a desexed subject that transcends the body and the feminine in particular. She also makes her annoyance at being treated as a 'girl' within the political domain explicit suggesting that in order to assume a political identity of their own, women had to disavow their sense of being a 'woman', and that their identities were split, as Supriya's story makes clear, as a result of their desire to be political agents.

Puwar (2004: 119) argues that the ontological denial of 'race', gender, and class is part of the process whereby racialized and gendered minorities become insiders in normatively male and white organizations. She further notes how naming oneself as an embodied subject, in such an environment, is not easily done. Naxalite women have begun to name gender—via sexism and sexual violence—as is evident in women's published memoirs. Gopa's professed awareness about these issues 'now' as opposed to her ignorance 'then' in the light of increased feminist consciousness suggests, as demonstrated later, that a pure non-identity with the experience of sexual violence is not entirely possible today. Gopa also indicates her slight suspicion towards these efforts in saying that now people talk a lot about 'these issues' and 'perhaps more than necessary'.

The narrative strategies employed by Roma in discussing sexual violence closely resemble those at work in the Gopa's account (and Maya's, described later). Her narrative as a whole strives hard to make one understand that revolution is ultimately an 'experiment' and that 'mistakes' *will* happen on the path toward revolution. When asked about gender discrimination in the party, Roma vehemently denied it and quickly moved to the narrativization of an incident when she was sexually threatened. As Summerfield (1998) notes of the dynamics of her own research, her denial could have also been prompted by her perception of me as a feminist researcher who was seen to be pressing her on issues of discrimination and sexism that she resented.

> No, I've never seen it. In my experience, I never saw this. Yes, it wasn't that a boy never ever behaved inappropriately towards a woman. This has happened, perhaps even with me, but that was 'immediately' taken care of. I saw it in one case, even though he was martyred later on. This young boy, we were sleeping at night and he did something at night. I told the others in the morning. It wasn't that he did something simple, his intention was to do more, so naturally, and due to some other incidents as well, they said to temporarily stop all 'connection' with him. But that boy, the 'feudal attitude' was inside him ... (Personal interview, Roma, August 2003)

I asked if she ever heard of it from other women:

> While at jail, I never heard of this from anyone ... Yes, I won't say that little incidents, look, coming from this society, at a personal level, a 'feudal attitude' wasn't there or a 'discriminatory mentality' wasn't there ... this was there. But 'in general', that the party 'nourished' this or didn't take any steps against this, that I have never heard of. In fact, the party has always taken steps when this has happened to anyone ... when we come from the old 'society', then we come with its vices along with the virtues. A true revolutionary is born through overcoming these vices.

Like Gopa, Roma refuses to name sexual violence or to recognize herself as a wounded subject even as she identifies with the experience of sexual aggression. She also makes a particular effort *not* to implicate the party in acts of sexual violence and gender discrimination. The party, according to her, was fairly vigilant and effective in responding to sexual offences. Sexual violence is rooted in a 'feudal attitude', and ascribed to only certain categories of oppressors, the state/ruling classes and some but not all activists. 'A true revolutionary is born through overcoming these vices', she says. Sexual aggression is then a 'vice' (or a 'mistake' as previously seen) that must be excluded for the emergence of the 'true' revolutionary subject. One cannot help but notice how close her words are to a leftist discourse of self-transformation or 'becoming declassed' to which sexuality was salient (see Chapters 2 and 3). She also displays a characteristic leftist mistrust of 'feminism' equating it with sexual permissiveness and 'living together', and accuses feminists of overdoing things. Finally, Roma's narrative shares with other women (and men) an investment in a particular construction of the 'old society' or mainstream bhadralok society against which movement participants attempted to define themselves. Repeatedly, I heard how members of the Naxalite community were also members of the 'old society', and thus it would be unnatural to presume that the contradictions of the old would not have to be confronted in their efforts to create the new. The pervasiveness of sexual aggression in the 'old society' works to render it unproblematic in the context of the movement besides precluding an engagement with the question as to why gender violence is pervasive in mainstream culture. As with the rapist state, the possibility of violence occurring within the community is precluded through a series of oppositions with an imagined other, here construed in the image of the 'old society'.

In the narrative negotiations of sexual violence discussed here, women appear to abject their own experiences of injury by privileging a disembodied, desexualized, and self-abnegating political subject of Left radicalism. While such acts of repudiation can be straightforwardly linked to the collective (and coercive) silencing of *some* forms of violence within radical political cultures or even to middle-class demands of honour and respectability, I have sought to locate them in women's conflicting identifications with a fantasy of revolution and their underlying costs. The threat of sexual violence powerfully disrupted, in Supriya's narrative, identification with this fantasy, undoing composure, especially along the lines of gender. It made evident the masculine nature of the images and identities on which such a fantasy relied in which women occupied specific (iconic) positions and performed limited roles. In the face of the fracturing of subjectivity that was engendered through this political culture, the recomposure of heroic identity *today* seems to entail a repudiation of past wounding together with the inability to identify oneself as an injured subject or even as a gendered one, as seen in Roma and Gopa's narratives. The 'bad' violence experienced in their pasts fails, however, to be safely contained by these narrative strategies. Subject positions always entail the loss of alternative identifications that are nevertheless not entirely lost. The subjective experience of violence cannot, it seems, be articulated as testimony but it cannot be 'forgotten' either.

Sexual Violence and Narrative Negotiations of Masculinity

Violence, I showed in Chapter 2, lies at the heart of Charu Mazumdar's redefined heroic masculinity. A new man is born in the exercise of violence. The official narrative of revolution thus effects two contradictory moves: on the one hand, it fuses male identity with violence in the public glorification of heroic masculinity; and on the other hand, it sublimates this violence by calling it heroism and self-sacrifice, thereby normalizing male violence or at least the relationship between masculinity and violence. What is left unacknowledged in this symbolic association is male sexual power and violence towards women.

For women activists and sympathizers, recognizing the possibility of sexual violence in male activists who are friends, even partners, is often difficult. Male activists clearly have more at stake in suppressing, from collective memory, stories of betrayal and violence that could potentially implicate them. Changing discourses around violence against women have, however, rendered it difficult to entirely deny issues of sexism and sexual harassment even as it becomes possible to claim ignorance. The perceived rarity of incidents of sexual violence in the context of the movement renders the issue, as a whole, unproblematic for some male leaders. This is a common double bind that feminists researching sexual harassment have drawn attention to: 'if it's commonplace, it isn't really sexual harassment; if it's rare, then it isn't really a problem. It has to be rare to be real; but if it's rare, then there's no need to worry about it' (Kitzinger and Thomas 1995: 42). Men and women's careful negotiations of the issue reveal underlying tensions surrounding gender, male sexuality, and class.

My exchange with Maya who identified as a sympathizer (see Chapter 6) can be seen as representative of one strategy of negotiating the tensions around revolutionary masculinity. Without being directly asked about issues of sexism or sexual aggression, Maya volunteered the following, drawing on tropes of benevolent communist masculinity.

> This much I can say—what I have seen in the Naxalbari politics, experienced it as well—that you can stay with them day after day in the same room, even then they won't ... I went to one meeting where there were many boys, about two–three women but there was no bad behaviour towards the women. This I really liked, liked it then and I like it even now, when I meet some of them today ... you can completely trust the house with them. (Personal interview, Maya, August 2003)

When I asked her (after she had made this statement) whether she had perceived any gender bias within the party, she emphatically denied it, and inquired into how other interviewees had responded: 'I don't know what others have said, those you have interviewed, but I don't think anyone will say this; everyone will have the same feeling that they were given enough respect, in terms of women. "Has anyone said this?" [The response has been mixed]. "One person or many?" [A few incidents] "What incidents?" ...' (Personal interview, Maya, August 2003). No doubt feeling a bit cornered by the examples I gave of other women, when Maya eventually admitted the possibility of sexual harassment, she allocated it to the realm of exceptionality: 'Everyone has come from this society so I can't say that everyone came in as a *mahapurush*. It can be that some people ... this can be there. I have never experienced it myself because I never really went to any meetings' (Personal interview, Maya, August 2003).

Maya's words carefully negotiate categories of maleness. She uses the word 'mahapurush', literally meaning a great man, to denote a form of masculinity that is not commonly available. Sexual violence is made part of an ordinary manliness since one can only expect exceptional men or a mahapurush not to indulge in acts of sexual violence towards women. Such a framing, which resonates in other women's accounts of sexual violence as a 'vice' or a 'mistake' that exists in some unfortunate men, implicitly naturalizes male sexual aggression. While Maya's narrative seemingly disrupts an idealization of Naxalite masculinity in equating it with innate sexual violence, it also reinforces an idealized benevolent masculinity (which includes trust and respect towards women) in assuming that all the men in the movement were, in general, mahapurush; only a few would give into their natural sexual instincts or would fail to control them. 'Bad' violence is thus attributed to some and not all male activists who represent an inferior manliness, a departure from the norm.

Let me end by considering a male narrative that draws attention to a hitherto unrecognized aspect of sexual violence—the sexual exploitation of adivasi women by middle-class revolutionaries. Saumen's discussion of sexual violence (as with his narrative on romance and marriage explored in the Chapter 4) is one of the few I encountered from a male activist:

> The boys who came from Presidency College (I won't give you any names but what I'm telling you is 'authentic')—many good, well-known Presidency College boys with 'good results', who went to Gopiballavpur, their 'method of integration' was to stay at peasant homes as man and wife. And under the influence of some famous Naxalite leaders, young, unmarried girls got 'pregnant' there, peasant girls. I can bring you a witness who has 'helped' one such girl. They would go and as man and wife, would be with this girl and that girl ... then at another place, they would also be husband–wife ... This 'reckless' behaviour that I can do anything and that it is 'justified' in the name of revolution ... (Personal interview, Saumen, September 2003)

Bhadralok comrades are known to have 'married' peasant and adivasi women in unions that, by and large, did not last. Saumen suggests that such unions were in the name of political efficacy, echoed by Sinha Roy (2011: 120) who observes how 'becoming declassed' came to include relations between middle-class (male) activists and peasant or working-class (female) activists. 'Becoming a Naxalite' relied not simply on sexual self-discipline, as previously noted (in Chapter 2), but in seemingly having 'political' relations with appropriate sexual subjects. 'Class struggle' is here enacted through sexuality, with subaltern female sexuality playing no small part in the production of a superior, authentic revolutionary masculinity. The fusing of political and erotic ends coexisted, however, with the possibility of exploitation and abuse in already unequal power relations, as Saumen emphasizes. Sexual freedoms for middle-class male revolutionaries occurred alongside a blurring of the distinction between sexuality and violence for peasant women (and middle-class activists as previously seen). The latter was also enabled by new normative visions of class and gender equality insofar as Saumen suggests that acts of male sexual violence remained couched within a (sexual) fantasy of revolution. The vulnerability of subaltern women to patriarchies, old and new, remained largely invisible within such a fantasy that required of them very specific signification.

Saumen's narrative is also part of his general condemnation of the 'brilliant students' of Presidency College who have been the chief beneficiaries of public recognition in the history of Naxalbari, as noted at the start of this book. The sexual exploitation of subaltern women is another way of putting their status of historical significance into question. Authentic revolutionary subjectivity is ascribed, throughout his larger movement story, to a lower middle-class/caste male community to which he belongs rather than the elite intelligentsia. As with Maya, the issue of sexual violence becomes a kind of currency that is employed to rank these different forms of masculinity. Such negotiations are also salient in accounts that tend to implicate peasants and workers of sexual crimes, thus absolving 'our boys' of any responsibility. There is a reversal in the construction of the male subaltern subject, the primary icon of the revolution, who becomes nothing less than a scapegoat in the present. Even as they demystify one icon of the movement (peasants/workers), these women and men's narratives choose to preserve another one in the image of the middle-class male revolutionary who continually strives to 'declass' himself by overcoming class differences, sexual instinct, and the body.

I have shown, through an engagement with women's testimonies of sexual violence and domestic abuse, the complex intermeshing of the violence that was 'external' to the revolutionary community and 'internal' to it. These forms of 'public' and 'private' violence mutually implicate one another suggestive of a continuum between everyday and so-called extraordinary expressions of violence. The very 'extraordinariness' of political conflict rendered invisible the underlying structures of power and vulnerability that constituted the quotidian life in the movement. The pervasiveness of the violence of the time also folded into interpersonal relationships in which desire and fear, trust and betrayal, and conjugality and violence were experienced concomitantly. Definitions of violence as exceptional, ascribable to certain bodies, and containable in certain (public) spaces were, however, far removed from this messy grey zone, and served, instead, to mask and normalize the violence that inhered *within* the community, at the hands of one's own.

Women's negotiations with the threat of sexual violence and the strategic forms of self-protection that they developed at the time were mediated through official perceptions of 'good' and 'bad' violence as well as middle-class concerns of sexual respectability. The rhetoric of self-transformation, especially of 'becoming declassed', recurs as a rationalization of and defence against illicit male sexual desire, employed by both men and women. Sexual violence simply becomes one other component of a bhadralok identity that needed to be shed in order to occupy the position of the normative revolutionary subject. This was merely one of the ways in which male sexual power remained embedded in the everyday life of the movement whose conspiratorial, familial, affective, and even erotic character placed structural conditions on the (im)possibility of female testimony to sexual crimes. The party played a significant role in the disqualification of this testimony and the normalization of violence against women by treating rape primarily as an index of class oppression, and the victim as a metonym for the violation of the community as a whole.

Female testimony to sexual violence continues to be articulated in the context of a normative silence. This is especially evident in the discussions of women who seem to be invested in *not* identifying sexual violence, even against their own experiences of abuse. Investment in a fantasy of revolution meant abjection of those experiences that were rooted in more fragmentary and vulnerable aspects of the self. The abject, for women, included that which was coded as feminine within primarily male (and disembodied) fantasies of heroic self-sacrifice. Such fantasies could not incorporate the full range of contradictions within the (gendered) social world from which they were largely divorced, and relied, in fact, on their containment. At least for some women here interviewed, identification with these imaginaries entails a *dis*identification with those experiences (like sexual violence) that seem to fracture the subject's coherency, resulting in a profound discomfort with regard to, and in some cases an outright denial of, one's own victimization. Women's investments in not identifying certain aspects of their past must, then, be thought less in terms of their 'complicity' with oppression than in terms of the 'ambivalent process' of identification itself (Butler 1993: 126). In naming sexism and sexual violence, Naxalite women effectively name themselves as embodied, as gendered (as meye); they name what was unnamable at the time of the movement in face of its privileging of a disembodied (male) political subject agent. Naming sexual aggression also means implicating comrades and party members in acts of illegitimate violence, and tends to become synonymous, in the aftermath of the andolan, with conflict and betrayal.

Sexual violence, it seems, is a pivot upon which conflicting narratives of the past are competing for supremacy in the movement's dissolution. Women's victimization at the hands of the state finds, instead, ready appropriation in the movement's cultural memory. However, as we see in a final discussion, this 'speaking' of women's trauma in testimony does not guarantee the alleviation of individual pain.

6

Political Violence, Trauma, and Healing

> I had known people of my own age, who had survived the Great Terror in the Calcutta of the sixties and the seventies, and I had at least a spectator knowledge of their courage.
>
> Ghosh 1988: 108

On 14 August 2003, whilst still in Kolkata on fieldwork, *The Times of India* reported a meeting to commemorate the Cossipore–Baranagar massacre of 1971 ('1970s massacre remembered').[1] A collective call for a non-official inquiry into the massacre was made at the meeting as it has been done in the past. Major Naxalite groups such as the 'above-the-ground' CPI(ML) Liberation have over the years raised a demand for a state-led enquiry into the massacre, which the Left Front government did not take up. The two commissions of inquiry that were set up by the government upon its election in 1977, the Sarma Sarkar Commission and the Haratosh Chakraborty Commission, produced reports detailing the misuse of state power and the illegal killings of persons in West Bengal during the period from the 20th March 1970 to May 1975. No action was taken on the basis of these reports.[2] Naxalite groups and political parties annually commemorate the Cossipore–Baranagar killings by holding rallies and meetings in the area as well as in other parts of the city. In scores of acts of memorializing Naxalbari, it is the horror of state repression that dominates, as in the legacy of the movement as a whole.

Stories of young idealistic men being brutally tortured and shot by the police has been the most sustained component of this legacy. Mahasweta Devi's work has been at the forefront of a tradition of Naxalite storytelling in which, Hutnyk notes, 'the graphic violence of police attacks becomes almost a traumatic catharsis' (Hutnyk 2000: 147). Political violence and the victimization of activists and sympathizers of the party is the subject of several other works of fiction and film.[3] Aside from the two memorials at Naxalbari and Baranagar for commemorating the massacres that took place there, I was told of pillars and memorial plaques in the various paras of Kolkata. These were said to be spontaneously erected by members of the neighbourhood to commemorate 'their boys' who were lost to the violence of the 1970s; what the writer Amitav Ghosh fittingly refers to as Kolkata's 'Great Terror'. Through these localized acts of commemoration, community members remember their young heroes who sacrificed their lives for the vision of a new world. The impulse to do so is all the more given that there is no official tribute to the lives lost, as with the Partition (Butalia 1998). In both cases, the state can hardly memorialize these events without recognizing its own complicity.

The memory of political violence is thus inscribed upon a community of survivors, including ex-activists, new and potential Naxalites, and smaller radical outfits. Political gatherings and publications, as with literature, songs, and poetry, of these fractured groups constitute a site for acknowledging and recording those who died during the violence of the 1970s in narratives of heroism and martyrdom. Public recognition of past injury and the restoration of justice is a core endeavour of these forms of commemoration. Demands have been made for the establishment of a Saroj Dutta memorial, and calls for official investigations into his death and that of Charu Mazumdar persist. Acts of memory also function as a testament to the past and ongoing brutality of the state. Given the internal differences within an ex-Naxalite community, memories of state repression do not constitute a singular oppositional narrative against state power. In a context of continuing political antagonism between the parliamentary Left and Naxalite and now Maoist groups, and within these groups as well, collective remembrance of past trauma helps to reproduce rather than reconcile 'the bitterness and hatred of violent conflict' (Dawson 1999: 189). These acts of memory are also sites for the enactment of party politics.

The imagining of revolution and its heroes has always been 'the historical occasion of unacknowledged traumas as well as utopian excitements, because these idealisations are founded upon manic triumphalism and its denial of psychic realities' (Dawson 1994: 285). When state repression was at its height in the 1970s, Mazumdar called for more martyrs to come forward in a public valourization of violence. His relentless optimism possibly guarded against feelings of insecurity and fear, once arrest and even death became imminent. Narratives of glorious struggle and sacrifice for the cause similarly negotiate feelings of trauma and loss in the aftermath of the movement. The memory of state repression is rewritten in these narratives, as obvious in the CPI(ML) Liberation group's English mouthpiece, as an overwhelmingly sacrificial one:

> Bathed in the blood of immortal martyr Comrade Dhaneswari Devi and others historical 25th May gave birth to the revolutionary India with the touch of the hands of the disciple of Chairman Mao—Immortal Martyr Respected Leader Comrade Charu Mazumdar. On that very 25th May the reactionary ruling class have leaped to silence the struggling peasants of Naxalbari with violence. But the brave peasants aroused with the international responsibility have not stepped back in scare, instead of that eight peasant women, two children, and one peasant by sacrificing their lives ... they are firm to grasp the spirit from the same, and for that they will fear no amount of self sacrifice. (CPI[ML] Liberation 2002)

Edkins (2003) identifies such a 'sacrificial memory' in forms of war commemoration as a way of silencing individual speech and forgetting trauma. A 'sacrificial memory' is endemic to the myth of the nation state in which death in war is reinscribed as a glorious sacrifice for the nation, and through which the state co-opts the bodies of dead soldiers and produces closure. In accepting the myth of self-sacrifice rather than the reality of death, remembrance becomes a way of forgetting violence and of domesticating its trauma. In the context of Naxalbari, practices of commemorating the dead as martyrs reinforce an imagined community held together by a comforting collective fantasy of revolution. The possibility of mourning the individual is delayed, or even lost, as the myth of the revolution takes precedence over 'the question of personal loss and bereavement' (Edkins 2003: 94). The human cost of sacrifice is also obliterated from collective memory.

While the trope of martyrdom comes most easily to 'official' and some forms of historical discourse, the trauma of political violence is inscribed in other sites of memory. Radical newspapers and periodicals of the time, like *Frontier*, bear testimony to the victimization of the activist community that occurred in the 'orgy of torture' (Guha 1971: 15) that was institutionalized by the state. In his observations on 'Torture and Culture', published in 1971 when state repression was at its height, Guha speaks of the normalization of a culture of political terror in Kolkata:

> Although most of the big 'national' dailies have not yet made up their mind about treating such information as 'news', some of the more outspoken periodicals are already shrieking in agony ... Besides, one has simply to ask the boy next door in almost any *para* of Calcutta, and he will produce oral—and if one has the stomach for it—visual evidence of broken wrists, roasted skin, mangled anus, bruised testicles—his own or those of his friends. (Guha 1971: 10)

In representing violence in its gruesome detail and not in abstraction, these sites of memory capture what is repudiated from a sacrificial one. Publications by radical journals and weeklies, and by civil liberties organizations such as the APDR and Amnesty International, have poignantly archived the violence of those times, documenting the nature of custodial violence, police torture, endless 'encounter' murders, the conditions for political prisoners in jail, and jail killings (see, for example, Chaudhuri 1977a, 1997b; editorials of *Frontier* from 1969 through to 1971; Goswami 1971; Kumar Ghosh 1993; Patwardhan 1978; and Sen *et al.* 1978).[4] The APDR (1999) has been at the forefront of the collection and publication of the testimonies of those who suffered custodial violence and torture, including the testimony of family members and sympathizers. What is remembered here is the individuality of the dead, supported by what Dawson, in the context of the political conflict in Northern Ireland, calls 'the desire to keep alive the name and value of the deceased in memory' (Dawson 1999: 195). These sites of memory also mount a full-scale challenge to the state. The writings in *Frontier* are the clearest examples: 'The period of silent killing and trying to explain away the bodies found here and there is drawing to an end. There will no longer be the problem of transporting them in dairy vans before break of dawn. They can now be carried in push-carts in daylight' (*Frontier*, 21 August 1971).

Another site in which the trauma of state violence is remembered is poetry. Much of this poetry was penned by activists while at prison and bore witness to the routinized brutality suffered besides the actual killings of fellow prisoners inside jails.[5] In fighting off prison guards and the police, prison was also the site of continuing rebellion against the state; it was, as in the case of other movements, 'the final front of struggle' (Hamilton 2007: 125). Songs were often the only means of communication that the prisoners had (Banerjee 1987: 96), and together with poetry, played a considerable role in the campaign to release political prisoners in 1977. Although largely inspirational, some of these poems evoke a darker, more brutal imagery of death. The last lines of a poem by a male activist, Shovan Shome, for instance, starkly represent the repression of an entire generation of youth whose wounded, violated bodies made a mockery out of a newly independent nation:

A generation lay on the road
Crying shame on all births (Banerjee 1987: 84)

These poems also signal the possibility of 'encircling' trauma, what Edkins, drawing on Žižek, identifies as a way of marking trauma, 'in its very impossibility' (Edkins 2003: 15) thereby resisting the inevitable depoliticization or 'gentrification' of trauma that takes place in its conversion into a linear narrative (see also Caruth 1995). Practices of memory and forgetting are crucial to this attempt to encircle the trauma rather than to obfuscate 'the true horror of a situation' (Žižek 1991: 6; see also Žižek 2000). Encircling or marking the trauma in this manner also opens up the possibility for individual mourning, the first step towards the healing of a wounded community. An anonymous poem written on the walls of a cell in Presidency Jail, Kolkata, commemorates the killing of 22-year-old Naxalite, Prabir Roy Choudhury, who died in a jail killing in 1975:

Silence!
Here sleeps my brother.
Don't stand by him
With a pale face and a sad heart ...
For, he is laughter!
Don't cover his body with flowers.
What's the use of adding flowers to a flower? ...
If you can,
Shed some tears
And –
All the blood of your body (Banerjee 1987: 18)

What is here remembered and mourned is the loss of an individual, a friend, a brother, and not simply a nameless, faceless foot soldier of the revolution. Inscribed on the walls of a prison, the poem is very much an act of witnessing state violence. The title of the poem, *Silence*, equally bears testimony to the power of violence to destroy language, and to the impossibility of fully capturing its trauma in language (Scarry 1985). It does not celebrate death as martyrdom but silently encircles trauma through the expression of sadness and grief. Sagar Chakravarty's poem,

Lying on the Terrace of a Police Station, similarly rejects the myth of sacrifice in remembering death *as death*, and in grieving its loss:

He's lying on the terrace of a police station.
He's dead now.
Gently touching his body,
I weep.
And some, in silence
Fume and ask–
Who have killed him?
Why? (Banerjee 1987: 85)

Death is marked, in these lines, in all its horror and futility. In asking, in rage and sadness, 'why', the poem renders the death of an individual incomprehensible. This is a question that cannot be raised within a politics of memory that co-opts the bodies of the dead for the sake of scripting an imaginary community of martyrs and heroes. The word 'why' marks the meaninglessness of death, not its triumph. Poetry, at least in the context of the few poems here reviewed, enables the 'public recognition of the individuality of the dead' that is integral to the 'emotional work of mourning' (Dawson 1999: 195).

The Female Subject of Political Violence

The female body occupies a distinctive place in the cultural memory of state repression even as it occupied an ambiguous position in the memorialization of the movement's everyday life, as previous chapters have shown. In the archive, the Naxalite as a gendered subject emerges in reports and documents detailing the horrific conditions in women's prisons, and later, in recounting the number and names of women tortured in police custody and at prison. An Amnesty International report on 'Detention Conditions in West Bengal Jails' published in 1974 contained details of the horrific conditions in women's prisons thereby underscoring the gendered nature of state violence (reprinted in APDR 1999). These and other reports (see Chaudhuri 1977b) publicly acknowledged, for the first time, women's participation in the struggle.

It is in Sumanta Banerjee's triumphalist account of state repression that the female Naxalite finally finds mention in the movement's historiography. What is notable is the highly sexualized nature of the torture that Banerjee describes: 'girls were "stripped naked", their bodies—

"the neck, the breast, the stomach and other private parts not excluded" burnt with cigarettes, "accompanied by every conceivable humiliation", often leading to rupture of the more sensitive organs' (Banerjee 1984: 345–6). In underlining the sexual nature of Naxalite women's victimization (see also Donner 2004b; and Kalpana Sen 2001), historiography seems to confirm the popular view that women activists and sympathizers were raped by state forces (see, for instance, films like *Anu*, and literary works like Devi's *Draupadi*, discussed later). The figure of the raped middle-class woman activist thus dominates in the memory of state terror even as it has no place in the memory of the underground. Rape is considered not exceptional but routine to the exercise of state power. Thus, in the journalistic, fictional, and historical imagination of state repression, rape, as Marcus argues in her influential analysis of the 'rape script', 'has always either already occurred and women are either already raped or already rapable' (Marcus 1992: 386). As De Mel notes in context of Sri Lanka, the iconic status attributed to acts of rape in these contexts do little to redress 'the wrongs committed by the security forces or to inaugurate a public discussion on women's bodies as sites of war' (De Mel 2001: 221). In film and fiction where rape becomes the predominant way of representing state brutality, there is very little negotiation of the rhetoric of shame and honour through which the trauma of rape is culturally understood. In official party discourse, there is, in fact, an appropriation of rape in order to further the revolutionary cause (see Chapter 2).

While popular memory is replete with images of Naxalite women as victims of state abuse, the female subject of violence is rewritten as a subject of resistance in women's own words. There is a slim albeit substantial body of writing by Naxalite activists on the memory of prison.[6] Middle-class women activists dominate within this literature with Joya Mitra's *Hanyaman* (Under the Shadow of Death, 1989), winner of the 1991 Ananda Puraskar, being the most prominent. Mitra's *Hanyaman* together with Minakhi Sen's *Jailer Bhitor Jail* (Jail Within Jail, 1994) and Tyler's *My Years in an Indian Prison* are deliberate attempts to testify to the state's disciplinary control over women's bodies. These texts rest on similar narrative strategies, that is, an effacement of the speaking subject in order to represent 'other' women, that is, non-political co-inmates, including a category of criminalized 'lunatic' women with whom these Naxalite women prisoners shared the overcrowded prison space. It is the everyday structural brutality of women's lives, supported by a patriarchal, paternalistic state, to which these prison memoirs bear witness. What also emerges in these texts is the staging of the female as both the subject of violence and of resistance to state power, as detailed by Punjabi (1997). Gender is thus a site not only of 'violability', as in the case of historical and popular memory, but also one of resistance. Prison memoirs of the Naxalite period contribute to a wider feminist scholarship that explores gendered memory as a form of political resistance (Cubilie 2005; Kaplan 2002; and Zur 1998).

Mahasweta Devi's story of a Naxalite Santhal woman, Dopdi Mehjen, titled *Draupadi*, enacts more powerful narrative strategies in fictionalizing police torture. Dopdi is gang raped by the police on the order of their chief, Senanyak. Yet, at the end, it is Senanyak who is afraid of Dopdi, 'an unarmed *target*'. She stands in front of him in all her nakedness, refusing to be clothed or cleaned, and mocks her aggressor: 'you can strip me, but how can you clothe me again? Are you a man?' (Devi 2002a [1997]: 36). In refusing to be clothed by male authority or to be shamed by patriarchal violence, Dopdi rewrites the 'rape script' by turning it into a farce. She deliberately rejects what Sunder Rajan (1999: 353) calls a 'shared sign-system' or the gendered logic of rape, and creates fear in her aggressor through the deployment of a different logic, mockery and laughter, instead of shame and fear (see also Misri 2011; and Spivak 2002).

To be sure, women are represented, even in Devi's oeuvre, as romanticized resisting subjects that political torture can never diminish. The female activist, Nandini, of *Hajar Churashir Ma* (Mother of 1084, discussed in Chapter 2) has been left blinded in one eye from prolonged interrogation; her skin bears the ritual cigarette burns that branded most Naxalite women at the time. She is bitter, cynical, and without grief, 'cold and almost indifferent' (Devi 2001 [1997]: 75). The trauma of state terror is starkly represented in this text, not robbed of its horror through the language of self-sacrifice or heroism. Yet, Nandini is constructed as being outside of 'normalcy' (Devi 2001 [1997]: 87), especially the bounds of conventional middle-class femininity. Nandini is closer to the idealized (masculine) Naxalite subject than she is to a Dopdi Mehjen who does not offer, in Sunder Rajan's (1999: 355) words, an ideal strategy of resistance. These cultural forms and processes of witnessing state violence are implicated in women's oral testimonies of political violence that I now turn to.

Women Witness State Terror

Of the women I interviewed, a majority was incarcerated for a period of three to five years. A close bond of friendship continues to exist amongst those who were incarcerated in Presidency Jail in Kolkata between 1971 to the end of the Emergency in 1977 when all political prisoners were released by the newly elected Left Front government. Almost all the women imprisoned at Presidency Jail suffered varying degrees of torture at the hands of a single police inspector within the confines of his 'special cell' created solely for interrogating Naxalite prisoners. Pressing lighted cigarette ends to parts of the female body was Inspector Runu Guha Neogi's favourite torture technique (there is significant recorded proof of such torture; see, for instance, Amnesty International's [1994] report on Archana Guha). In addition to custodial violence of this nature or that witnessed on others while at prison, most women were incarcerated for a prolonged period of time, which saw the denigration of the human body through malnutrition and disease. Some have lost close comrades, even partners, as a result of state repression; others live with husbands whose bodies have been permanently damaged by police brutality. The organization of domestic lives has been irrevocably altered in these cases, not least because of the inability to secure some form of financial stability since being released from prison.

Outside of the community, there has been very little space for the public articulation of women's testimonies of state terror, largely attributable to the official silencing by the state. The community itself chose not to seek any legal reparation immediately after the movement given their ideological rejection of the juridical system (though some are doing so today). The Archana Guha case against police torture has been a significant force in propelling the issue of police torture onto civil society, symbolizing, as Dasgupta (1998) writes in *The Telegraph*, 'a tormented generation's yearning for justice'. The national and international attention drawn by this two-decade long legal battle has made 'Archana Guha' a metonym for human rights violations in India. It is not uncommon for Kolkata newspapers to compare contemporary acts of state abuse with the degree of brutality suffered by 'an Archana Guha'. Unlike Archana (and her sister-in-law, Latika, who I discuss later), the women who told me their stories of political abuse have not occupied the position of a legal witness in a court of law. Rather, they occupy the position of the survivor, someone who has lived through something and can therefore bear witness to it (Agamben 2004: 438). Their testimonies circulate within a community of survivors like themselves or within other communities that some of these women are now members of, such as women's groups and human rights organizations.

The unspeakable terror of physical torture is made to speak in different ways in women's narratives (Aretxaga 1997; Cubilie 2005; Hamilton 2007; Jelin 2003; Kaplan 2002; Motsemme 2004; Ross 2003; and Zur 1998). While the traumatic event has been safely integrated into some life stories, in others, it is a continuing source of pain, an open wound. In narrating the fragmentation of the self in torture, these memories remain tied to the body, as memories of atrocity and violence are often said to (Bakare–Yusuf 1997; Cubilie and Good 2003; Scarry 1985; and Todeschini 2001). The maimed, bruised, and torn female body is carried from the *thana* to the prison where it survives as a wounded, diseased body that is also open to the inscription of new wounds. The memory of torture suffered in police custody almost invariably leads to the recollection of prison years. Themes of friendship and domesticity reinscribe the experience of incarceration as one filled with warmth, camaraderie, and resistance, in sharp contrast to the isolation, fear, and pain that characterizes the memory of police custody. If the self was 'unmade' in the violence of the 'interrogation', it was 're-made' through its integration into a community of sufferers in prison (Brison 2002).

Maya, Latika, and Rukmini were detained from anything between three to five years at different and overlapping periods of time at Presidency Jail in Kolkata. Of the three, Rukmini alone was a full-time member of the party at the time of her arrest. As 'sympathizers', Maya and Latika were hardly exempt from arbitrary detention and even torture at the hands of the police. For all three women, this was their first direct encounter with state violence, and the pattern of their arrest, torture, imprisonment, and eventual release resonates with that of others, both male and female, who were arrested at the time. Their post-prison lives have, however, unfolded in significantly different ways, attributable, as I later discuss, to differences in class and age. These social structures not only shape one's experience of wounding but also the afterlife of survival (Arif 2007; and Das 1992). Today, Rukmini describes herself as a journalist with a special interest in women's issues. Maya, too, is active in people's movements, having worked with prominent civil liberties and women's groups. Latika's post-prison life has been remarkably different from the other two women given her role as the lead witness in the Archana Guha legal case. In considering their oral testimonies in turn, I focus on the distinct modes of witnessing that the 'event' of torture and its aftermath has produced, raising questions around recovery or 'healing' in lives touched and transformed by violence. I also point to some of the underlying complexities of the articulation of traumatic memory in testimony, especially, as I have analysed elsewhere (S. Roy 2010), around the assumed political and palliative nature of rendering trauma 'tellable' in testimony.[7]

The Body Remembers

A refugee from the 1947 Partition and of a lower middle-class background, Maya was, at the time of her arrest, teaching at a school in Kolkata. She was imprisoned, like most Naxalites, under anti-terrorist legislation (the Maintenance of Internal Security Act or MISA) in Presidency Jail for three years. For women like Maya (and Latika), remembering is anchored around this 'moment of transformation' (Arif 2007: 36) in which their relationship with 'normalcy' breaks. The past is relived from this moment while 'the future appears trapped as an afterlife of the event itself rather than as an accumulated unfolding of time', as Arif (2007: 29) writes of survivor narratives of the 1984 anti-Sikh riots in Delhi. In her interview with me, Maya moved quickly to a narration of the time of her arrest and torture at Lalbazar (the Kolkata Police Headquarters where political activists were interrogated). Subsequent life events and narrative responses to particular questions were also structured in terms of these events in her life. It was obvious that she had spoken of this experience at other forums; she, in fact, noted the public recognition awarded to her as a survivor of political violence at her place of work and within the public domain more generally. The recognition that Maya drew from her friend (in whose house the interview was being conducted) further confirmed her status as an injured subject. It seemed that suffering had conferred upon Maya a special status (Das 1992), one that not only privileged but also preserved her victimization.

While the body, especially the female body, is ambiguously recollected if not 'forgotten' in narratives of political activism, it is here continually revisited as the very repository of the memory of torture. Thus, Maya says:

> Runu said 'come on, lift her up on the table; so much courage? Put her on the table quickly'. After that what they did, I didn't understand, they made me lie on top of a table and covered me with blankets, my legs and all. Then, then they, they held my hands so that I didn't fall. Then it was from top to bottom; it's still there, the havoc they caused, it's still there. The way it swelled up, my body was like this much [gestures with hands]. I was just nothing; I mean I was just silent. Just felt like throwing up. In an hour I was unconscious ... They gave me some water and Runu said 'come on, lift her up again' [pause]. Sometimes my senses would come back then I could see what they were doing ... I can't understand what's happening, why? (Personal interview, Maya, August 2003)

Later she recalls:

> On the fifth day [voice dips] ... everyone was yelling at the police that why have you done this. You know when you pull the *sari* what happens, the entire body is in a state, *sari* and all, and my hair was upset [*Did they pull your sari?*] What was there to pull my *sari* when Runu was throwing me against the wall by my hair?! Held my hair and then let it go, was beating me on my hands, my legs. That had already happened. They were doing these things; I mean, they couldn't think of what more to do! They were telling me to speak, what will I say? I don't know anything. There's nothing for me to say. What do I know that I can tell you? [*I thought they hit you on your legs?*] They hit me my on my legs and here [gestures to her buttocks and hips], these areas. It's still there. (Personal interview, Maya, August 2003)

Speech seems inadequate to represent the memory of violence that Maya tries to evoke. Language fails her as her voice dips; her speech becomes elliptical, even metaphorical at certain moments. The inscription of torture on the hips and buttocks can only be gestured at; it cannot be spoken of. Particular objects of attack—the sari, hair, hips, buttocks—are repositories of female identity that are particularly vulnerable to a gendered process of shaming. In reducing selfhood to the body, to mere physicality and nothingness ('I was nothing'), gendered torture humiliates its victim and tries to shame her into silence (Kaplan 2002). This sense of shame renders the task of giving words to violence that is inscribed on women's bodies, in their loss of dignity and in their humiliation, a near impossible one. What verbal speech fails to represent is communicated in the use of the body, in bodily gestures that speak where words cannot. In gesturing to the wounds located in various parts of the body (the buttocks, legs, even a broken finger), pain is represented in the very corporeality of the body. The pain of torture is literally inscribed on the body where it leaves its mark, and it is the body that remembers 'long after the infliction [has] ceased' (Bakare–Yusuf 1997: 178; on 'body memory', see also Mallot 2006). For Maya, her wounding still exists: 'it's still there', she says more than once, using her maimed wounded body as testimony to violence. If intense physical pain is 'language-destroying', in Scarry's (1985) words, and left to reside in the body, then it is the body that bears witness to trauma.

Like other women, Maya remarks how past sites of injury are beginning to reappear—in persistent leg aches, pain, and fatigue—with old age. The memory of torture continually invades the present in its literal inscription on the body; it cannot be reduced to Nora's (1989) *lieux de memoire* where memory is a site to be visited. As Cubilie notes of testimonies of state terror, Maya's testimony is not memorial in tone; it does not speak of an event that is definitely past, neither for the individual survivor nor for society at large. For Maya, as with several interviewees, the situation from the time of Naxalbari has in no way changed in the present, demonstrated (at the time of the interview) by an undemocratic and oppressive Left Front government. Given this larger social context, her narrative assumes an 'interventionist tone' (2005: 161), committed to a critique of state oppression and the pursuit of justice. So, when asked whether it was necessary for so many young comrades to have lost their lives, Maya evokes the victimization that is inscribed not just on her own body but also on that of her husband to assert the following:

> That was necessary. My husband and I have both become lame. If you see the man you'll be amazed. His height has decreased by this much [gestures with hands]. What they did to him, it's unspeakable. It is unspeakable. You know they put iron sticks up men's, you know what I mean ... What I was saying was that I never felt ill but I feel lots of pain in my body now. I walk slowly ... my movement has been restricted so much that it cannot be spoken of. My strength has diminished. And my husband is just about alive and his state [refers to her friend], you've actually seen what has happened to the man ... I mean, what can I say? And there is nothing more to say about all this. Nothing has been done for the masses but I have this little faith, this deep belief that we can raise awareness amongst the masses—this is the only thing that's real to me. (Personal interview, Maya, August 2003)[8]

In a sharp departure from traditional paradigms of heroic resistance and survival that write against the grain of torture and dehumanization,

Maya speaks not only of her own broken body but also of the sexualized torture suffered by male activists like her own husband. As in the case of conflicts elsewhere, it is not surprising that men too were subject to torture as a 'gendered and sexualised performance' (Hamilton 2007: 138). In a further reversal of gender roles, here it is the woman who bears witness to the manner in which torture 'emasculates' men. The violation suffered by both husband and wife is not one that can be mourned privately, not as long as loss and injustice have a broader social effect. The testimonial imperative is not simply to bear witness to personal injustice but to intervene in ongoing forms of social injustice on behalf of the *jonogon* or the masses. It seems that the possibility of recovery, closure, or even healing is also tied to the idea of justice, not in a narrow legal sense but as ascribing legitimacy to pain, privately felt and socially structured.

The pursuit of a just closure is what also compels Maya's continued investment in forms of Left politics, including those that are violent. As indicated in Chapter 3, she was one of the few interviewees who resolutely defended the Naxalite 'line' of individual annihilation ('personally I think it was right') as a response to the injustices of the state but also on the basis of personal loss and injury. In the face of gross human rights violations, the strong retributive emotions that Maya expresses are not uncommon. There is, however, a danger that the call for justice as revenge could work against the need for reconciliation and healing in the aftermath of violence, preserving rather than liberating the survivor from a state of victimhood. Suffering, as Veena Das notes, 'can also lead to the belief that, having suffered, one has acquired a right to impose suffering upon others' (1992: 33). In what follows, we consider more closely how, while testimony might reinvest agency in the survivor, it does not necessarily (or unproblematically) 'heal' the survivor of trauma, as is often assumed.

The Burden of the Witness

In 1974, Latika, her sister in-law, Archana, and a close family friend, Gauri, were arrested from their home. Physical torture, particularly the use of *falanga* or the systematic beating of the soles of the feet, left Archana's lower limbs completely paralysed. Latika's husband, Saumen, who was a middle-ranking activist, was arrested soon after and tortured as well. Although Latika suffered much less physical torture than the other two women, she bore the solitary burden of being witness to this entire ordeal and took upon herself the responsibility of nurturing the wounded. Latika, along with the two other women and her husband, was incarcerated in Presidency Jail from 1974 to 1977. Since their release from jail, the entire Guha family has been involved in a case against the policemen for the torture inflicted upon Archana. The legal battle against custodial violence is nothing short of historic in West Bengal; it has no precedent, and has inaugurated a new chapter in the civil rights movement in the state.[9] In the last year of trial, Saumen appeared as the defence counsel on behalf of his sister, the plaintiff, Archana. Amnesty International subsequently sent Archana to Denmark for rehabilitation where she continues to live. In a landmark victory in 1996, after nineteen years of struggle, Runu Guha Neogi, the primary accused, was sentenced to a year's imprisonment.

Not only has Latika been the lead witness in what proved to be a very long and arduous legal battle but she also bore the sole responsibility of providing financial security to a family that was collectively crippled. Besides Archana who was left lame from police torture, Saumen's mother suffered a stroke in the course of the legal struggle and died soon after. Much like Maya, Latika has had to cope with extreme material insecurity through much of her post-prison life as well as having to adopt caring roles vis-à-vis ailing family members, including her own husband who too was left 'emasculated' by the state. Relations between the couple and former Naxalites, including Archana, have also soured over the case, attributable to their belief that no one came to their aid (one that was repeatedly refuted by other interviewees).

I interviewed Latika and Saumen over several meetings that spanned a few months. As the interview progressed and in subsequent meetings with Latika, I realized how it was practically impossible to elicit a conventional life story from her given that her memory remained tightly tethered to certain key moments that unite in a single, dominant story. The story begins with her marriage to Saumen in 1973, her subsequent arrest and torture in 1974, followed by a period of incarceration to an afterlife of loss and insecurity that left her with few (material or psychological) resources to 'work through' her traumatic past, let alone begin the work of mourning. Needless to say, the legal battle is the pivot upon which not only the narration of this afterlife but that of her entire story hinges. The 'Archana Guha case' that Saumen describes as 'the most beloved baby in the bosom of the then childless couple' (S. Guha 1997: xiii) has imbued the memory of the 'event' with new significance, besides transforming Latika's status from a victim of torture to a crusader against human rights violations. The event and the case comprise a master narrative that pervades Latika's speech, memory, and sense of self. As she puts it: 'This, in my life has been a major event, you know, I mean, you can say, the last event in my life, the impact of which I will have to carry till my death' (Personal interview, Latika, July 2003).

In the legal battle against custodial violence, Latika has been the key eyewitness to the torture inflicted upon Archana. Much like her legal testimony, her interview with me was structured around the precise temporal and spatial coordinates of her arrest; her movements within the Lalbazar police station; a detailed description of the people encountered—names, faces, and designations; and finally, the moment of torture itself.

> We had to walk half a mile to the main Dum Dum Road where the van was parked. It was drizzling. We walked all the way, getting wet. They took us straight to Cossipore *thana* where they kept us waiting ... There was one officer and two constables. Then after a while they came back, past 3–3:30 ... Then they took us to Lalbazar at 4:30. (*You remember the exact time?*) Yes, morning was approaching ... [At Lalbazar] The officer, Manas called us and asked mother's, father's name, husband's name, where does he live, do you do politics or not, all that ... They kept us waiting. Runu Guha had created a special cell only for Naxalites, just for their torture. We sat outside this room. There was a huge, long corridor [detailed description of the building] ... it [the 'special cell'] was part of the detective department but only for the repression of the Naxalites. Then it became morning, between 10–10:30. First Archana was called in ... (Personal interview, Latika, July 2003)

What follows is the subsequent, turn-by-turn torture of the three women in Inspector Runu Guha Neogi's infamous 'special cell'. As with other Naxalites, the three women were repeatedly subjected to police interrogation and torture, sometimes with a gap of only a few hours. Again, in common with the experience of other women, they were illegally detained in police custody for twenty-seven days and were never physically produced before a magistrate (Ganguly 1997: 300). Latika's published memoir conveys a similar depth of detail while bearing witness to the collective strength shared by the women in the face of humiliating torture: 'My body trembled with anger. I would not weep in the face of such tremendous uncertainty. I would not shrivel up. I would listen quietly, watch, I would bear everything. I didn't tremble the slightest. I didn't get perturbed. None of us did' (Guha 2001: 28).

Evoking the burden of the witness that Felman (1995: 15) describes, Latika emphasizes how she feels that it is her 'responsibility' to speak out against custodial violence even though the process itself makes her feel 'very bad': 'But then I feel that writing is my responsibility, so I continue to write. What I've seen, there's a need to write that ... this is a responsibility. The whole of history has to be recorded and the event definitely has a place there' (Personal interview, Latika, July 2003). Such a sense of responsibility is common to survivors of state terror who adopt a representative rather than personal voice in bearing witness to past injuries. As Cubilie notes of Alice Partnoy's testimonial to political oppression in Argentina: 'she is not writing as the autobiographical individual narrating a private life but as a member of a collective of voices that have shared and are sharing an experience of oppression for which she can provide a testimonial voice' (Cubilie 2005: 156). Unlike Partnoy, however, Latika's testimony does not refuse a representation of the moment of torture itself. On the contrary, she seems compelled to speak the 'unspeakable'.

The force of this trauma is also salient in the manner in which she seems unable to bear witness to her own suffering while, at the same time, speaking on behalf of the suffering of an other, namely, Archana. There is a slow erasure of the speaking subject or, as Caruth observes, drawing on Dori Laub's work with Holocaust survivors, '[an] ability to witness the *event* fully only at the cost of witnessing oneself' (Caruth 1995: 7). Latika almost always takes recourse to the collective, impersonal 'we' (referring to herself, Archana, and Gauri) when speaking of her experience of police custody and jail. Common to such 'judicial models of witnessing' (Das and Kleinman 2001: 26), emotions and subjective interpretations of events are also kept to a minimum. I often forgot, in my interactions with Latika, that she too was beaten, slapped, and verbally abused while in police custody. Even where the individual voice is employed, as in her memoir, the experience of physical torture is narrated as a record of happenings, a series of events that the victim passively undergoes: '... Runu's cohorts pushed me up against the wall and began to madly slap my left cheek. I realized the cheek had swollen up' (Guha 2001: 27). Such a mode of writing does not reveal a personal side of pain, or any personal truths, in its emphasis on historical truth.

It not uncommon for a trauma survivor to feel alienated from her own words in such ways (see Greenberg 1998). There is, however, an important gendered dimension to this biographical effacement that bespeaks more than a sense of alienation. In the written version of Latika's story, self-identity is constructed through the self-effacing and self-sacrificial qualities of motherhood that are traditionally valourized and that the movement itself propagated (see Chapter 2). All three women are presented as showing no weakness, remaining resolute, and bearing suffering for the sake of others (namely, Saumen, who they were questioned about). The only time they break down is when they think of their ailing mother (in-law) alone at home. A beacon of will, patience, and love, she inspires them to bear suffering and 'not to break'. Pain is here construed as weakness to the extent that the very expression of physical pain is derided as a sign of possible betrayal. In newspaper reportage, Latika's representation is governed by similar terms: 'Particularly Latika, less severely tortured stood like a rock by the side of the other two ignoring her own injuries' (Ganguly 1997: 302). Such representations have been noted in the gendering of torture in the context of other radical movements (Aretxaga 1997; and Hamilton 2007) where women are meant to endure pain on behalf of an other (male) in their association with motherhood and silence.

Latika's self-identity as a witness to someone else's pain has also meant a circumscribed role for her in the public domain since the only 'story' that she deems worth sharing is her testimony; all other life experiences and opinions are subsumed under the voice of Saumen, who speaks on her behalf. This dynamic might be attributable to their differential roles with regard to the legal case: while Latika has been the key witness in the case, Saumen has been its public voice throughout. This division of labour structured their interviews with me where Saumen dominated and Latika spoke primarily to give her testimony.[10] Saumen's oral discourse is also remarkably different from that of his wife's. It is not overdetermined by the experience of torture and pain and comes closer to a life story in its evocation of multiple pasts and life experiences.

The structure of Latika's testimony is part of a juridical mode of witnessing, one that demands a very specific epistemic stance and elicits a cognitive rather than an emotional attitude towards the 'truth'. Outside the legal imperative, the political force of testimony equally entails a conceding of the autobiographical voice on behalf of a collective of sufferers. While some have thought this as imparting a degree of political agency to the survivor (Cubilie 2005), it might also complicate the process of individual recovery and healing. For, does Latika's testimonial act not preserve her inability to speak of her own trauma except through patriarchal modes of speech/silence? Does this juridical mode of witnessing not prevent her trauma from being discharged, and eventually preserves traumatic memory in an endless demand for reparation? In both Maya and Latika, while the memory of violence might fulfil the ethical demand for justice, I am uncertain to what extent it responds to the need for personal healing. But in lives touched by violence, what could create the possibility for healing?

Narratives of Survival

In 1973, when she was just eighteen, Rukmini and her fellow comrades attempted a jailbreak to free Naxalite prisoners at Alipore Jail, including Sanjeev, her then husband. The plan involved a coordinated attack on jail personnel from the inside and the outside, involving the use of a few bombs and one revolver, which eventually and quite accidentally ended up in Rukmini's hands (a point that was emphasized in media reports of the event). The jailbreak failed, and Sanjeev and Rukmini both suffered bullet wounds (Rukmini in her leg) and were mercilessly kicked and beaten by the police. Sanjeev died soon after. After a brief hospitalization, Rukmini was taken into police custody where she was repeatedly tortured for a period of fourteen days by Runu Neogi. She was then shifted to Presidency Jail but made to return to police custody for further 'interrogation'. She was imprisoned for four years.

A return to normal life has been possible in Rukmini's case in ways that it has not for the other women. This difference can be understood through considerations of class, and can, to this extent, be thought of as a form of what Arif (2007: 30) calls a 'material recovery' in accounting for differences in survivor narratives. Since her release from prison, Rukmini has lived a life of material comfort and security attributable to her upper middle-class background. She has children from a second marriage with someone who was not involved in the movement. Not only did he replenish the violent loss of a partner but also aided her re-entry into everyday life. Her parents, who were unusually supportive right through her involvement in the movement, equally enabled the creation of a 'new normality', so hard in the aftermath of terror and loss, as Das and Kleinman (2001) have noted. Rukmini was able to return to her studies and complete her graduation, something that most women activists were unable to given the urgency to earn a living or the care work that they had to undertake. Material security also brought with it the repair of a wounded body. Her legs were particularly weak after suffering a bullet wound, worsened by periods of torture and debilitating prison conditions. She recalls how much acupuncture helped regain strength in her legs and more touchingly, how the acupuncturist refused any payment from her. Healing and a reclaiming of everyday life were made possible within these structures of care found within family and friendship networks. Indeed, as shown next, the recreation of an inhabitable world begun much earlier, in prison itself.

A degree of closure has ascribed to Rukmini's memory a different temporal ordering, 'a different kind of excavation of the past' (Arif 2007: 29), than that found in the narratives of Maya and Latika. Her narration of time spent in the movement and the period of incarceration that followed has a sense of 'pastness' that cannot be attributed to the two other women for whom the 'event' cannot be contained in the past. Unlike Maya, Rukmini's narrative does not seek (at least not overtly) to politically intervene in an ongoing state of social oppression and is, in Cubilie's (2005) terms, more memorial than interventionist. It includes, however, a critical and reflexive stance towards the past through which loss and atrocity can be given meaning even if not entirely rationalized. The past informs rather than invades the present (Jelin 2003: 51), and is an acknowledged part of the work of self-(re)creation. Rukmini describes her four years in prison as a process of gaining maturity, as 'part of my growing up' from which 'I've learnt a hell of a lot', which 'I cannot deny' (Personal interview, October 2003).

What stands out in her memory of prison life is the experience not of suffering and violation but of survival in the face of dehumanizing violence. Her narrative moves away from recounting scenes of wounding and victimization to the manner in which these were endured, accommodated, and even resisted. Survival is here presented not as a dramatic resistance to or transgression of everyday life but in terms of its recreation in a context where it seems least possible. Importantly, it is learnt: as Rukmini says, 'you learn to survive'. One learns to survive through daily rituals of forcing oneself to eat, of being alert to the gestures, even the silences that surround you, of developing your senses and relying on your intuition: 'because of survival, you're like an animal, you know'. Key to survival is the collective of sufferers that one finds oneself in; a collective that transforms into a community based on a shared sense of vulnerability, injury, and loss (Butler 2004; see also Das 1995).

Women's memories of state terror tend to privilege communities forged out of a shared gendered vulnerability but also out of camaraderie and domesticity through which a daily life-world is created and maintained in the shadow of violence. The Naxalite experience bears the same gender distinction: male Naxalites recall the individualizing and alienating aspects of incarceration (see, for example, Bandyopadhyay 2000), while women emphasize bonds of friendship that were key to their survival. It was within this 'mutually supportive community of women' (Cubilie 2005: 97) that Rukmini's wounded body was cared for, 'remade' to whatever extent possible, and her spirit restored. The possibility of resistance was only conceivable within these communal structures of support, and Rukmini uses humour to speak of this limited possibility:

> After the second time, after Lalbazar, they [other women prisoners] made me wear two petticoats so that the beating is less. Can you believe it? [Laughs] ... and then they made me wear the drabbest sari, gray color. They thought I was very beautiful so they made me wear a gray sari so I wouldn't look good! (Personal interview, Rukmini, October 2003)

In foregrounding a community forged out of vulnerability but also female solidarity and camaraderie, Rukmini's speech draws on the conventions of Naxalite women's prison writings with some distinctions. Her narrative does not reproduce paradigms of heroic (female) resistance and triumph over tragedy that, at times, underpin the writing of these texts, and are part of their politically interventionist agenda. The latter is explicit in the acclaimed memoir of this period, Joya Mitra's *Hanyaman*, where the self is effaced in order to bear witness on behalf of non-political 'ordinary' prisoners. Rukmini's prison memory similarly effaces the singular voice. Yet this effacement does not take place at the cost of bearing witness to one's own place in past events. The experience of daily beatings, torture, and isolation suffered in prison is not erased from memory, nor is it memory's anchor. Perhaps it is because it is freed from a grand narrative of resistance or even justice that Rukmini's memory can turn to the banalities of routine prison life through which trauma could be endured, if not healed.

The Afterlife of Violence and the Possibility of Healing

In spite of the fact that all three women have undergone similar horrific events, their memories of state terror are fairly distinct. Rukmini appears to have been able to reclaim a normal life through the privileges of class and through the structures of care and support provided by family members. In the lives of Maya and Latika, by contrast, the failure of such a mode of recovery, and the healing that comes with it, cannot be reduced to class differences alone. For one, the family and even wider community to which these women returned, post their incarceration, was one that had been profoundly altered, almost crushed under the force of state power. It was left to them, as is usually the case in periods of violent rupture (Das 2007), to piece together what remained at the cost of their own recovery and well-being. Their post-incarceration lives have, moreover, inscribed new forms of vulnerability upon existing ones such that subjectivity remains temporally frozen in the moment of violence and in a permanent state of victimhood (Arif 2007). This was the general and gendered pattern of lives in the aftermath of the Naxalite uprising: Maya and Latika form the rule rather than the exception.

The specific contexts in which the afterlife of violence and survival has unfolded has entailed distinct ways of relating to the past and elicited different modes of remembering. Thus, Latika's narrative seems tied up with judicial ideas of what counts as truth even as it moves outside the legal domain and invades everyday speech. As a vehicle for communicating the truth, her testimony relies on an effacement of the biographical self and bears witness, instead, to 'a stance or a dimension *beyond [her]self*' (Felman 1995: 15; emphasis in original). This biographical effacement is part of the profoundly political (and gendered) nature of testimony—to speak 'for another, to another' (Butler 2004: 25). Both Maya and Latika's testimonials fulfil what Ricoeur (1999, 2004) calls the duty of memory as the duty to do justice. Does the testimonial act recover, in this manner, the agency of the survivor, liberating her from a state of trauma and victimhood? Does it thereby act not simply as a means of historical transmission but also as one of healing (Felman 1995)?

Remembering state violence, in both public and private acts of commemoration, is an occasion for multiple forms of dis/identification. While the memory of political violence, as opposed to certain other forms of violence, is afforded a high degree of recognition in cultural forms and processes of remembrance, these can end up obscuring its trauma, as in the case of an official sacrificial memory of the movement. The unacknowledged costs of heroic martyrdom are preserved in other sites of memory like poetry, fiction, reportage, and personal testimony. The gendered nature of such forms of cultural remembrance is evident in the predominance they afford to the figure of the raped woman as a metonym of state terror. There is here a danger of fetishizing personal injury and reproducing female victimization in frozen and fixed terms. In contrast, women's prison memoirs and fictional works stage a wounded female subjectivity in more complex and nuanced ways.

In women's oral narratives reviewed in this chapter, the event of trauma is not always separable from its aftermath which, in many cases, has inscribed new forms of vulnerability upon existent ones. The long afterlife of political violence complicates, in this instance, ideas around recovery and healing, especially those that are pivoted on the giving of 'voice' to trauma in testimony. As with public acts of commemoration, the 'tellability' of state terror is not automatically therapeutic or empowering for the subject in pain. It is certainly not obvious to me that Latika's drive to testify, within and beyond the legal domain, has 'cured' the injury inflicted on her mind. I have encountered her testimony not as a coherent, comprehensible story but as the very structure of traumatic memory—'bodily, fragmented, sensory, intrusive, recurrent, uncontrollable' (Brison 2002: 31)—one that is preserved in the testimonial act itself. It is also not surprising that testimony can privilege victimhood over other forms of subjectivity in ways that could work against the need for reparation and healing, as in Maya's case. Rukmini's memory of state terror can be contrasted with that of the other two women insofar as it ceases to be tethered to the moment of terror and an accompanied state of victimhood, foregrounding, instead, a discourse of survival, agency, and healing. It can, to this extent, be considered an instance of recovery. Yet, the seamless manner in which a traumatic past is integrated into her larger life story seems to be interrupted by the way in which she almost always takes recourse to the third person to recount prison life. In all three, a transformation of the 'wound' into modes of testimony, whether legal, social, or political, attempts to establish order upon traumatic experience by means of re-entering normalcy and resuming one's place in the social order. Perhaps such a domestication of traumatic experience is the inevitable cost of recovering in the shadow of violence and devastation, of being healed.

Conclusion

Mourning Revolution

State-sponsored terror in West Bengal is, once again, in the news. The Left Front government's violent repression of popular protest against forcible land acquisition in Nandigram in March 2007, which led to the death of fourteen people, was reminiscent of the original event at Naxalbari in more ways than one (see Menon and Nigam 2007). Nandigram has been compared to Naxalbari, except that this time, the CPI(M) had been in power for thirty long years. Its actions found no available rationalization even amongst some of its most ardent supporters (Nigam 2010). While many viewed the parliamentary Left's most recent recourse to violence as foreshadowing its death knell in a historic electoral defeat in 2011, others recommended mourning 'rather than celebration or vindication' (Sarkar 2007).

In this concluding chapter, I want to explore some of the implications of this study of women in the Naxalbari movement for theorizing a range of issues that go beyond the bounds of India/South Asia. These include: feminist political theorizing of women's involvement in radical or even 'terrorist' movements; analyses of violence and its afterlife (in which issues of speech and silence have become salient); an appreciation of the affective life of social movements; and the work of individual and collective memory in a globally pervasive context of mourning and (Left) melancholia. For Brown (1999: 19), pace Walter Benjamin, the contemporary crisis of the Left is symptomatic of a melancholic inability to let go of 'a particular political analysis or ideal' that might be past, even lost. Attachment to such an ideal, even to its failure, supersedes the desire to move beyond it, to seize new possibilities, and forge connections in the present, rendering the Left not merely anachronistic but also a conservative force. Left melancholia of the kind Brown describes is evident in the nostalgia that pervades post-Nandigram condemnations of the Left Front through an implicit call to return to 'a purer leftism of earlier decades' or to a 'real' Left. It is also implicit in current assessments of the Indian 'far left' as being, in the face of the many failures of the parliamentary Left, 'the only true, authentic face of left wing politics in India', as noted and critiqued by Sarkar (2007).

Represented today by the Maoists, the far left emerges in such conversations as the only available voice for/of the poor and marginalized, its violence only and ever derivative of the violence of the neoliberal state. To critique the Maoists, as some Left intellectuals are now doing, is to betray the cause of the Left ('the people') and to endorse the routinized violence of the state in collusion with that of corporate capitalism. Debates came to a head with the publication of writer–activist Arundhati Roy's (2010) long essay, 'Walking with the Comrades', an eyewitness account of the everyday lives of cadres of the CPI (Maoists) in Chhattisgarh's Dantewada district, an epicentre of the war between the state and the revolutionaries. Critics accused Roy of aestheticizing the revolution, reifying the 'adivasi', and glorifying the everyday culture of violence and militarization that she witnessed (Nigam 2003). What is striking in Roy's text is that the literal and visual figure of revolution is female in ways that are continuous with other media representations (see Chapter 1). Her endorsement of Maoist politics finds legitimacy in the feminist credentials of the party that, she argues, are a distinct improvement from the Naxalites of yesteryears. Whatever their misgivings, patriarchal or otherwise, Naxalite leaders like Charu Mazumdar founded, she writes, 'the dream of revolution real and present in India. Imagine a society without that dream. For that alone, we cannot judge him too harshly' (Arundhati Roy 2010).

Feminists are not exempt from Left melancholia (see Roy 2009b), often manifest in their purchase of the 'dream of revolution'. In critical assessments of the far left, Indian feminists have invariably separated the problem of Left traditionalism (particularly with respect to sexuality) from the normalization of violence and the militarization of everyday life. This feminist separation that I noted at the start of this book is not a matter of casual oversight. It stems from a long, deeply melancholic investment in the moral worth of revolutionary struggles and resistance—even violent resistance—to colonial and state oppression. While Third World feminists have been mostly suspicious of political violence, especially that of the state, they have not completely ruled out its use, as Hutchings (2007a) has detailed in her discussion of the feminist ethics of political violence. As I have argued elsewhere (Roy 2009a), this opens up the possibility for feminism in a post-colonial mode to support the use of political violence in certain, very exceptional circumstances, such as for national liberation or under the banner of 'class struggle'. It makes it possible for feminists to ethically discriminate between forms of violence, and to share radical Left understandings of violence as a politically progressive 'good' violence against the 'bad' violence of the (patriarchal) state. 'Good' violence of this sort is not only seen to fulfil anti-oppressive ends but also feminist ones, evident in current appraisals of anti-state political violence as a site of female empowerment, even agency. For many feminists in South Asia today, anti-state movements (unlike nationalist ones) are seen to provide the opportunity for women's politicization, especially in military or combatant roles, that have been historically unavailable to them (see, for instance, Alison 2004; Manchanda 2004; Pettigrew and Shneiderman 2004; and Rajasingham–Senanayake 2004).

Violence: Continuities, Meanings, Ethics

The analysis in this book serves as a caution against such feminist evaluations of radical politics at several levels. It suggests, for a start, that conceptual distinctions between forms of violence, based on the ethical ends that they seek to achieve, are largely unsustainable in practice. This is obvious when we consider how political violence tends to give rise to other violence, besides the high probability that violence against oppressors may be used against those who are not directly responsible for oppression (Hutchings 2007b). Social activist and left-wing intellectual, Balagopal (2006) notes of today's Naxalites that the killing of ones' own (comrades, civilians) greatly exceeds the killing of the purported enemy. Less obvious is the manner in which such violent politics actively produce rather than simply enable other violences, including violence against women. The ideology and ritual of political violence also structures the subjective experience of violence, besides determining the possibilities of witnessing and resisting violence.

Remembering Revolution shows how, much like the state, the violence of the revolutionary was continuous with forms of everyday, especially gender-based and sexual, violence against women. Against official and historiographic discourse in which political terror exhausts the potential for recognizing violence in the movement, I have turned to the everyday that was transformed by the 'exceptional' political violence of the time. The very extraordinariness of political conflict, including the construct of a rapist state, transformed the spaces of the underground and the shelter into ones of safety, rendering invisible or exceptional the forms of violence and vulnerability that occurred in these spaces. For women activists, spaces of safety were often part of the 'routinisation of violence' (Pandey 2006: 15), and the community of trust to which they belonged lost its taken-for-granted quality. Rigid divisions and taxonomies of violence—particularly between the state and the revolutionary—are especially hard to sustain once we consider the manner in which the extremity of political violence reverberated in the dynamics of everyday interpersonal relationships, as revealed in Chapters 3 and 5. The preceding chapters have paid particular attention to the ideological and structural conditions, on the one hand, and the 'pervasiveness of the spirit of violence' (Pandey 2006: 12), on the other, that enabled intimate forms of violence to go unchallenged, remain invisible, and even normalized.

In an important reminder of the continuities between progressive anti-state struggles and the (patriarchal). ideologies of the state, the CPI(ML) (mis)recognized the existence of violence against women only within certain qualified spaces and in ideological categories of victims and perpetrators. Its actions served, however inadvertently, to normalize some forms of sexual violence, which are constituted in the afterlife of the movement as an aberration of a benevolent communist masculinity. I have shown how working-class or peasant women were plausible victims of sexual violence deserving of the party's protection in ways that middle-class women activists were not always deemed to be. Similarly, middle-class male activists were plausible perpetrators of sexual violence, while the aggression of lower middleclass males was condoned in the name of peasant purity.

As shown in Chapter 5, such axiological understandings of violence masked, and thereby normalized, the complex idioms through which male power operated in context-specific ways: through the production of new ('declassed') political identities, in a deification of the male subaltern; through friendship, (male) protection, and intimacy; and through the disqualification of women's speech. Even when it sought to punish sexual offences, the party's sanctioning of retributive violence reinforced the logic of patriarchal violence and failed to challenge wider assumptions about rape as rooted in community identity and honour. As elsewhere, rape was understood in the context of this progressive Left-led movement as a violation of the codes of sexual honour and shame (see Chapters 2 and 5). Responses to and silences around rape were in complete conformity with middle-class codes of sexual respectability.

Throughout the discussion of this book, we have seen the acceptance of conventional certainties about gender and sexuality in Bengali bhadralok culture by a movement that saw itself as defiant of this culture's norms. The radicalization of conjugal relations within the movement was, for instance, deeply reiterative of the hegemonic gender norms and sexual moralities of the 'old' society that the revolutionaries were trying to dismantle. Against the historical silence on heterosexual (or even homosocial) intimacies produced through political spaces and ideologies, Chapter 4's discussion of love, intimacy, and conjugality in the everyday life of the movement emphasized affective and erotic investments in the imagining of the revolution. It also pointed to its potential to enable new normative visions around gender, romance, and sexuality. These possibilities were thwarted given the overwhelming consideration of sexual propriety, a sacrosanct marker of respectability for the Bengali middle classes and one that was seemingly under threat in the anarchy of the underground.

Women's discussions of both Chapters 3 and 4 emphasize the new modes of regulation and control—the new patriarchies—that were developed in a revolutionary but respectable political domain. These were primarily in aid of restoring middle-class codes and expectations of womanhood in political activity that is considered unconventional for middle-class women, the subjects of this study. They were also in aid of transforming class identity such that the lived practice of 'becoming declassed' served to reinforce gender inequalities and even to normalize male sexual violence in some instances. Chapter 5 showed that the enactment of class politics on the terrain of sexual politics brought sexual freedoms for middle-class male activists while leaving middle-class and subaltern women, at times, more vulnerable to sexual abuse and domestic violence in conditions of extreme insecurity. Such forms of violence even found sanction in the promise of revolution. The large literature on the general history of the Naxalbari movement has not only ignored troubling questions of such inner violence but also the question of how a culture of violence generated in the name of 'class struggle' slowly becomes impossible to restrain.

The recognition of a continuum of violence at the time of Naxalbari flies in the face of the distinction between ethical and unethical uses of violence upon which revolutionary action (like state power) relies. The revolutionary acts with a high degree of moral certainty with respect to actions and ends that are, per force, judged to be right, rendering violence, as noted in women's discussions on khatam, in Chapter 3, a matter of course rather than a complex ethical choice (Hutchings 2007b: 126). Commentators in India are increasingly reflecting on the disappearance of the 'middle ground' in the pitted battles between the state and the revolutionary where, 'you can either be one or the other—and this choice is forced on us equally by the state as by the "revolutionaries"' (Nigam 2008). The reading of resistance mirrors this logic, inviting us to view individuals and actions on the basis of absolute moral binaries 'as either all bad or all good, sinful or virtuous, noble or ignoble' (Bourgois 2002: 222). What tends to get lost in this demand to take sides is precisely the grey nature of revolutionary and indeed all violence and the ambiguity under whose sign revolutionary relations are lived in the course of such struggles, as this book has endeavoured to show.

Problematizing Power

Ethical distinctions between good and bad violence were secured, at least in the context of this movement, through particular presumptions of femininity, masculinity, and class–caste. Chapter 2 showed how the justificatory discourses of good violence relied on constructions of women's sexuality and virile masculinity. Class struggle was itself configured in party discourse as a battle for the sexual honour of subaltern women. The fact that gender plays a major part in representing violence (and even war) as 'legitimate, honourable or desirable' (Treacher *et al.* 2008: 1) poses, Hutchings (2007a: 102) argues, a deep challenge to those feminists who defend the use of violence in advance. As noted earlier, post-colonial feminists not only keep open the possibility of the use of violence in certain (exceptional) circumstances but also see radical politics as a space of emancipatory and agentive potentialities for women (even if these are rarely actualized). In a classic liberal sense, they posit power as a positive social good that is unequally distributed amongst women and men. Women's taking up of political roles, even one of violence, is thus one step in the redistribution of power in the name of equality and agency.

The problem with such a redistributive model of power (as Iris Marion Young has called it) is that it tends to view questions of empowerment and agency largely in abstraction, outside of their imbrication in wider 'historically specific networks of power relations' (Gedalof 1999: 53). It thus asks that women be included in structures and institutions of power leaving their normative and gendered nature largely unchallenged. Such a move is all the more problematic in the context of militarized resistant struggles in South Asia where the entry and presence of women, while initially empowering to the women involved, is regulated by rigid conformity to the masculinist and patriarchal ideologies of these organizations (Menon 2004). A related problem with this feminist stance is, as Young has noted of the use of 'woman's liberation' in legitimizing humanitarian intervention, that it does not 'have principled ways of distancing itself from paternalist militarism' (Young 2003: 230). For Young (2003: 231), a concern for the well-being of women is not a sufficient condition of feminism, which also requires a commitment to democratic values and citizenship on a global scale. It cannot, in other words, be concerned with gender or sexual difference alone at the cost of addressing a more complex moral economy of rationalizing and reproducing violence and war to which 'woman' is central.

In the preceding chapters, we have seen how the category of 'woman' as it intersected with those of class and sexuality was foregrounded, made visible and useful in the constitution of normative political identity and in the legitimation of political violence. Gender, I argued in Chapter 2, was scarcely absent from the cultural imaginary of the Naxalbari movement; it was employed to signify power relations that may or may not have had to do with women. Oppositions between masculinity and effeminacy served, as in the colonial context, to politicize or even militarize revolutionary subjectivity for wider patriotic ends. The very practice of 'becoming a Naxalite' entailed specific transformations to the gendered and sexualized (and not merely classed) self, even as it involved a deliberate repudiation of feminine domesticity. Sexual difference emerged as a primary way of constructing and legitimizing other (class) differences in the political domain obvious in the regulation of the body of the bhadramahila observed in Chapter 3. The manner in which 'politics constructs gender and gender constructs politics' (Scott 1986: 1070) is also evident in the normative utility of motherhood, especially through the religiously coded language of sacrifice. Together with maternal sacrifice, the trope of feminine sexual vulnerability was used to not only legitimate Naxalite violence at the time of the movement but also in its afterlife, where rape at the hands of the state keeps alive the demand for retributive violence. Rape 'mobilizes and gives agency' to the revolution, as Mookherjee (2008: 50) notes of nationalist narratives in Bangladesh.

In showing through an engagement with the Indian feminist scholarship on the gendered dynamics of community and national identity constitution, Gedalof (1999) argues that women are made useful and visible to the constitution of these identities through processes that at once render them invisible. Their 'curious visibility' cannot be understood, she argues, through an exclusionary model of power in which women are always excluded and abjected, but through a Foucauldian one in which 'woman' emerge as simultaneously enabled and constrained. Indeed, the foregrounding of women in the context of the Naxalbari movement did little to assuage middle-class male privilege, serving, on the contrary, to reproduce a culturally specific and classed patriarchal order. Women were made visible through historically resilient and culturally specific constructs of the feminine associated with culture, (hetero)sexuality, affectivity, sacrificial motherhood, domesticity, and body work. Their 'conspicuous bodies' had to occupy 'specific slots' (Puwar 2004) as wives, mothers, and widows of male revolutionaries.

Similarly, the peasant was a fixed signifier for validating class struggle and producing its normative subject in the middle-class male activist who could 'declass', 'desex', and 'regender' at will. For Puwar, 'women and non-whites are ... highly visible as deviations from the norm and invisible as the norm' (Puwar 2004: 59). Indeed, albeit in distinct ways, both the subaltern and the woman were invisible as political agents in the imagined and actual life of the Naxalbari movement. Normative political identity was itself constructed in this and other movements through transcendence of that which 'woman' stands for, namely, the body, affectivity, and the private domestic sphere. For middle-class women activists, being a political agent required a transgression of the female body constituted as a problem to be overcome, as 'matter out of place', in a political domain where the male body was the norm. Their own sense of agency rested on a denial of sexual difference and the successful performance of idealized (male) revolutionary identities and scripts.

The analysis of the book thus suggests that women in politics are not in/visible in straightforward ways. A model of power that rests on women's exclusion alone ignores how 'woman' and gender are central to the moral economy of radical political violence. Consequently, and in a liberal feminist mode of rendering hitherto invisible 'woman' visible, it problematically associates women's *visibility* in cultures of violent politics with a foregrounding of women's rights, empowerment, and agency.[1] It thereby perpetuates the gendered and patriarchal images on which the rhetoric of revolutionary ideology relies, such as the male protector and the feminized protectee.

Beyond Dichotomies

Women are thus neither fully passive nor active, entirely visible nor invisible, victims nor agents of politics. Political identities and spaces are not produced through the mere exclusion of women's (and subaltern) bodies, in need of inclusion and visibility. In any case, as Puwar has persuasively shown, the exclusion of women from politics or power cannot be resolved by mere inclusion: 'given that women are in a rather tenuous situation as "space invaders" ..., the expectation that their mere presence as individuals will be enough to shift the political style of the place is unrealistic' (Puwar 2004: 105). In order to undo the historic and institutionally embedded privilege of the unmarked normative male body, what is required is 'a huge overhaul of the political imagination'. I have shown, after Puwar (2004) writing about the British civil service, how the transformation from being political outsiders to insiders remains a tenuous process for those who have been historically excluded from the sphere of politics.

Even as urban middle-class women Naxalites left the sphere of the family and the household to go underground, a rigid 'ideological separation of spheres of activism' (Hamilton 2007: 93) pervaded their everyday lives in the underground just as it structured the revolution in an imagined sense. As in the case of the Indian nationalist struggle, political activity was constituted, for middle-class women Naxalites, as an extension of their traditional gender roles, even as 'the equality of choice and work in the political sphere makes a mockery of the language of traditionalism' (Sarkar 2001: 267). These women entered the public/political domain via the movement, but the code by which they were inevitably judged was that of the private, as Kannabiran and Lalitha (1989: 193) have noted of the Telangana people's struggle. Like nationalist and communist women before them (and not in India alone), the experiences of Naxalite women cannot be captured in a dualism of exclusion or inclusion, passivity or agency; they were both insiders and outsiders in political space.

A way of moving beyond such dichotomies is available in a more complex theory of power that addresses the ambiguous, even paradoxical nature of power that simultaneously enables and constrains subjects. For Butler (1993), the power relations that constitute identity categories like 'woman' are inherently unstable. Agency emerges 'in part from the instabilities of those normative power relations, whose results are not always predictable and which can therefore produce unintended consequences' (Gedalof 1999: 107). The manner in which radical ideology produces 'woman' as a non-traditional, masculinized subject, *and* as a carrier of tradition and collective sexual propriety, is one instance of the manner in which the instability of 'woman' opens up the possibility of 'political resignification' or the possibility of signifying a different set of meanings from normative ones. The recent feminist stress on women's *ambivalent* agency in the realm of armed conflict (see Manchanda 2004; and Rajasingham–Senanayake 2001, 2004) can be seen as opening up the possibility of exploring the manner in which identities are constituted through the productive and repressive capacity of power. Beyond dichotomies of inclusion and exclusion, such a model of power might effectively free up feminists from viewing revolutionary moments as spaces of liberation *or* subjugation to map, instead, how the rhetoric of revolution (and war) articulates itself through gendered power, enabling as well as constraining the subject.

Remembering Revolution takes us beyond these dominant polarizations to consider the various modes of subjectivities made available to women by the discourse of Left radicalism. It also moves beyond their consideration at the discursive level alone to explore individual women's identifications with and investments in them, and how it makes available modes of 'subjective composure'; a term that evokes the sociocultural dimensions of the work of memory as well as its irreducibly individual and personal quality. In Chapter 2, I delineated official and popular constructions of revolutionary masculinity and heroic femininity that were important sources of identification for men and women. True to a nationalist legacy, the ideal revolutionary subject was a strictly male and middle-class one, constructed in relation to what it excluded, such as the feminine (to which subaltern masculinity was invariably reduced) and domestic or private concerns. Unlike revolutionary masculinity which provided middle-class men with a coherent, recognizable, and hegemonic identity in the Naxalite movement, politicized femininity rendered women's bodies visible in particular ways while rendering them invisible as political agents.

Middle-class women activists, for their part, employed traditional femininity as a political resource (in courier work), but also repudiated any sign of female 'weakness' (such as the prioritizing of children over the just cause) and downplayed gender differences to live up to male standards. But given that women cannot straightforwardly don the political costume, which Pateman (1995, cited in Puwar 2004) notes has been made with men in mind, their attempt to do so marked them as gendered 'other'. Their complex location within the public and the private, along with their symbolic function as preservers of cultural identity, made it hard for women to 'take up' (male) revolutionary identities and to 'compose' themselves in their terms. Their achievement of composure also rested on their repudiation of 'natural' desires and other markers of feminine (and class) difference that were perceived, in the context of this and other political movements, as 'otherness'. Cultural forms of revolutionary masculinity and heroic femininity that were themselves contradictory and not easily reducible to archetypes of 'victim' and 'agent' also constitute, as demonstrated throughout the book, important resources in the 'composure' of individual subjectivity, for both male and female activists.

Identification, Idealization, and Denial

Remembering Revolution has explored the ways in which individuals do not just passively inhabit the discursive spaces afforded to them. It has pointed to interviewees' unconscious attachments to dominant typologies of self-sacrifice and heroic resistance in ways that negotiate the tensions of gender, class, and changed personal and social circumstances. Summerfield argues that the 'psychic turn' in oral history has enabled an important focus on 'the personal and collective meanings of silences concerning certain subjects, of defensiveness and denial of others, and of repeated emphasis upon some aspects of the past at the expense of others' (Summerfield 2000: 92). She suggests, however, that the practice of oral history is more likely to produce instabilities, or what she calls *dis*composure of both the narrators and their life story. Arguing against the idea of narrative as a site of coherence and comfort, she points to the inevitable lack of composure in the face of the inherent fragility of the constituted subject and the need to defend against perceived threats and anxieties. In personal narratives of former Naxalites, the composure of a self-abnegating subject of leftist discourse invariably relied upon the disavowal of more vulnerable aspects of the past/self, serving what Hollway and Jefferson (2000) call a 'defensive function'. The interview situation itself might have given rise to these anxieties in forcing women to revisit painful memories of violence and loss.

For at least some of the women interviewed, the (gendered) contradictions implicit in past political lives, especially in the demands of political subjectivity, have become evident in the decades that have passed. Middle-class Naxalite women's published memoirs (Bandyopadhyay 2001; and Sanyal 2001) employ the language of feminism to name some of the underlying contradictions of revolutionary identities, such as the exclusion of womanhood from the domain of the political, the fetishization of the subaltern subject in ways that made naming its aggression or vulnerability impossible, and the pervasive need to silence sexism and sexual violence for the purposes of political agency. These resonate with oral narratives reviewed in Chapters 3 and 4 that emphasized, in turning to intimate histories of marriage and motherhood, the tension between the demands of a disembodied rationality in the public sphere and those who were incapable of transcending their embodiment and were thus synonymous with the private and the affective (Lister 1997, cited in Puwar 2004). Experiences of sexual violence recounted in Chapter 5 forcefully revealed the unmarked masculine nature of political space in which the bodies of women were a liability.

But as Dawson asks, what 'of the cases where the contradictions cannot be named as such—where the conflicting identifications are not worked through to some fuller understanding?' (Dawson 1994: 280). Even as Naxalite women are today able to name what was unnameable in the past, their investments in revolutionary subjectivities and cultures have not entirely been abandoned. I have repeatedly been struck, in the course of this study, by the pleasures that at least some Naxalite men and women continue to draw from a romanticized political past in response to the psychic and social tensions of lived experience.

The persistence of such a pleasure culture, that is fairly pervasive if we consider the elite intellectual support for contemporary Maoist struggles, partly explains the resilience of radical political cultures and identities that 'acquire their subjective purchase by becoming parts of the self' (Dawson 1994: 234).

Notwithstanding the contradictions that idealized heroic subjectivity posed for Naxalite women and the psychic and social conflicts that these gave rise to, identification with it also came with the promise of resolving these very conflicts and of providing a coherent sense of self. Such identifications were ambivalent in that they entailed a disidentification with, even repudiation of, more contradictory aspects of the self. Narrative negotiations with sexual violence exemplify women's continuing conflicting identifications with revolutionary identities that were split along gendered lines and largely divorced from the contradictions of a gendered social world. As with the cultural constitution of the soldier hero that Dawson details, we can recognize this as a 'peculiarly masculine form of splitting' (Dawson 1994: 286) that involved the forced separation of the work of revolution from feminized domesticity, and the attendant sacrifice of 'private' everyday concerns to some abstract 'world–historical' responsibility (Nigam 2007). In showing, in his reading of a recent film on Naxalbari (*Kalbela* discussed in Chapter 2), how women had to confront 'the most ordinary and aggressively nonpolitical concerns' thrown up by daily life towards which the male 'Agent of History' showed little inclination or agency, Nigam (2007) is one of the few to note the extent to which women are the bearers of the costs of such masculine splitting.

Given that women have been historically and conceptually excluded from the public realm, and marked as 'other' even upon inclusion, political participation entails varying degrees of 'ontological complicity' (Puwar 2004), including acquiescing in the power hierarchies within which they are located. In the specific context of the andolan, it is not surprising that most women could not recognize the patriarchy that was intrinsic to its structure and ideology; even today, the price of political agency and belonging is an inability to see or hear sexism and sexual violence. For both Dawson and Butler—speaking from the different but not divergent theoretical traditions that this book has drawn on—the achievement of self-identity through processes of disidentification and repudiation raises the political question of what is at stake in attaining 'composure' through normative (political) identities, especially those that are grounded in the containment of real life contradictions and conflicts, and in the essentializing of (gendered, classed, and caste-based) identities.

Psychic mechanisms of idealization and denial underlie the cultural imaginary of biplab itself, as they do the narration of any military enterprise as 'an adventure' (Dawson 1994). I have shown, in Chapter 2, how the heroism of the revolutionary Naxalite was dependent upon the denigration of significant others (the state, landowners, political 'reactionaries') into objects worthy *only* of violence, while the violence of the self was idealized in the service of heroic patriotic ends. Even in the aftermath of Naxalbari, which still reverberates in personal and familial biographies, violence can be misrecognized as not being violence but as something necessary, even good. Amongst the women interviewed for this project, not all equally condemned the violence of their past, and for at least one, violence constituted a source of redress. This discrepancy in sociocultural as well as personal memory is just as telling of the ideologically charged usage of political violence at the time of the movement as it is today.

The party's misrecognition of violence is also revealing of the extent to which the very structures of everyday interpersonal relations were abstracted within a reified language of class struggle. Nowhere is this more obvious than in the party's deification of the subaltern subject which could not be implicated in a discourse of sexual violence. While anthropomorphizing the subaltern, women's narratives also seek to preserve the myth of bhadralok male heroism against accusations of sexual violence today. Male sexual violence undercuts the potency of this myth, taking away from the heroic and righteous dimensions of waging a war against the state from which individuals can draw pleasure. This pleasure is contingent upon the distancing and defending of war-as-adventure from 'real life' anxieties, whether around the terrors of imprisonment, torture, and even death, or the personal vulnerabilities of those who are implicated in a narrative of 'class struggle'. The cultural imaginary of revolution and its fetishized hero can only be sustained, as Dawson (1994) has persuasively shown, through such interpretive and imaginative linkages and separations, especially the holding apart of different forms of violence (political, sexual, everyday), and by idealizing some and 'forgetting' others.

NAMING

Women's naming of violence *against women* is always contentious. It is even more so in Kolkata's leftist political field as noted in preceding chapters. The 'metaphor of the family' (Stree Shakti Sanghatana 1989: 269) that best describes the ideologies and practices of the democratic *and* revolutionary Left makes it difficult for women to 'speak out' against patriarchy and sexual violence as against other forms of (political) violence. For all the recent interest in radical politics in the subcontinent, feminists have had little to say about women's experiences of sexual violence at the hands of male party members. Allegations of the rape of female activists by Maoists have recently come in, which feminists have read through the idiom of 'personal vendetta'.[2] Even when feminists are not explicitly sympathetic to Maoists, the radical Left inheritance of the women's movement implicates how violence is understood and named in ways that render some forms of violence and their effects as 'exceptional/political' and others as 'everyday/personal'. The allocation of rape to a realm of exceptionalism in the context of radical Left politics is particularly troubling given the routine manner in which sexual violence has come to accompany acts of political violence in contemporary India. This confluence was most recently witnessed in the sexual violence that marked the repression of land struggles in Nandigram and Singur, allegedly by CPI(M) workers (*Singur Andolan* 2007).

In the case of Naxalbari, women that have named sexual violence and implicated male comrades have done so with trepidation, evident in Krishna Bandyopadhyay's published confessional, and in the need for anonymity. The discussion in Chapter 5 dwelt on women and men's complex feelings around the issue of sexual violence within the movement, creating a contentious terrain for the tellability and hearability of women's testimony to such violence. In naming sexism and sexual violence by fellow revolutionaries, women also mark the embodied nature of the political domain and gender its privileged subject. They identify and articulate the gendered economies that governed their exclusion in the political domain; they name, in other words, gendered power. Puwar (2004: 153–4) remarks how acts that name can be difficult when institutions disavow cultural and corporeal specificity and difference. It is particularly difficult for those who are constituted as different to name their difference. The force of naming not just gender violence but also the violence entailed in the imagining of revolutionary class struggle in particular (split) ways cannot be underestimated. Dawson suggests that 'naming the damage done in the name of adventure to ourselves as well as to others becomes a precondition of working through to the composure of a more integrated narrative form, founded upon the acknowledgment rather than the denial of psychic realities' (Dawson 1994: 287).

Naming requires allies and solidarity, Puwar (2004) says, which is all the more pressing in the current context where women activists (like Krishna Bandyopadhyay) who have spoken out and named have done so under the threat of being 'isolated'. Solidarity has been available to these women in the form of contemporary feminist discourses and activism, which several are actively engaged with today. Yet women interviewees—even those who identified as feminists—did not always take recourse to the language of feminism to make sense of past trauma, drawing instead on the discursive terms of the movement as well as middle-class codes of respectable sexuality. The feminist narrative seemed to be subsumed, in accounts of violence in Chapters 3 and 5, by a leftist one, suggestive of the manner in which feminism has travelled to Kolkata as well as the Maoist legacies of Indian feminism. In naming violence (or not), Naxalite women thus drew on distinct discourses, underscoring the extent to which their memories were cultural constructs, reconstructed and narrated through intervening events and meanings over the decades. Their memories were also intersubjectively produced, especially through the cultural and feminist values represented by the interviewer.

Trauma and the Affective Afterlife of Naxalbari

The untellability of stories of sexual violence suffered *within* the revolutionary community must be linked to the ways in which stories of state terror faced by activists, including rape, have become highly tellable, and have assumed a pre-eminent role in the cultural memory of Naxalbari. Stories of *victims* of Naxalite violence, such as landlords, policemen, and middle-class families, including my own (see Introduction), are also entirely absent from the movement's broader cultural memory. The analysis of this book takes place within and not outside of these politics of trauma and testimony. While women's testimonies have been privileged throughout, they are articulated by visible 'activist' women, not by those bystanders who might have got caught up in the chaos of the time (think, for instance, of 'Gauri' in the Archana Guha case discussed in Chapter 6 who was arrested along with Latika and Archana Guha but remains invisible in this highly publicized case). The routinized experiences of betrayal and abuse suffered by women like Supriya have also not been theorized under the category of trauma in the same way that the experiences of women survivors of custodial violence have been.

The gendered memories of violence explored in this book trouble the forced separation between 'unusual' forms of violence and its more quotidian expressions whose effects do not necessarily or always appear to be traumatic. Supriya, for instance, says she went 'mad' for a brief period when the andolan was breathing its last, although she was never arrested. Her 'madness' immediately followed the incident which comrade 'S' recounted in Chapter 5, and was only cured, she says, with the resumption of routine everyday life in the form of undertaking a typewriting course. Like Supriya, whom I have identified as someone who lies relatively outside the dominant clique of Naxalite women, Lata narrated episodes in the aftermath of the movement that had involved her entirely losing consciousness and finding herself in a strange place with no recollection as to why or how she got there or what she was doing.[3] Early in 2003, she suffered a cerebral stroke but recovered quickly. Just before I left the field, she told me that she had suffered another minor stroke and had to give up her job. In my field notes, I identified Lata as a 'victim of a certain type of mental trauma', though I have struggled since to explicate my meaning, especially in terms of current mobilizations of the term 'trauma', whether cultural or in its more clinical form of post-traumatic stress disorder.

Like many recent studies, *Remembering Revolution* asks for an urgent re-examination of the affective and political force of 'trauma'. Hodgkin and Radstone (2003) are not the first to note the many problems in the use of this category around questions of classification (how do we classify a traumatic experience/event?), the privileging of psychic response to suffering over structural ones, and the easy slippage between individual trauma and collective suffering. For the South Asian scholar, these problems are compounded by the Eurocentric character of cultural trauma studies, which largely remains despite a commitment to cross-cultural solidarity. It has not always found easy translation to South Asian sites of violence, leading some (for example, Argenti–Pillen 2003; and Saunders and Aghaie 2005) to question if not altogether reject a Western paradigm of trauma as Eurocentric and particularist, in spite (or rather because) of its universalizing tendencies. However, like Mallot (2006: 168), I am wary of stretching a 'cultural alterity reasoning' or using 'culture' as shorthand to confound varied and complex issues (such as the medicalization and pathologization of trauma). I am also wary of a wholesale rejection of 'trauma' given its potential to address pain as psychic and not just physical. Feminist critiques like Cvetkovich (2003) push for a much-needed expansion of the field of trauma studies in ways that fundamentally rethink 'trauma', rather than fulfil the promise of cross-cultural engagement which might not respond to the gendered dynamics of vulnerability and suffering.

Insidious trauma, as described by Brown (1995) in referring to the effects of routinized sexual assault in North America, best captures Naxalite women's heightened self-awareness of their own vulnerability in the underground life of the movement. Defensive strategies of 'denial and disidentification' (Brown 1995: 108) observed in some Naxalite women's responses to sexual aggression can also be read as a way of avoiding manifestations of this everyday trauma, which took place in the secrecy and silencing of the andolan. Women like Supriya and Lata, who arguably suffer the continuing effects of insidious trauma, might themselves construct its effects as 'normal' in the face of the 'real' trauma of political terror to which neither was exposed. If Supriya's memoir makes evident the everydayness of violence, then her interviews with me (recorded over several sessions spanning many months) speak of the 'subtle manifestations of trauma' (Brown 1995: 108). The act of publicly naming violence in her memoir suggests that Supriya has moved away from the disidentification with violence that was required of her political identity to 'identification and action' in the long aftermath of the movement.

Traumatic Speech and Silence

The discussion of Chapter 6 explored some of the difficulties involved in either shattering or keeping the silence of trauma. The first of these is commonly equated with liberation, at the level of the individual and the collective. Consequently, testimony has moved centre stage in understanding and addressing trauma as a means through which the wounded subject cannot only be heard but also healed (see S. Roy 2010). The conversion of women's silence into speech through the act of testimony is also 'a specific attribute of feminist politics' (Sunder Rajan 1993: 84); feminism itself has been partly forged out of 'speaking' pain. However, the analysis of public and personal memories of state repression, presented in Chapter 6, suggests that the mere tellability of stories of political violence and survivor testimony should not be seen as inherently empowering to the individual or to an injured collective. While the memory of political violence is afforded a high degree of recognition in cultural acts of commemoration and testimony, these can end up domesticating its trauma. Within the victimized community itself, political violence has been reinscribed as heroic resistance and self-sacrifice, thereby marginalizing alternative forms of witnessing and mourning violence. Even women's testimonies of state terror can, on the one hand, become a call for revenge (and not redemption), and reproduce, on the other, female victimization in gendered if not patriarchal terms. For some of the women I met, the event of torture and incarceration is not temporally containable in the past, given its continual unfolding in their daily lives and in that of their families. In such a context of continuing social and economic struggle, to speak of the memory of violence in psychic terms of trauma and its recovery through testimony alone seems inadequate, if not unjust.

In post-colonial cultures of memory, speech has come most easily to those who have sought to 'recover' women's bodies in the service of national honour, and for the sake of establishing political legitimacy in the aftermath of crisis (see Das 2007). As Mallot (2006) and Mookherjee (2008) have shown, events like the Partition of the Indian subcontinent and the Bangladesh war have made all the more obvious the manner in which the spectacle of gendered and sexualized trauma has been instrumentally employed for the sake of nation-building. The limitations of representing *gendered* pain have led scholars to acknowledge silence as meaningful and as a 'legitimate discourse on pain' (Ross 2003: 49). In the context of the Partition, silencing has been thought of as a way of keeping something within the self as opposed to bringing it to a surface that had literally been inscribed by a brutal nationalist imaginary (Das 2007: 84); as a way of protecting women since it was dangerous to remember (Butalia 1998: 357). Against the predominance of Western models of Freud's 'talking cure', Argenti–Pillen (2003) argues for silence to be seen as beneficial and curative for women, such as the ones she encountered in Sri Lanka's conflict zones.

These recent ruminations on the politics and power of silencing resonate with my concerns in this book, given that the narratives I encountered were structured by varying degrees of silences and omissions (especially when it came to intimate relationships and experiences). On the whole, women chose to speak about certain experiences and not others, exemplified, perhaps, in one of my earliest conversations on the phone with Kalyani, when she simply said, 'there are many things I won't talk about anyway'.[4] The idea that these women were silencing certain past experiences as a conscious act of agency is an attractive way of moving beyond their victimization, or from perceiving them as having been *silenced*. Yet, I have found it difficult to view gendered silences of this sort as straightforwardly agential. Women's need to silence certain experiences repeatedly alerted me to the wider contexts in which these silences were produced. Silences on 'marriage', for instance, suggested normative middle-class expectations in rendering unspeakable those experiences that failed to fulfil them. At least for Das (2007), it would seem that the gaps and silences in women's narratives are grounds not for the romantic idealization of silences as female resistance, but more about the collective failure to acknowledge the pain of an other. While speech might be a 'contaminated area for research into women's subjectivities' (Sunder Rajan 1993: 89), silence no less signifies the depth of women's exclusion and alienation from the world.

Mourning as Political Praxis

Silencing is, for me, another cost of remembering and mourning revolution in particular (largely celebratory) ways. In melancholic attachment to a vision of revolution and the identities and possibilities that it made available, one is also silencing the possibility of recognizing how fractured and inadequate this vision was, the personal and collective costs that its completion relied on, and its traumatic impact and afterlife. So, too, one is silencing the possibility of working through loss to allow something new to emerge and begin. The acceptance of loss in mourning enables a moving forward, beyond a pathological attachment to the past that is fashioned in melancholia. This process could begin, as it has in the legacy of Naxalbari, with women's acts of naming violence, a major step in a truly critical reappraisal of the movement from within. Naming, to recall Dawson (1994), is a first step towards a more integrated, tolerant mode of composure that is built on 'working through' rather than repudiating contradictory aspects of the self as well as the self's relation to others, both imagined and real. Even as the discussion of this book has pointed to the significant limits and costs of attaining composure in culturally available identities, composure can effect a temporary resolution to the divisions in the psychic and social world that are configured and reconfigured in interaction with one another (Redman 1999). As against a splitting of parts of the (gendered, classed) self and an idealization of some as opposed to an abandoning of others, composure could entail, to paraphrase Dawson (1994: 44), recognition of oneself as a multifaceted and contradictory subjectivity founded upon the realities of the contemporary world.

Besides underscoring the intersubjective dimension of subject formation—the fact that self-identity is dependent upon its relation to others and the world at large—this idea of composure as a way of 'working through' evokes the Freudian concept of memory as work. In distinction from melancholic 'acting out', mourning can be a mode of 'working through' past loss, of reconciling oneself with lost objects and ideals rather than being possessed or haunted by them (see LaCapra 2001; and Ricoeur 2004). It also recalls the Kleinian language of reparation, which, at least for Dawson, involves a 'working through' of the contradictions of the social world that might otherwise be experienced in split, disavowed, and essentialized ways. Whether reconciliatory or reparative, the work of memory as mourning becomes an important precondition of the resumption, post-loss, of social life which allows one to begin anew. Historical loss, LaCapra (2001: 66) says, calls for mourning of this kind that can potentially rewrite the past and reimagine the future (Eng and Kazanjian 2003), but also for critique and transformative sociopolitical practice. Indeed, the psychic categories of mourning, melancholia, and composure here speak to principles of mutuality, democracy, and cultural pluralism that form the basis of progressive and democratic politics. Dawson (1994: 287) rightly notes that these political values cannot be realized at the psychic level alone without a corresponding transformation of concrete sociopolitical conditions.

But let us also not be too quick to dismiss the psychic and affective dimensions of political life, or the subjective purchase of political values. These are nothing if not part of our fantasy life, as Rose (1996) has persuasively shown. After all, Naxalites and Maoists are, for

Arundhati Roy (2010) and several others, those who keep the dream of revolution 'real and present', synonymous with the promise of the Indian Left. That an 'idealisation of that romantic left promise' (Brown 1999: 22) must be sustained at whatever cost, even at the risk of rendering the Left into an anachronistic and authoritarian force in the present, suggests the need for a closer scrutiny of 'the feelings and sentiments ... that sustain our attachments to left analyses and left projects' (Brown 1999: 22). This is particularly urgent at a time of feminist and Left melancholia where the failure to provide 'either a deep and radical critique of the status quo or a compelling alternative to the existing order of things' (Brown 1999: 22) has led many 'progressives' to uphold armed revolutions over the kind of everyday struggles that have brought the most success, including a measure of feminist success, and not in India alone. However, as Nigam (2007) rightly points out in the context of Naxalbari, the revolutionary is a stranger to the everyday, just as an attachment to the 'dream of revolution' is grounded in a refusal of its realities.

What this book has at least in part tried to do—and I hope will inspire others to take further—is to unpack these complex investments in and attachments to political ideology as the subjective fuel that drives 'real' political passions, practices, and, dare I say, 'real' political change. In destabilizing (as Rose, Brown, and Dawson have done) forced divisions between 'inner' fantasy world and 'outer' public political life, the analysis of political subjectivity offered in this book suggests that a much more sustained engagement is needed with the imaginaries, the narratives, the fantasies and phantasms, and the economy of emotions and desires that sustain utopian political discourses. A detailed examination is required, in other words, of the psychic life of political cultures, of the emotionally charged images that circulate in them and congeal into particular archetypical formulations (of martyr/mother), the forms of dis/identifications that these create, and their relation to discursive practices (of remembering, forgetting, witnessing, testifying, and silencing) and to 'lived' (gendered, classed, and caste-based) subjectivities. A 'wounded attachment' (Brown 1993) to leftist ideals and values at a time when they appear to be in deep crisis has meant that political spaces and subjects have come to be constituted in overwhelmingly split and dichotomous terms obscuring the middle ground, the grey zone, the messiness of the everyday. Foucault's (1984) question—'how does one keep from being a fascist, even (especially) when one believes oneself to be a revolutionary militant?'—bespeaks these hidden interstices. The significance of this question cannot be underestimated if we, as feminists, continue to draw sustenance from leftist ideals and promises. Our attachments to these ideals can only be sustained by grappling seriously with the nature and costs of the imaginaries through which transformative politics express their visions of utopian change, and with the possibility of imagining otherwise.

Notes

Remembering Revolution: An Introduction

1. Even though the events that this book recalls took place in Calcutta in the 1960s and the 1970s, I use the new name of the city, Kolkata, and what it has always been referred to in Bengali for the sake of uniformity.

2. In contrast to sociological understandings of identity as external to the individual, I use the term identification in a psychoanalytic sense to emphasize the manner in which the individual gets constituted in the emotive investment in social objects in a process that Freud called cathexis.

3. Contemporary usages of memory in the social sciences are usually traced to the work of Halbwachs (1992), one of the earliest theorizations of personal recollections as socially produced. Recent scholarship on memory has taken up the observations of Halbwachs and psychologist Bartlett (1995) to (re)define memory as a process rather than a mere 'registration or recording of the "happened"' (Radstone 2000: 9). See Antze and Lambek (1996); Klein (2000); Misztal (2003); Olick and Robbins (1998); Radstone and Hodgkin (2003); Zelizer (1995); and the Routledge Studies in Memory and Narrative for recent overviews of the disciplinary history of contemporary memory studies. Scholars are already beginning to caution against an 'overextension' of the concept of memory and a consequent loss of meaning (Berliner 2005; see also, Confino 1997).

4. Studies on cultural memory are concerned with an expansion of the field of history writing away from formal historical discourses to popular forms and shared cultural narratives (see, for instance, Antze and Lambek 1996; Bal *et al.* 1999; Klein 2000; Sturken 1997; and on cultural memory and gender, see Hirsch and Smith 2002; Leydesdorff *et al.* 1996).

5. Members of the Group began to study the popular memory of the Second World War and its relation to British nationalism. Much of the broader canvas of work that draws on its theoretical insights is also located in war memory. See Ashplant *et al.* (2000); Dawson and West (1984); Evans (1997); Noakes (1998); and Redman (1999).

6. In his study of a peasant riot in northern India, Amin (1995) observes the manner in which individual peasant's recollections relied for coherence on the narratives of established historical accounts. Mayaram (1997: 9) has similarly observed in her study on Meo narratives of resistance that '. . . the subaltern world is hardly an autonomous realm'.

7. See Garton (2000) and Roper (2000), who make similar critiques of popular memory theory.

8. Feminist debates on sexual violence have long been concerned with questions of memory, trauma, and testimony (see Brison 2002; Gilmore 2001; Haaken 1998; Herman 1994; Sturken 1999; Tal 1996). While these have been mostly limited to the recovered memory debate, they have more recently included the study of gender and political violence (Kaplan 2002; Zur 1998), commissions on truth and reconciliation (Motsemme 2004; Ross 2001), and war memory (Giles 2002; Summerfield 1998) besides women's Partition memories in the Indian subcontinent, already referred to.

Chapter I

1. 'Mainstream' here refers to the two parliamentary communist parties, namely, the Communist Party of India (CPI) and the Communist Party of India (Marxist) or CPI(M), of which only the latter remains an important political player (often referred to as the parliamentary or democratic Left). As against this 'Old Left', Menon and Nigam (2007: 115) use the 'New Left' to designate several, non-unified Left articulations and formations which have 'grappled with the issues that the mainstream Old Left has failed to confront'. Contemporary Naxalite and Maoist groups, especially those that reject parliamentary participation for an exclusive reliance on armed struggle, are characterized as the 'far left' by these and other authors.

2. The politics of revolutionary terrorism emerged as a significant force around the time of the Swadeshi movement in Bengal (1905–8) to protest

the first partition of Bengal. The two main underground organizations that came to dominate the terrorist movement were the Anushilan Samiti and later, Jugantar. The groups were almost entirely composed of upper-caste Hindu men with their activities confined to the assassination of British officials. The Chittagong armoury raid brought in a new phase of revolutionary activity in the 1930s. The raid made household names of the revolutionaries involved, including women like Kalpana Dutta and Pritilata Waddedar, 'the most celebrated female martyr of the freedom movement' (Sen 2000: 19). Many Bengali 'terrorists' later converted to communism, including M.N. Roy who helped found the CPI. The revolutionary terrorist tradition—the first to uphold violence as a political tool—is important for understanding leftist politics in Bengal, including the Naxalites who are often viewed as its direct successors (see Franda 1971; Sarkar 1983; and Sarkar 1987).

3. Birbhum district, however, experienced heightened Naxalite activism in 1971 and 1972. Banerjee (1984) identifies Birbhum as a principal centre of Naxalite activism from 1970 onwards; and Sinha Roy (2011) focuses on the dynamics of the movement in Birbhum.

4. In 1966, a major campaign took place at Presidency College over the administration of college hostels, which is referred to as the Presidency College movement (see Acharya 1994; Banerjee 1984). A leading figure in this campaign was Ashim Chatterjee who played an important role in the Naxalite movement, emerging as one the leaders of the rural rebellion at Debra–Gopiballavpur.

5. In an edited volume that brings the Nepalese and Indian Maoists into a singular frame for the first time, the editors, Shah and Pettigrew (2009), observe that the former emerged out of intimate dialogue and debate with their Indian counterparts.

6. Chhattisgarh is also where the state created armed vigilante groups called the Salwa Judum from the local tribal population to counter the Maoists. The Salwa Judum is reported to have displaced at least 30,000 people, and killed many suspected Maoists and civilians. In 2011, it was declared unconstitutional by India's Supreme Court.

7. See also, Nirmalangshu Mukherjee's open letter to Noam Chomsky and other intellectuals in India and abroad (posted on the political blog, *Kafila*, on 21 October 2009) in the wake of their endorsement of

a statement against the government's military response to the 'Maoist problem'. By addressing, head-on, the issue of Maoist violence and its complicity with state violence, the letter exposes the elisions upon which the middle-class intellectual support of Maoism relies. See also, Banerjee (2009); Jha (2007); and Simeon (2010).

8. Satyajit Ray's 'Calcutta trilogy' includes *Pratidwandi* (The Adversary, 1970), *Seemabaddha* (Company Limited, 1971), and *Jana Aranya* (The Middleman, 1975). Mrinal Sen's *Interview* (1970), *Calcutta 71* (1972), and *Padatik* (The Foot Soldier, 1973), also centre on the city of Kolkata, capturing an important mood of rebellion and providing contemporary Bengali cinema some of its most iconic moments in representing the angry Bengali youth of the 1970s (Nigam 2007). These, especially the films of Sen, form part of a particular tradition of radical political Bengali cinema that Nigam turns to in exploring a recent film based on Naxalbari (discussed in the next chapter).

9. Media coverage of the arrest of Maoist ideologue, Kobad Ghandy, in 2009, reiterated popular stereotypes of the middle-class if not elite revolutionary as sacrificing, together with his wife, his life of privilege for the sake of the poor. Blockbuster Bollywood films like *Rang de Basanti* (Paint in Saffron, 2006) and *Hazaaron Khwaishein Aisi* (A Thousand Dreams Such As These, 2005), which draw on the Naxalite experience, equally reinstate the metropolitan middle-class attraction to extreme radical politics. On aestheticizing and romancing the 'revolution'—of which these media representations are a part—and the appeal of Naxalite revolutionaries as cultural matter, see Hutnyk (2000).

10. Words in quotation marks were said in English (all translations from the Bengali are mine). Interview excerpts have been edited for the sake for readability.

11. Sukanta Bhattacharya—a romantic, revolutionary poet who died a tragic youthful death in 1947—along with Khudiram Bose, an anti-colonial revolutionary who was arrested and executed when he was only 14 years, are key icons for the Bengali middle classes.

12. Autonomous women's groups that self-identified as feminist emerged in the aftermath of Naxalbari; many of these deliberately breaking away and asserting their autonomy from Left groups even as their feminist ideologies remained indebted to the Left. For the location of feminism

in Kolkata's political milieu, see Ray (1999); and for a short history of the feminist movement from the 1980s in West Bengal, see Chatterji (2000). It is important to point out that 'feminism' is a highly contested term in India (and especially in Kolkata; Ray 1999) given its continued association with 'Western feminism' (Chaudhuri 2004: xi).

13. Omvedt (1980) speaks of the way in which it had become natural, amongst communists in the western state of Maharashtra, for 'political' women to take up full-time employment (besides maintaining the household) after marriage, given that their activist husbands could not support them. Consequently, they had little or no time to devote to political theorizing or activity, and lost their claim to decision-making within the party. Kalpana Sen (2001) writes that the Naxalites broke down this model of 'political husbands' and 'working housewives', although in my own research, I have found several couples who still ascribe to it.

Chapter 2

1. 'Renunciative celibacy' is key to the achievement of hegemonic Hindu masculinity, as a number of studies have noted (Alter 1994; Chopra *et al.* 2004; Monti 2004; Nandy 1988). Such hegemonic masculinity was put in service of Indian nationalism, especially its more violent variant such as revolutionary terrorism.

2. In his *Anandamath* (1882), Bankim Chandra Chatterjee stages this model in the figure of the political *sanyasin* or monk who is the ideal Hindu warrior against alien rule, both British and Muslim. This book is considered to be important for the contemporary Hindu Right in India. See Bagchi's (2000) and Sarkar (1996) readings of the novel from the perspective of gender.

3. The grandiose language of revolution with its shades of 'apocalyptic conflict' has not at all been absent from the literary (especially poetic) repertoire of the Bengali Left. A vision of imminent revolution was common to the revolutionary poetry of Bengali stalwarts like Nazrul Islam and Sukanta and Subhash Mukhopadhyay, as detailed by Dasgupta (2005).

4. All party quotations (most of these are by Charu Mazumdar) are, unless otherwise stated, from Suniti Kumar Ghosh (ed.) (1993).

5. The rhetoric of martyrdom was also seen in the public valourization of violence amongst New Left radicals such as the Baader Meinhof and the Weather Underground, where politics was sometimes reduced to a 'fatalistic end game, consummated in death' (Varon 2004: 183). The cult of martyrdom has been an enduring feature in the self-conceptualization of 'terrorist' groups closer to home like the Sri Lankan Tamil Tigers (De Mel 2001), Sikh militants (Das 1995; and Mahmood 1996), and more recently, the Nepalese Maoists (Lecomte–Tilouine 2009).

6. Mazumdar's excessive emphasis on martyrdom drew criticism from within the CPI(ML) (from the likes of Ashim Chatterjee). Such forms of internal criticism were condemned as 'revisionist thinking'. Historian Banerjee writes that 'from Mazumdar's repeated stress on the need for self-sacrifice in his writings and speeches in 1970 and 1971, one has the feeling that he was trying to shape an elite of self-immolators' (Banerjee 1984: 360). This is true of his immediate successors like Mahadeb Mukherjee who summoned all imprisoned Naxalites for a mass suicide.

7. *Frontier* was formed in the wake of the uprising at Naxalbari and was edited by prominent left-wing Bengali poet–intellectual Samar Sen. The weekly included debates between the different factions of the Left (especially the Maoists); discussions and reviews of new film, literature, and art; and reports of local agrarian struggles and of human rights violations by the state, 'which no bourgeoisie paper was likely to print' (Guha 2004).

8. These are the lines of the male protagonist of Mukhopadhyay's *Brishtir Ghran* (1985) on receiving a revolver from his Naxalite friend. I quote from the English translation, *Waiting for Rain* (2003: 148).

9. Ray (1998) associates the Naxalite fetishization of violence, in the excessive usage of the idiom of *rọkto* or blood in CPI(ML) writings, with virility.

10. Mazumdar was averse to the use of arms by peasants in the initial stages of guerrilla warfare and insisted on the use of traditional weapons. It was only at an advanced or a 'higher' stage of struggle that firearms could be used, which formed the rationale of the rifle-snatching campaign. The middle-class comrade was, however, entitled to the possession of small pistols when carrying out revolutionary work in rural areas. See Mazumdar's 'A Few Words about Guerrilla Actions' or the 'murder manual', reprinted in Ghosh (1993: 68–73).

11. For a useful summary of the cultural meanings of izzat, see Chakravarti (2003).

12. Although in this section, I limit my discussion to autobiographical tracts by activists published in various *patrikas*, motherhood forms a dominant discursive image in the literary and poetic imagination of the movement. The most obvious example is that of Devi's *Hajar Churashir Ma* (Mother of 1084, 2001[1997]). Several short stories inspired by the andolan (see, for instance, the collection of stories edited by Bandopadhyay and Chattopadhyay 1999; and Samaresh Basu's *Shahider Ma* [A Martyr's Mother], recently translated and published in Basu 2003) centre upon the symbolic force of motherhood. See also the collections of poetry edited by Banerjee (1987) and Dasadhikari (1998) for poetry that mobilizes the emotive force of motherhood for political purposes.

13. This collection of auto/biographical writings published by the journal, *Jalark*, also includes letters from imprisoned activists to their mothers and eulogies written by women in memory of their dead Naxalite sons.

14. Nirmala Krishnamurthy was killed in the Naxalite struggle in Andhra. Ahalya, a peasant woman, was killed by the police during a communist-led upsurge in Chandanpiri, West Bengal, in 1949 (Banerjee 1987).

15. One of India's foremost writers, Mahasweta Devi's work has found its way into the ambit of First World cultural studies through the sustained translations by Gayatri Spivak. Besides *Hajar Churashir Ma* (Mother of 1084, 2001 [1997]), *Operation Bashai Tudu* (2002b[1990]) and her short story, *Draupadi* (2002a[1997]), are two of her other recognizable 'Naxalite' works, although these sharply depart from the middle-class focus of *Hajar* to the contemporary politics of adivasi existence to which Devi, the activist and the writer, has a long-standing commitment (see Basu Ray 1994; and Spivak 2002).

16. Popular Bengali novelist, Samaresh Majumdar's *Kalbela* is one of the most critically acclaimed novels in the last decade, and forms the second part of his tripartite documentation of the life of political radical, Animesh. It has recently been made into a film by the same name by Gautam Ghose, discussed by Nigam (2007) and Sinha Roy (2011).

17. See, for instance, *The Statesman*, 31 October 1973; an interview of hers by Saeed Naqvi in *The Sunday Statesman Magazine*, 30 September 1973;

and also an interview by Anand Patvardan which appears in his documentary *Prisoners of Conscience*, 1978. She spent five years in prison, which forms the basis of her memoir, *My Years in an Indian Prison* (1977).

18. In his interview, Saibal Mitra, a well-known ex-Naxalite and a fairly established contemporary writer, revealed to me how the character of Katherine and the novel at large is a fictionalized account of Mary Tyler. The book's title, *Manabputri*, can be loosely translated as 'daughter of a human', which is itself a provocation since there is no feminine for '*putra*', meaning son.

Chapter 3

1. From my interview with Supriya, though in this chapter and elsewhere, I draw on her published memoir (Sanyal 2001), and my analysis moves between the two sources.

2. This is not to suggest that women voice a unanimous critique of their marginalization within the party. Some women identify themselves as 'organizers' rather than as couriers, thus ascribing to themselves a more affirmative political role. There are others who emphasize that courier work was not perceived as 'women's work', in an attempt to revoke the subsidiary status afforded to it.

3. Interviews with Rukmini and Bulbul were, as previously noted, conducted primarily in English.

4. On the manner in which 1930s 'terrorist' women subverted *and* confirmed the expectations of Bengali womanhood, see Ghosh (2006); Mukherjee (1999); and Sarkar (1984); and see also Dutta's (1945) own reminiscences.

5. See also Stree Shakti Sanghatana (1989: 264) on the experience of the Telangana struggle where the party found it difficult to welcome women who were seen as burdensome (because they were physically 'weak') and a risk to the party's reputation (because of the 'problem' of sexuality).

6. While others have referred to instances when men and women lived together as man and wife for the purposes of camouflage, in Lata's case, an actual marital alliance between two party workers was instituted for the purposes of political expediency, to create families for providing shelter. See the discussion on marriage within the movement in Chapter 4.

7. One of the incidents that Sen narrates is one that I heard from different quarters—a tragic incident in which a woman lost her newborn child while being on the run. A similar incident took place during the Telangana struggle, where a woman activist was forced to give up her newly born child. The Stree Shakti Sanghatana (1989: 265) argues that it was precisely because the party never took up questions of reproduction and childbirth politically that a situation like this was created.

8. Some parents, including mothers of activists, were also, I was told, more willing to 'sacrifice' daughters rather than sons for similar economic reasons. Complexities of class, economic survival, and son preference complicate ideological constructs of mothers as ever willing to nurture and sacrifice their sons as soldiers of the revolution.

9. Arendt's (1970) critique of the New Left's use of violence was rooted in her belief that violence and power are opposites: violence is based on strength and force, while power is a function of human relations; violence can always destroy but never create power. Like de Beauvoir (1976), Arendt also showed the impossibility of knowing in advance the outcomes or consequences of the use of violence for political ends. For both, means cannot be clearly distinguishable from the ends they serve. In the context of political struggles, means also tend to overtake ends such that violence becomes an end in itself (see Roy 2009a). See also Nigam's (2007) discussion of Arendt in the context of the politics of revolutionary violence in relation to the current Maoist movement in India.

Chapter 4

1. This poem (in Banerjee 1987:61), as with some others cited in other chapters, is from the *Thema Book of Naxalite Poetry*, edited and translated into English by Sumanta Banerjee.

2. Most activists use the term marriage or biye to characterize male–female relationships at the time even when these did not conform to the prescribed bounds of marriage, as I go on to describe.

3. 'Love marriage' refers to self-chosen unions (*nijer* biye) amongst middle-class Bengalis (and Indians) as an advancement over the more conventional (and still predominant) arranged marriage, a distinctively Indian practice. Donner (2008) shows how in contemporary Bengali middle-class society

(as elsewhere in the country), the two forms of conjugality inevitably blur into one another, and cannot be straightforwardly read, as also emphasized in Majumdar's (2009) historical study on Bengali marriage, as markers of 'tradition' or 'modernity'. On 'love marriages' in North India, see Mody (2008).

4. For commentaries on Naxalbari poetry, see Banerjee's (1987) introduction to the *Thema Book of Naxalite Poetry*, and various essays that accompany poetry published in Dasadhikari (1998).

5. Young middle-class male activists wrote the fragments of poetry I here consider. Both Murari Mukhopadhyay and Dronacharya Ghosh were killed in the course of the movement. Leading party ideologues like Saroj Dutta (who is also said to have been killed by the police) also wrote a substantial amount of poetry. Besides young activists, established literary personalities have also produced poetry inspired by Naxalbari such as Nabarun Bhattacharya and Nabanita Debsen.

6. See also Kannabiran and Lalitha (1989:183) on the promise of a new, socialist society, 'where women and men would be equal' in personal narratives of the Telangana people's struggle.

7. Basu's *Antarghat* has been recently translated into English as *The Enemy Within* (2002). While the protagonist of the novel is a female activist, the novel itself—a psychological thriller which explores the dark underbelly of the movement much after its demise—is not particularly concerned with the movement, and certainly not from the perspective of gender.

8. Kapur defines 'motherhood, wifehood', domesticity, marriage, chastity, purity, and self-sacrifice as constituting a normative sexuality in India, which were also 'colonial constructs used to mark the distinction between the colonial power and the colonial subject' (Kapur 2005: 55).

9. On constructions of chastity as the most valorized womanly virtue in nineteenth century Bengal, see Chowdhury (1998).

10. The use of sexual shaming to denigrate women activists has been noted of militant nationalist and revolutionary movements elsewhere (see, for instance, De Mel 2001; and Kannabiran and Lalitha 1989).

11. Omvedt (1980: 48) remarks of the communists in western India that their marriages were half prompted by personal choice and half arranged by the party for practical purposes, and sometimes, to discourage attraction to non-party persons.

12. See Mody (2008) for the violent repercussions of 'love marriages' across caste and community boundaries. A recent inter-community love marriage of this kind in Kolkata led to the death of the husband, Rizwanur Rahman, and public outrage at the possibility of police complicity in his murder.

Chapter 5

1. Sexual violence refers to the range of abuses and threats that women faced within the political field, including acts of physical assault, rape, acts that stopped short of rape, unwanted gestures, sexually inflected and sexist comments, and domestic abuse.

2. Levi's (1998) 'grey zone' captures the central ideology of the Nazi concentration camps where victims, victimizers, and witnesses found themselves in a web of complicity to the extent that it became impossible to attribute moral responsibility to a clearly defined group of 'perpetrators' alone. My usage of the term in the very different context of radical politics counters the moral absoluteness in which the revolutionary and the state are usually placed.

3. Although Supriya mentions this incident in her published memoir, I quote from her oral interview with me given the greater detail and depth. The manner in which oral and written material here compliment each other only goes to show how both are fragmented and neither wholly reliable, as Hershatter (2011) notes in her oral history of 1950s rural Chinese women.

4. It is significant that the state has recently employed 'Naxal' as one of the signifiers by which women are rendered 'unrapable', as was seen in the rape and murder of 16-year-old Meena Khalkho in Chhattisgarh in July 2011. Feminists were outraged by the state's dismissal of this act of violence on the basis that the woman was a Naxalite, besides being perceived as 'habituated' to sexual intercourse.

5. See also the narrative of 'Deepa' in Kalpana Sen (2001: 178) who speaks of the party's insensitivity to the sexual violence that women activists like her faced.

6. Such 'mock trials' and 'kangaroo courts' are part of the policing function of most revolutionary movements, such as the Farabundo Marti National Liberation Front (FMLN) in El Salvador, the Irish Republican

Army (IRA) in Northern Ireland, the Liberation Tigers of Tamil Eelam (LTTE) in Sri Lanka, and contemporary Maoists in India.

7. These internal acts of betrayal also compose a form of risky memory. I was asked, on at least two occasions, to turn my tape recorder off when they were discussed, however briefly.

8. Two male comrades participated in the murder along with Molina, and were sentenced to death as well. All three were later released under general amnesty by the Left Front government.

9. Rege (1998: WS43) has also shown how the Indian women's movements' major campaigns around dowry-related deaths and rape in the 1970s ignored the 'caste hierarchies and patriarchies' that shape such forms of violence in tune with the 'class framework' that Indian feminists had inherited from the Left.

10. This is akin to the manner in which Aretxaga (1997) describes the use of menstrual blood by Armagh women in Northern Ireland's Dirty Protest as bringing to the surface the gender and sexual difference that had otherwise been erased for the sake of political identity and participation.

Chapter 6

1. To recall from Chapter 1, around 100–50 young men were butchered in the span of two days, over 12–13 August 1971, in Cossipore in north Kolkata. Such 'mass murders' were all too common at the time with reports of similar incidents occurring at Howrah, Diamond Harbour, Beliaghata, and Barasat where eleven bodies ridden with bullet marks were found strewn over several miles on the outskirt of the city in Barasat (Chaudhuri 1977c). While it is commonly known that many of these massacres were orchestrated by the police (or at least with their full knowledge), no action was ever taken.

2. For details of these commissions, see Amnesty International's (2001) report and Chaudhuri (1977c). The Bandimukti-O-Ganabadi Prastuti Commission was one of the first to make an attempt at collecting cases of police atrocities, although it failed to produce a final report. Its initial report suggested that the police, under the Congress government, had resorted to 'systematic liquidation' of political activists between 1970–6.

Seventy-six political prisoners were reported to be killed in jails alone. Besides such jail killings, official sources have estimated 202 encounter deaths between March 1971 and October 1971 alone. The article from which this data is drawn provides a partial list of 'political activists killed by police and parliamentary forces in West Bengal' (Chaudhuri 1977c: 1135), which includes leaders, cadres, and sympathizers, men and a few women.

3. The violence of the late 1960s–70s forms the backdrop if not the substantive content of a number of short stories and novels by prominent writers (in Bangla) such as Sunil Gangopadhyay, Samaresh Basu, Samaresh Majumdar, Sirshendu Mukhopadhyay, and Ashim Ray, amongst others. Political violence is also the subject of several of the films inspired by the movement which includes Mrinal Sen's Calcutta Trilogy, and Ritwik Ghatak's *Jukti, Takko aar Gappo* (Reason, Discussion and a Tale, 1974). More recently, the brutal repression of the Naxalites has found its way into Booker Prize-winning novels like *The God of Small Things* by Arundhati Roy (1997), and Hindi films like *Hazaaron Khwaishein Aisi* (A Thousand Dreams Such As These, 2005).

4. One of India's most well-known documentary filmmaker, Anand Patwardhan's *Prisoners of Consciousness* (1978) is a unique chronicle of state repression and of political prisoners during the Emergency. See a recent piece evaluating the contemporary relevance of the film by a filmmaker, Paromita Vohra (2009).

5. Banerjee (1987: 95) observes in his introduction to an edited volume of Naxalite poetry, including prison poems, how firings inside jails became quite common from 1970, and between the end of that year and 1972, no less than 100 prisoners were killed and hundreds of others injured in jail firings. In documenting jail 'disturbances' in West Bengal in the period between December 1970 and May 1975, Chaudhuri (1977c) reported the death of sixty-eight prisoners and the wounding of 310. A 100-odd prisoners managed to escape in 'jailbreaks' that had become a key political strategy at the time.

6. I am referring to prison memoirs by Mitra (1989), Sen (1994), and Tyler (1977). Mitra's *Hanyaman* has been recently translated into English as *Killing Days: Prison Memoirs* (2004). See Punjabi (1997) for a discussion of *Hanyaman* in relation to women's testimonies of state

violence in India and Latin America. For a discussion of prison memory in both *Hanyaman* and *Jailer Bhitor Jail*, see S. Ghosh (2001).

7. On the curative function of narrative memory or testimony as a means of healing, see Brison (2002), Felman and Laub (1992), and Herman (1994). For critiques of the 'narrative cure', see Caruth (1995), Edkins (2003), and Robson (2001).

8. Maya's interview was conducted, on her request, in the house of a friend. It is interesting to note that throughout the interview, Maya addressed her friend (who was relatively non-interfering), and that her narrative is punctuated with 'are you listening x?' and 'did you know that x?'. Presumably, her friend acted as a source of recognition for a version of the past and the self that is already widely in circulation.

9. For details regarding the historic nature of the case and its significance in judicial history in Bengal, see Ganguly, reprinted in a book written by Saumen Guha, and jointly published by the couple (Ganguly 1997). Latika's legal testimony appears in full here as well (S. Guha 1997). See also Chatterji (2000) and Dasgupta (1996) for the significance of the case in relation to the women's movement in Kolkata. Information on the case appears on the Amnesty International website as well. Available at http://www.amnestyusa.org/countries/india/document.do?id=900CA7C25DBC8313802569A60060485D.

10. Here, it must be made clear that it was practically impossible to interview Latika on her own and not in the presence of her husband. Even though I always chose to fix up an appointment with Latika, Saumen would invariably be present.

Conclusion

1. This is explicit in Sinha Roy's recent analysis of radical politics in India, starting with Naxalbari, which she concludes by noting how the 'greater visibility of women in the Maoist movement . . . —from propaganda to armed action—has the potential to redefine the "woman question", with the only impediment being the sexual conservatism of these groups' (Sinha Roy 2011: 168).

2. See the Sanhati report (Women against Sexual Violence and State Repression [WSS], 2011) on rape and molestation by security forces

during combing/search operations in villages in Jharkhand. This independent fact-finding mission comprised of women also investigated allegations of rape at the hands of Maoists. It concludes by calling for greater party scrutiny of sexual violence that is rooted in 'personal vendetta' (as opposed to sanctioned party action).

3. She was arrested twice, spent about twelve months in prison, but was never physically tortured.

4. Given that most women know one another within this sample, they sometimes referred to the self-censorship that others had resorted to with respect to their lives in the andolan. A male activist remarked how even something as public and revelatory as Bandyopadhyay's (2001) article was ridden with the unspoken and unsaid, and how her self-censorship was (he felt) perhaps due to the pressures and obligations of maintaining a family.

Glossary

Adda	to indulge in informal and friendly talk with others
Adivasi	scheduled tribes in the Indian constitution
Andolan	movement
Attotyag	self-denial or self-abnegation
Baba	father
Bandimukti	freedom of prisoners
Bandimukti-O-Ganabadi Prastuti Commission	commission to free prisoners and reinstate democracy
Bari	home
Bau	wife
Bhab	behaviour
Bhadra	respectable
Bhalo	good
Bhadra	respectable
Bhadralok	respectable man
Bhadramahila	respectable woman
Bhakti	devotion
Bhalobasha	love
Biplab	revolution
Biplabi	revolutionary
Biye	marriage
Boudi	wife of elder brother
Bustee	slum
Chakri	salaried job
Chotolok	lower caste–class
Choto Meye	little girl
Dada	elder brother
Danab	demon
Debi	goddess

Desh	country
Didi	elder sister
Falanga	the systematic beating of the soles of the feet
Gram	village
Jonogon	masses
Kapurush	faliure of manliness
Kharap	bad
Khatam	annihilation
Ma	mother
Madhyabitta	middle class
Mahapurush	great man
Mahila	woman
Mashi/Mashima	maternal aunt
Matribhumi	motherland
Memshahib	European/Western woman
Meshomoshai	uncle
Moshaal	flaming torch
Meye	girl
Naxalponthi	followers of Naxalbari politics
Nijer Biye	self-chosen union/marriage
Nimno Madhyabitta	lower middle-class
Para	neighbourhood
Patrika	newspaper/magazine
Premika	lover (female)
Probashi	Bengali who lives outside of West Bengal
Rajniti	politics
Rokto	blood
Sanyasi	ascetic (male)
Sanyasin	ascetic (female)
Satyagraha	non-violent resistance
Shakti	strength
Sindoor	vermillion worn by married Hindu women
Songothon kaaj	organizational work
Tebhaga	agitation
Tek Naam	technical name or activist pseudonym
Thakuma	grandmother
Thana	police station

References

Acharya, Anil (ed.), 1994, *Shottor Dasak* [The Seventies Decade], Kolkata: Anushtup.

Agamben, Giorgio, 2004, 'The Witness', in Nancy Scheper–Hughes and Philippe Bourgois (eds), *Violence in War and Peace: An Anthology*, Malden, MA: Blackwell Publishers, pp. 437–42.

Ajitha, 2008, *Kerala's Naxalbari: Ajitha, Memoirs of a Young Revolutionary*, trans. by Sanju Ramachandran, New Delhi: Shrishti.

Alison, Miranda, 2004, 'Women as Agents of Political Violence: Gendering Security', *Security Dialogue*, 35(4): 447–63.

Alter, Joseph S., 1994, 'Celibacy, Sexuality, and the Transformation of Gender into Nationalism in North India', *The Journal of Asian Studies*, 53(1): 45–66.

Amin, Shahid, 1995, *Event, Metaphor, Memory: Chauri Chaura, 1922–1992*, Berkeley: University of California Press.

Antze, Paul and Michael Lambek, 1996, 'Introduction: Forecasting Memory', in Paul Antze and Michael Lambek (eds), *Tense Past: Cultural Essays in Trauma and Memory*, London: Routledge, pp. xi–xxxviii.

Arendt, Hannah, 1970, *On Violence*, New York: Harcourt.

———, 1990 [1962], *On Revolution*, Harmondsworth: Penguin.

Aretxaga, Begoña, 1997, *Shattering Silence: Women, Nationalism, and Political Subjectivity in Northern Ireland*, Princeton; NJ: Princeton University Press.

Argenti–Pillen, Alex, 2003, *Masking Terror: How Women Contain Violence in Southern Sri Lanka*, Philadelphia, PA: University of Pennsylvania Press.

Arif, Yasmeen, 2007, 'The Delhi Carnage of 1984: The After Life of Violence and Loss', *Domains: The Journal of the International Centre for Ethnic Studies*, 3: 14–37.

Ashplant, T.G., Graham Dawson, and Michael Roper, 2000, 'The Politics of War Memory and Commemoration: Contexts, Structures and Dynamics', in T.G. Ashplant, Graham Dawson, and Michael Roper (eds), *The Politics of War Memory and Commemoration*, London: Routledge, pp. 3–86.

Association for the Protection of Democratic Rights (APDR), 1999, *Bharatiya Ganatantreyer (?) Swarup* (A True Picture of Indian Democracy [?]), Kolkata: APDR.

Bacchetta, Paola, 2004, *Gender in the Hindu Nation*, New Delhi: Women Unlimited.

Bagchi, Jashodhara, 1990, 'Representing Nationalism: Ideology of Motherhood in Colonial Bengal', *Economic and Political Weekly*, 20–7 (October): WS 65–71.

———, 2000, 'Positivism and Nationalism: Womanhood and Crisis in Nationalist Fiction—Bankimchandra's *Anandmath*', in Alice Thorner and Maithreyi Krishnaraj (eds), *Ideals, Images and Real Lives: Women in Literature and History*, Mumbai: Orient Longman, pp. 176–91.

Bagchi, Jashodhara and Subhoranjan Dasgupta, 2003, 'Introduction', in Jasodhara Bagchi and Subhoranjan Dasgupta (eds), *The Trauma and the Triumph: Gender and the Partition in Eastern India*, Kolkata: Stree, pp. 1–14.

Bakare–Yusuf, Bibi, 1997, 'The Economy of Violence: Black Bodies and the Unspeakable Terror', in Ronit Lentin (ed.), *Gender and Catastrophe*, London: Zed Books, pp. 171–83.

Bal, Mieke, Jonathan Crewe, and Leo Spitzer Hanover (eds), 1999, *Acts of Memory: Cultural Recall in the Present*, New Hampshire and London: University Press of New England.

Balagopal, K., 2006, 'Maoist Movement in Andhra Pradesh', *Economic and Political Weekly*, 41(29): 3183–7.

Bandyopadhyay, Krishna, 2001, 'Abirata Larai' [Relentless Struggle], *Khonj Ekhon* [Search Today], 1(May): 86–100.

———, 2008, 'Naxalbari Politics: A Feminist Narrative', *Economic and Political* Weekly, 43(14): 52–9.

Bandyopadhyay, Raghab, 2000, *Journal Shottor* [Journal Seventies], Kolkata: Mitra and Ghosh.

Bandyopadhyay, Parthapratim and Sadhan Chattopadhyay (eds), 1999, *Pratibader Galpo: Naxalbari* [Stories of Protest: Naxalbari], Kolkata: Radical Impression.

Banerjee, Sikata, 2003, 'Gender and Nationalism: The Masculinisation of Hinduism and Female Political Participation in India', *Women's Studies International Forum*, 26(2): 167–79.

Banerjee, Sukanya, Angana Chatterji, Lubna Nazir Chaudhry, Manali Desai, Saadia Toor, and Kamala Visweswaran, 2004, 'Engendering Violence: Boundaries, Histories, and the Everyday', *Cultural Dynamics*, 16(2–3): 125–39.

Banerjee, Sumanta, 1984, *India's Simmering Revolution: The Naxalite Uprising*, London: Zed Books.

——— (ed.), 1987, *Thema Book of Naxalite Poetry*, Kolkata: Thema.

———, 2002, 'Naxalbari: Between Past and Future', *Economic and Political Weekly*, 37(21): 2115–16.

———, 2006, 'Beyond Naxalbari', *Economic and Political Weekly*, 41(29): 3159–62.

———, 2009, 'Reflections of a One-time Maoist Activist', *Dialectical Anthropology*, 33(3–4): 253–69.

Bannerji, Himani, 1995, 'Attired in Virtue: The Discourse on Shame (Lajja) and Clothing of the Bhadramahila in Colonial Bengal', in Bharati Ray (ed.), *From the Seams of History*, New Delhi: Oxford University Press, pp. 67–106.

Bartky, Sandra Lee, 1990, *Femininity and Domination: Studies in the Phenomenology of Oppression*, London: Routledge.

Bartlett, Frederic C., 1995, *Remembering: A Study in Experimental and Social Psychology*, Cambridge and New York: Cambridge University Press.

Basu, Amrita, 1992, *Two Faces of Protest: Contrasting Modes of Women's Activism in India*, Berkeley and London: University of California Press.

Basu, Amrita and Patricia Jeffery (eds), 1998, *Appropriating Gender: Women's Activism and Politicized Religion in South Asia*, New York; London: Routledge.

Basu, Bani, 2002, *Antarghat* [The Enemy Within], trans. by Jayanti Datta, New Delhi: Orient Longman.

Basu, Pradip, 2000, *Towards Naxalbari, 1953–1967: An Account of Inner-party Ideological Struggle*, Kolkata: Progressive Publishers.

Basu, Sajal, 1982, *Politics of Violence: A Case Study of West Bengal*, Kolkata: Minerva.

Basu, Samaresh, 2003, *Selected Stories (Vol. 1)*, trans. by Sumanta Banerjee, Kolkata: Thema.

Basu, Srimati, 2001, 'The Blunt Cutting-Edge: The Construction of Sexuality in the Bengali "Feminist" Magazine *Sananda*', *Feminist Media Studies*, 1(2): 179–96.

Basu, Subho and Sikata Banerjee, 2006, 'The Quest for Manhood: Masculine Hinduism and Nation in Bengal', *Comparative Studies of South Asia, Africa and the Middle East*, 26(3): 476–90.

Basu Ray, Iraboni, 1994, 'Shottor Dashaker Bangla Uppanyash', in Anil Acharya (ed.), *Shottor Dasak* [A Socioeconomic, Political, and Cultural Evaluation of the Senenties], Kolkata: Anushtup, pp.174–200.

Baxi, Pratiksha, 2005, 'The Social and Juridical Framework of Rape in India: Case Studies in Gujarat', Unpublished PhD thesis, Delhi School of Economics, University of Delhi.

———, 2010, 'Justice is a Secret: Compromise in Rape Trials', *Contributions to Indian Sociology* 44(3): 207–33.

Berliner, David, 2005, 'The Abuses of Memory: Reflections on the Memory Boom in Anthropology', *Anthropological Quarterly*, 78(1): 197–211.

Bhasin, Kamla and Ritu Menon, 1998, *Borders and Boundaries: Women in India's Partition*, New Delhi: Kali for Women.

Bhatia, Bela (2000) *The Naxalite Movement in Central Bihar*, Unpublished PhD Thesis, University of Cambridge.

———, 2006, 'On Armed Resistance', *Economic and Political Weekly*, 41(29): 3179–83.

Bhattacharya, Debashish, 2000, *Shottorer Dinguli* [Days of the Seventies], Kolkata: Ekhon Bisngbad.

Borthwick, Meredith, 1984, *The Changing Role of Women in Bengal 1849–1905*, Princeton, NJ: Princeton University Press.

Bourdieu, Pierre, 2001, *Masculine Domination*, trans. by Richard Nice, Cambridge: Polity.

Bourgois, Philippe, 2001, 'The Power of Violence in War and Peace: Post-Cold War Lessons from El Salvador', *Ethnography*, 2(1): 5–34.

_______, 2002, 'The Violence of Moral Binaries: Response to Leigh Binford', *Ethnography*, 3(2): 221–31.

_______, 2004, 'The Continuum of Violence in War and Peace: Post-Cold War Lessons from El Salvador', in Nancy Scheper–Hughes and Phillipe Bourgois (eds), *Violence in War and Peace: An Anthology*, Malden, MA: Blackwell Publishers, pp. 425–34.

Brison, Susan, 2002, *Aftermath: Violence and the Remaking of a Self*, Princeton, NJ: Princeton University Press.

Broomfield, J.H., 1968, *Elite Conflict in a Plural Society: Twentieth Century Bengal*, Berkeley: University of California Press.

Brown, Laura, 1995, 'Not Outside the Range: One Feminist Perspective on Psychic Trauma', in Cathy Caruth (ed.), *Trauma: Explorations in Memory*, Baltimore, MD, and London: Johns Hopkins University Press, pp. 100–12.

Brown, Wendy, 1993, 'Wounded Attachments', *Political Theory*, 21(3): 390–410.

_______, 1999, 'Resisting Left Melancholia', *Boundary 2*, 26(3): 19–27.

Butalia, Urvashi, 1998, *The Other Side of Silence: Voices from the Partition of India*, New Delhi: Penguin.

Butalia, Urvashi and Tanika Sarkar (eds), 1995, *Women and the Hindu Right: A Collection of Essays*, New Delhi, India: Kali for Women.

Butler, Judith, 1990, *Gender Trouble: Feminism and the Subversion of Identity*, New York and London: Routledge.

_______, 1993, *Bodies that Matter: On the Discursive Limits of 'Sex'*, New York and London: Routledge.

_______, 1997, *The Psychic Life of Power: Theories in Subjection*, Stanford, CA: Stanford University Press.

_______, 2004, *Precarious Life: The Powers of Mourning and Violence*, London and New York: Verso.

Byrne, Bridget, 2003, 'Reciting the Self: Narrative Representations of the Self in Qualitative Interviews', *Feminist Theory*, 4(1): 29–49.

Caruth, Cathy (ed.), 1995, *Trauma: Explorations in Memory*, Baltimore, MD, and London: Johns Hopkins University Press.

Chakrabarty, Dipesh, 1996, 'Remembered Villages: Representation of Hindu-Bengali Memories in the Aftermath of the Partition', *Economic and Political Weekly*, 10(August): 2143–51.

_______, 2000, *Provincializing Europe: Postcolonial Thought and Historical Difference*, Princeton, N.J.; Oxford: Princeton University Press.

———, 2004, 'Romantic Archives: Literature and the Politics of Identity in Bengal', *Critical Inquiry*, 30(3): 654–82.

Chakrabarty, Prafulla, 1990, *The Marginal Men: The Refugees and the Left Political Syndrome in West Bengal*, Kalyani: Lumière Books.

Chakravarti, Uma, 1998, 'Inventing Saffron History: A Celibate Hero Rescues an Emasculated Nation', in Mary E. John and Janaki Nair (eds), *A Question of Silence?: The Sexual Economies of Modern India*, New Delhi: Kali for Women, pp. 243–68.

———, 2003, *Gendering Caste: Through a Feminist Lens*, Kolkata: Stree.

Chatterjee, Partha, 1983, 'Introduction', in Promode Sengupta, *Naxalbari and Indian Revolution*, Kolkata: Research India Publications.

———, 1989, 'The Nationalist Resolution of the Women's Question', in Kumkum Sangari and Sudesh Vaid (eds), *Recasting Women: Essays in Indian Colonial History*, New Delhi: Kali for Women, pp. 233–53.

———, 1993a, *The Nation and Its Fragments: Colonial and Postcolonial Histories*, Princeton, NJ, and Chichester: Princeton University Press.

———, 1993b, 'A Religion of Urban Domesticity: Sri Ramakrishna and the Kolkata Middle Classes', in Partha Chatterjee and Gyanendra Pandey (eds), *Subaltern Studies VII*, New Delhi: Oxford University Press, pp. 40–68.

———, 1998, *The Present History of West Bengal: Essays in Political Criticism*, New Delhi and Oxford: Oxford University Press.

———, 2001, 'Democracy and the Violence of the State: A Political Negotiation of Death', *Inter-Asia Cultural Studies*, 2(1): 7–21.

Chatterji, Maitreyi, 2000, 'The Feminist Movement in West Bengal: From the 1980s to 1990s', in Mandrakanta Bose (ed.), *Faces of the Feminine in Ancient, Medieval and Modern India*, New York and Oxford: Oxford University Press, pp. 322–34.

Chatterji, Roma and Deepak Mehta, 2007, *Living With Violence: An Anthropology of Events and Everyday Life*, New Delhi: Routledge.

Chattopadhyay, Kunal, 2001, 'Tebhaga Andolane Krishak Meyera' [Peasant Women in Tebhaga Movement], in Maitreyi Chatterji (ed.), *Esho Mukto Koro: Nareer Adhikar o Adhikar Andolan Bishayak Prabandha Sankalan* [Let Us Be Free: A Collection of Essays on Women's Rights and Movements], Kolkata: People's Book Society, pp. 145–58.

Chaudhuri, Kalyan, 1977a, 'The Howrah Prison Killings: Story of a "Jail Break"', *Economic and Political Weekly*, 23 April: 673–5.

———, 1977b, 'Women Prisoners in Presidency Jail', *Economic and Political Weekly*, 7 May: 755–6.

———, 1977c, '"Law and Order" Killings', *Economic and Political Weekly*, 16 July: 1134–42.

Chaudhuri, Maitrayee, 2004, 'Introduction', in Maitrayee Chaudhuri (ed.), *Feminism in India*, London and New York: Zed Books, pp. xi–xlvi.

Chenoy, Anuradha M., 1998, 'Militarization, Conflict and Women in South Asia', in Lois Ann Lorentzen and Jennifer Turpin (eds), *The Women and War Reader*, New York: New York University Press, pp. 101–10.

Chopra, Radhika, Caroline Osella, and Filippo Osella (eds), 2004, *Masculinities in South Asia: Context of Change, Sites of Continuity*, New Delhi: Women Unlimited.

Chowdhury, Indira, 1998 *The Frail Hero and Virile History: Gender and the Politics of Culture in Colonial Bengal Delhi*, Oxford: Oxford University Press.

Confino, Alon, 1997, 'Collective Memory and Cultural History: Problems of Method', *American Historical Review*, 102(5): 1386–403.

Cubilie, Anne, 2005, *Women Witnessing Terror: Testimony and the Cultural Politics of Human Rights*, New York: Fordham University Press.

Cubilie Anne and Carl Good (guest eds), 2003, 'Introduction: The Future of Testimony', Special Issue: The Future of Testimony, *Discourse*, 25(1–2), Winter: 4–18.

Cunningham, Karla, 2003, 'Cross-Regional Trends in Female Terrorism', *Studies in Conflict and Terrorism*, 26(3): 171–95.

Custers, Peter, 1987, *Women in the Tebhaga Uprising: Rural Poor Women and Revolutionary Leadership (1946–47)*, Kolkata: Naya Prokash.

Cvetkovich, Anne, 2003, *An Archive of Feelings: Trauma, Sexuality, and Lesbian Public Cultures*, Durham, NC, and London: Duke University Press.

Da Costa, Dia, 2010, *Development Dramas: Reimagining Rural Political Action in Eastern India*, New Delhi: Routledge.

Damas, Marius, 1991, *Approaching Naxalbari*, Kolkata: Radical Impression.

Das, Anirban, 2001, 'In(re)trospection: Suturing of Selves Past', *Margins*, February: 64–75.

Das, Anirban and Ritu Sen Chaudhuri, 2007, 'The Desired "One": Thinking the Woman in the Nation', *History Compass*, 5(5): 1483–99.

Das, Veena (ed.), 1992, *Mirrors of Violence: Communities, Riots and Survivors in South Asia*, New Delhi: Oxford University Press.

———, 1995, *Critical Events: An Anthropological Perspective on Contemporary India*, New Delhi: Oxford University Press.

———, 1996, 'Sexual Violence, Discursive Formations and the State', *Economic and Political Weekly*, 31(35/37, Special Number): 2411–23.

———, 2007, *Life and Words: Violence and the Descent into the Ordinary*, Berkeley: University of California Press.

Das, Veena and Arthur Kleinman, 2000, 'Introduction', in Veena Das, Arthur Kleinman, Mamphela Ramphele, and Pamela Reynolds (eds), *Violence and Subjectivity*, Berkley: University of California Press, pp. 1–18.

———, 2001, 'Introduction', in Veena Das, Arthur Kleinman, Margaret Lock, Mamphela Ramphele, and Pamela Reynolds (eds), *Remaking a World: Violence, Social Suffering, and Recovery*, Berkeley: University of California Press, pp. 1–30.

Dasadhikari, Swapan (ed.), 1998, *Shottorer Shahid Lekhok Shilpi* [Martyr[s], Writers, Artists of the Seventies], Kolkata: Adhuna Jalarka Parishad.
Dasgupta, Biplab, 1975, *The Naxalite Movement*, Bombay: Allied Publishers.
Dasgupta, Rajashri, 1996, 'Cry Freedom', *The Telegraph*, 9 June, pp. 14–15.
———, 1998, 'Freedom', *The Telegraph*, 29 March.
———, 2003, 'Marxism and the Middle-class Intelligentsia: Culture and Politics in Bengal 1920s–1950s', Unpublished DPhil thesis, Oxford University.
———, 2005, 'Rhyming Revolution: Marxism and Culture in Colonial Bengal', *Studies in History*, 21(1): 79–98.
Dasgupta, Rajeshwari, 2006, 'Towards the "New Man": Revolutionary Youth and Rural Agency in the Naxalite Movement', *Economic and Political Weekly*, 41(19): 1920–7.
Dave, Naisargi, 2011, 'Activism as Ethical Practice: Queer Politics in Contemporary India', *Cultural Dynamics*, 23(1): 3–20.
Dawson, Graham, 1994, *Soldier Heroes: British Adventure, Empire and the Imagining of Masculinity*, London: Routledge.
———, 1999, 'Trauma, Memory, Politics: The Irish Troubles', in Kim Lacy Rogers, Selma Leydesdorff, and Graham Dawson (eds), *Trauma and Life Stories: International Perspectives*, London: Routledge, pp. 180–204.
Dawson, Graham and Bob West, 1984, 'Our Finest Hour: The Popular Memory of World War II and the Struggle over National Identity', in Geoff Hurd (ed.), *National Fictions: World War Two in British Films and Television*, London: BFI Publishing, pp. 8–13.
De Alwis, Malathi, 1998a, 'Motherhood as a Space of Protest: Women's Political Participation in Contemporary Sri Lanka', in Amrita Basu and Patricia Jeffery (eds), *Appropriating Gender: Women's Activism and Politicized Religion in South Asia*, New York and London: Routledge, pp. 185–201.
———, 1998b, 'Moral Mothers and Stalwart Sons: Reading Binaries in a Time of War', in Lois Ann Lorentzen and Jennifer Turpin (eds), *The Women and War Reader*, New York: New York University Press, pp. 217–54.
———, 2002, 'Changing Role of Women in Sri Lankan Society', *Social Science Research*, 69(3).
De Beauvoir, Simone, 1976[1948], *The Ethics of Ambiguity*, trans. by Bernard Frechtman, New York: Citadel Press.
De Mel, Neloufer, 2001, *Women and the Nation's Narrative: Gender and Nationalism in Twentieth Century Sri Lanka*, Lanham, MD: Rowman and Littlefield.
———, 2007, *Militarizing Sri Lanka: Popular Culture, Memory and Narrative in the Armed Conflict*, LA; London; New Delhi; Singapore: Sage Publications.
Devi, Mahasweta, 2001[1997], *Hajar Churashir Ma* [Mother of 1084], trans. by Samik Bandyopadhyay, Kolkata: Seagull Books.
———, 2002a[1997], 'Draupadi', in *Breast Stories*, trans. Gayatri Chakravorty Spivak, Kolkata: Seagull Books.

Devi, Mahasweta, 2002b[1990], *Bashai Tudu*, trans. by Samik Bandyopadhyay and Gayatri Charkavorty Spivak, Kolkata: Thema.

Dirlik, Arif, 1998, 'The Third World', in Carole Fink, Philipp Gassert, and Detlef Junker (eds), *1968: The World Transformed*, Cambridge and New York: Cambridge University Press, pp. 295–320.

Donner, Henrike, 2004a, 'The Significance of Naxalbari: Accounts of Personal Involvement and Politics in West Bengal', Occasional Paper No. 2, Centre of South Asian Studies, Cambridge: University of Cambridge.

———, 2004b, 'The Legacy of the Maoists in West Bengal', Paper presented at the panel discussion on 'The Legacy of Maoism in China and India', LSE Asia Research Centre Seminar.

———, 2008, *Domestic Goddesses: Maternity, Globalisation and Middle-class Identity in Contemporary India*, Aldershot: Ashgate.

———, 2009, 'Radical Masculinity: Morality, Sociality and Relationships through Recollections of Naxalite Activists', *Dialectical Anthropology*, 33: 327–43.

———, 2011, 'Locating Activist Spaces: The Neighbourhood as a Source and Site of Urban Activism in 1970s Kolkata', *Cultural Dynamics*, 23(1): 21–40.

Duyker, Edward, 1987, *Tribal Guerrillas: The Santals of West Bengal and the Naxalite Movement*, New Delhi: Oxford University Press.

Edkins, Jenny, 2003, *Trauma and the Memory of Politics*, Cambridge and New York: Cambridge University Press.

Elshtain, Jean, 1995[1987], *Women and War*, Chicago: Chicago University Press.

Eng, David L. and David Kazanjian, 2003, 'Introduction: Mourning Remains', *Loss: The Politics of Mourning*, Berkeley, CA; London: University of California Press, 324–43

Engels, Dagmar, 1996, *Beyond Purdah? Women in Bengal, 1849-1905*, New Delhi: Oxford University Press.

Enloe, Cynthia, 1983, *Does Khaki Become You? The Militarization of Women's Lives*, Boston, MA: South End Press.

———, 1989, *Bananas, Beaches and Bases: Making Feminist Sense of International Politics*, London: Pandora.

———, 2004, *The Curious Feminist: Searching for Women in a New Age of Empire*, Berkley: University of California Press.

Evans, Harriet, 1992, 'Monogamy and Female Sexuality in the People's Republic of China', in S. Rai, H. Pilkington, and A. Phizacklea (eds), *Women in the Face of Change: The Soviet Union, Eastern Europe and China*, London: Routledge, pp. 147–63.

———, 1997, *Women and Sexuality in China: Dominant Discourses of Female Sexuality and Gender since 1949*, Cambridge: Polity.

Featherstone, Mike, 1992, 'The Heroic Life and Everyday Life', *Theory, Culture and Society*, 9(1): 159–82.

Felman, Shoshana, 1995. 'Education and Crisis, or the Vicissitudes of Teaching', in Cathy Caruth (ed.), *Trauma: Explorations in* Memory, Baltimore, MD, and London: Johns Hopkins University Press, pp. 13–60.

Felman, Shoshana and Dori Laub, 1992, *Testimony: Crises of Witnessing in Literature, Psychoanalysis, and History*, New York: Routledge.

Felski, Rita, 1999–2000, 'The Invention of Everyday Life', *New Formation*, 39: 15–31.

Fentress, James and Chris Wickham, 1992, *Social Memory*, Oxford: Blackwell.

Foucault, Michel, 1980, *Language, Counter-memory, Practice: Selected Essays and Interviews*; edited (with an introduction) by Donald F. Bouchard, trans. by Donald F. Bouchard and Sherry Simon, Ithaca, NY: Cornell University Press.

———, 1984, 'Preface', in Gilles Deleuze and Félix Guattari, *Anti-Oedipus: Capitalism and Schizophrenia*, trans. by Robert Hurley, Mark Seem, and Helen R. Lane, London: Athlone, pp. xi–xiv.

Franda, Marcus, 1971, *Radical Politics in West Bengal*, Cambridge, MA, and London: MIT Press.

Frontier, 1970, 'A Naxalite Who Died', 15 August, pp. 13–15.

Frontier, 1969, 'Shoot to Kill', *Frontier*, 2(36): 1–2, 13 December.

Gangopadhyay, Sunil, 2005, *Pratidwandi*, trans. by Enakshi Chatterjee, New Delhi: Orient Longman.

Ganguly, Subhas, 1997, 'The Forgotten Decade: Archana Guha Case', in Saumen Guha (ed.), *The Battle of 'Archana Guha Case'*, Kolkata: Human Justice in India, pp. 297–326.

Ganguly, Suranjan, 2000, *Satyajit Ray: In Search of the Modern*, Lanham, MD, and London: Scarecrow.

Ganguly–Scrase, Ruchira and Timothy Scrase, 2009, *Globalization and the Middle Classes in India: The Social and Cultural Impact of Neoliberal Reforms*, Oxon and New York: Routledge.

Garton, Stephen, 2000, 'Longing for War: Nostalgia and Australian Returned Soldiers after the First World War', in T.G. Ashplant, G. Dawson, and M. Roper (eds), *The Politics of War Memory and Commemoration*, London: Routledge, pp. 222–39.

Gautam, Shobha, Amrita Banskota, and Rita Manchanda, 2001, 'Where There are No Men: Women in the Maoist Insurgency in Nepal', in Rita Manchanda (ed.), *Women, War, and Peace in South Asia: Beyond Victimhood to Agency*, New Delhi and Thousand Oaks, CA: Sage Publications, pp. 214–51.

Gedalof, Irene, 1999, *Against Purity: Rethinking Identity with Indian and Western Feminisms*, London: Routledge.

Geetha, V., n.d., 'The Story of a Marriage: Being a Tale of Self-Respect Unions and What Happened to Them', *Landmarks in Women's Studies in India*, 4.

Ghosh, Amitav, 1988, *The Shadow Lines*, London: Bloomsbury.

Ghosh, Devleena, 2001, 'Water Out of Fire: Novel Women, National Fictions and the Legacy of Nehruvian Developmentalism in India', *Third World Quarterly*, 22(6): 951–67.

Ghosh, Durba, 2006, 'Revolutionary Women, Nationalist Heroes: Kalpana, Kalyani, Kamaladevi and the Narratives of Violent Resistance,' paper presented at the Association of Asian Studies Annual Meeting, April 6–9, San Francisco.

Ghosh, Swati, 2001, 'Prison Memory: Retrieval of the Silent Other', *Margins*, February: 50–63, Kolkata.

Gilmartin, Christina Kelley, 1995, *Engendering the Chinese Revolution: Radical Women, Communist Politics, and Mass Movements in the 1920s*, Berkeley and London: University of California Press.

Gilmore, Leigh, 2001, *The Limits of Autobiography: Trauma and Testimony*, Ithaca; London: Cornell University Press.

Goodwin, Jeff, James M. Jasper, and Francesa Polletta, 2001, *Passionate Politics*, Chicago: Chicago University Press.

Goswami, T., 1971, 'The Hounds of West Bengal', *Frontier*, 17 April, pp. 11–13.

Greenberg, Judith, 1998, 'The Echo of Trauma and the Trauma of Echo', *American Imago*, 55(3): 319–47.

Griffin, Roger, 1993, *The Nature of Fascism*, London: Routledge.

Guha, Latika, 2001, 'Narak Prokash Hok' [Let Hell be Revealed], *Poricboy*, February–July: 27–8, Kolkata.

Guha, Ranajit, 1971, 'On Torture and Culture', *Frontier*, 23 January, pp. 9–15.

———, 1997a, *Dominance without Hegemony: History and Power in Colonial India*, Cambridge, MA, and London: Harvard University Press.

———, 1997b, 'Introduction', to Ranajit Guha (ed.), *Subaltern Studies Reader 1986–1995*, Minnesota: University of Minnesota Press; pp. ix–xv.

Guha, Saumen (ed.), 1997, *The Battle of 'Archana Guha Case'*, Kolkata: Human Justice in India.

Haaken, Janice, 1998, *Pillar of Salt: Gender, Memory, and the Perils of Looking Back*, New Brunswick, N.J.; London: Rutgers University Press.

Halbwachs, Maurice, 1992, *On Collective Memory*, edited, trans., and with an introduction by Lewis A. Coser, Chicago and London: University of Chicago Press.

Hamilton, Carrie, 2007, *Women and the ETA: The Gender Politics of Radical Basque Nationalism*, Manchester: Manchester University Press.

Haq, Farhat, 2007, 'Militarism and Motherhood: The Women of the Lashkar-i-Tayyabia in Pakistan', *Signs: Journal of Women in Culture and Society*, 32(4): 1024–46.

Haque, Ajijul, 1991, *Karagere Athero Bochhor* [18 Years in Prison], Kolkata: Dey's Publishing.

Harriss, John, 2011, 'What Is Going On in India's "Red Corridor"? Questions about India's Maoist Insurgency', *Pacific Affairs*, 84(2): 309–27.

Hasso, Frances, 2005, 'Discursive and Political Deployments by/of the 2002 Palestinian Women Suicide Bombers/Martyrs', *Feminist Review*, 81(1): 23–51.

Herman, Judith, 1994, *Trauma and Recovery: From Domestic Abuse to Political Terror*, London: Pandora.

Hershatter, Gail, 2011, *The Gender of Memory: Rural Women and China's Collective Past*, Berkeley: University of California Press.

Hirsch, Marianne and Valerie Smith, 2002, 'Feminism and Cultural Memory: An Introduction', *Signs: Journal of Women in Culture and Society*, 28(1): 1–19.

Hodges, Sarah, 2005, 'Revolutionary Family Life and the Self Respect Movement in Tamil South India, 1926–49', *Contributions to Indian Sociology*, 39(2): 251–77.

Hodgkin, Katherine and Sussanah Radstone, 2003, 'Introduction to Remembering Suffering: Trauma and History', in Katherine Hodgkin and Sussanah Radstone (eds), *Contested Pasts: The Politics of Memory*, London: Routledge, pp. 1–22.

Hollway, Wendy and Tony Jefferson, 2000, *Doing Qualitative Research Differently: Free Association, Narrative and the Interview Method*, London: Sage Publications.

Honig, Emily and Gail Hershatter, 1988, *Personal Voices: Chinese Women in the 1980's*, Stanford, CA: Stanford University Press.

Hutchings, Kimberly, 2007a, 'Feminist Ethics and Political Violence', *International Politics*, 44(1): 90–106.

———, 2007b, 'Simone de Beauvoir and the Ambiguous Ethics of Political Violence', *Hypatia*, 22(3): 111–32.

Hutnyk, John, 2000, *Critique of Exotica: Music, Politics, and the Culture Industry*, London: Pluto.

Jackson, Sue, 2001, 'Happily Never After: Young Women's Stories of Abuse in Heterosexual Love Relationships', *Feminism and Psychology*, 11(3): 305–21.

Jacoby, T.A., 1999, 'Feminism, Nationalism, and Difference: Reflections on the Palestinian Women's Movement', *Women's Studies International Forum*, 22(5): 511–23.

Jasper, James M., 1997, *The Art of Moral Protest: Culture, Biography and Creativity in Social Movements*, Chicago: University of Chicago Press.

Jeganathan, Pradeep, 2000, 'A Space for Violence', in Partha Chatterjee and Pradeep Jeganathan (eds), *Community, Gender and Violence: Subaltern Studies XI*, New Delhi: Permanent Black, pp. 37–65.

———, 2002, 'Walking through Violence: "Everyday Life" and Anthropology', in Diane Mines and Sarah Lamb (eds), *Everyday Life in South Asia*, Bloomington: Indiana University Press, pp. 357–65.

Jelin, Elizabeth, 2003, *State Repression and the Struggles for Memory*, trans. by Judy Rein and Marcial Godoy–Anativia, London: Latin America Bureau.

John, Mary E., 1996, *Discrepant Dislocations: Feminism, Theory, and Postcolonial Histories*, Berkeley, CA: University of California Press.

John, Mary E., 2004, Review of 'Militarism and Women in South Asia', by Anuradha Chenoy, *Interventions*, 6: 304–6.

John, Mary E. and Janaki Nair (eds), 1998, *A Question of Silence? The Sexual Economies of Modern India*, London: Zed.

———, 1999, 'Sexuality in Modern India: Critical Concerns', *Voices for Change: A Journal on Communication for Development*, 3(1): 4–8.

Johnson, Richard, 1982, 'Popular Memory: Theory, Politics, Method', in Richard Johnson, David Sutton, and Gregor McLennan (eds), *Making Histories: Studies in History-writing and Politics*, London: Hutchinson in association with Centre for Contemporary Cultural Studies, University of Birmingham, pp. 205–52.

Joshi Dutta, Kalpana, 1979, *Chittagong Armoury Raiders: Reminiscences*, Delhi: People's Publishing House.

Kakar, Sudhir, 1992, 'Some Unconscious Aspects of Ethnic Violence in India', in Veena Das (ed.), *Mirrors of Violence: Communities, Riots and Survivors in South Asia*, New Delhi: Oxford University Press, pp. 135–45.

———, 1996, *The Colors of Violence: Cultural Identities, Religion, and Conflict*, Chicago and London: University of Chicago Press.

Kannabiran, Kalpana, 2002, 'A Ravished Justice: Half a Century of Judicial Discourse on Rape', in Kalpana Kannabiran and Vasanth Kannabiran, *De-Eroticising Assault: Essays on Modesty, Honour and Power*, Kolkata: Stree, pp. 104–69.

Kannabiran, Kalpana and Vasanth Kannabiran, 2002, *De-Eroticising Assault: Essays on Modesty, Honour and Power*, Kolkata: Stree.

Kannabiran, Vasanth and K. Lalitha, 1989, 'That Magic Time: Women in the Telengana People's Struggle', in Kumkum Sangari and Sudesh Vaid (eds), *Recasting Women: Essays in Indian Colonial History*, New Delhi: Kali for Women, pp. 180–203.

Kannabiran, Vasanth, Volga, and Kalpana Kannabiran, 2004, 'Women's Rights and Naxalite Groups', *Economic and Political Weekly*, 39(45), 4874–7.

Kaplan, Temma, 2002, 'Acts of Testimony: Reversing the Shame and Gendering the Memory', *Signs: Journal of Women in Culture and Society*, 28(1): 179–99.

Kapur, Ratna, 2005, *Erotic Justice: Law and the New Politics of Postcolonialism*, London and Portland: Glass House Press.

Karlekar, Malavika, 1982, *Poverty and Women's Work: A Study of Sweeper Women in Delhi*, New Delhi: Vikas Publishing.

———, 1991, *Voices from Within: Early Personal Narratives of Bengali Women*, New Delhi and Oxford: Oxford University Press.

Kaviraj, Sudipta, 1992, 'The Imaginary Institution of India', in Partha Chatterjee and Gyanendra Pandey (eds), *Subaltern Studies VII*, New Delhi: Oxford University Press, pp. 1–39.

Kelly, Liz, 1988, *Surviving Sexual Violence*, Cambridge: Polity.

Kelly, Liz, 2000, 'Wars against Women: Sexual Violence, Sexual Politics and the Militarized State', in Susie Jacobs, Ruth Jacobson, and Jennifer Marchbank (eds), *States of Conflict: Gender, Violence and Resistance*, London: Zed Books, pp. 45–65.

Kitzinger, Celia and Alison Thomas, 1995, 'Sexual Harassment: A Discursive Approach', in Sue Wilkinson and Celia Kitzinger (eds), *Feminism and Discourse: Psychological Perspectives*, London: Sage Publications, pp. 32–48.

Klein, Kerwin Lee, 2000, 'On the Emergence of Memory in Historical Discourse', *Representations*, 69: 127–50.

Kudva, Neema, 2005, 'Strong States, Strong NGOs', in Raka Ray and Mary Katzenstein (eds), *Social Movements in India: Poverty, Power, and Politics*, Lanham, MD: Rowman and Littlefield, pp. 233–65.

Kuhn, Annette, 1999, 'A Journey through Memory', in Susannah Radstone (ed.), *Memory and Methodology*, Oxford: Berg, pp. 179–96.

Kumar, Radha, 1993, *The History of Doing: An Illustrated Account of Movements for Women's Rights and Feminism in India 1800–1990*, New Delhi: Kali for Women.

Kumar Ghosh, Suniti (ed.), 1993, *The Historic Turning Point: A Liberation Anthology*, Kolkata: S.K. Ghosh.

Kumari, Abhilasha and Sabina Kidwai, 1998, *Crossing the Sacred Line: Women's Search for Political Power*, New Delhi: Orient Longman.

Lacapra, Dominick, 2001, *Writing History, Writing Trauma*, Baltimore: Johns Hopkins University Press.

Lahiri, Abani, 2001, *Postwar Revolt of the Rural Poor in Bengal*, Kolkata: Seagull Books.

Lawler, Stephanie, 2002, 'Narrative in Social Research', in Tim May (ed.), *Qualitative Research in Action*, London: Sage Publications, pp. 242–58.

———, 2008, *Identity: Sociological Perspectives*, Cambridge: Polity.

Lecomte-Tilouine, Marie, 2009, *Hindu Kingship, Ethnic Revival, and Maoist Rebellion in Nepal*, New Delhi: Oxford University Press.

Lefebvre, Henri, 1971, 'Everyday Life in the Modern World: An Inquiry, and Some Discoveries', in Tony Bennett and Diane Watson (eds), (2002) *Understanding Everyday Life*, Oxford: Blackwell Publishers, pp. 317–19.

Legg, Stephen, 2011, 'Violent Memories: South Asian Spaces of Postcolonial Anamnesis', in M. Heffernan, P. Meusburger, and E. Wunder (eds), *Cultural Memories*, Dordrecht: Springer, pp. 287–303.

Levi, Primo, 1998, *The Drowned and the Saved*, trans. by Raymond Rosenthal, London: Joseph.

Leydesdorff, Selma, Luisa Passerini, and Paul Thompson (special eds), 1996, 'Gender and Memory', *International Yearbook of Oral History and Life Stories, Vol. 4*, Oxford: Oxford University Press.

Mahmood, Cynthia, 1996, *Fighting for Faith and Nation: Dialogues with Sikh Militants*, Philadelphia: University of Pennsylvania Press.

Majumdar, Rochona, 2009, *Marriage and Modernity: Family Values in Colonial Bengal, 1870–1956*, Durham, NC: Duke University Press.

Majumdar, Samaresh, 1983, *Kalbela* [The Omnious Hour], Kolkata: Ananda.

Mallick, Ross, 1994, *Development Policy of a Communist Government: West Bengal since 1977*, New York: Cambridge University Press.

Mallot, Edward J., 2006, 'Body Politics and the Body Politic', *Interventions*, 8(2): 165–77.

Manchanda, Rita, 2004, 'Maoist Insurgency in Nepal: Radicalising Gendered Narratives', *Cultural Dynamics*, 16(2–3): 237–58.

Mandal, Pulakesh and Joya Mitra, 1994, (eds), *Shei Dashak* [That Decade], Kolkata: Papyrus.

Mandal, Tirtha, 1991, *The Women Revolutionaries of Bengal, 1905–1939*, Kolkata: Minerva Associates (Publications).

Mankekar, Purnima, 1999, *Screening Culture, Viewing Politics: An Ethnography of Television, Womanhood, and Nation in Postcolonial India*, Durham, NC, and London: Duke University Press.

Manimala, 1995, 'Women of the Killing Belt of Bihar', in Jasodhara Bagchi (ed.), *Indian Women: Myth and Reality*, London: Sangam, pp. 59–70.

Marcus, Sharon, 1992, 'Fighting Bodies, Fighting Words: A Theory and Politics of Rape Prevention', in Judith Butler and Joan W. Scott (eds), *Feminists Theorise the Political*, New York and London: Routledge, pp. 385–403.

Mayaram, Shail, 1997, *Resisting Regimes: Myth, Memory and the Shaping of a Muslim Identity*, New Delhi and Oxford: Oxford University Press.

Mazumdar, Charu, 2001, *Rachana Sangraha* [Collected Works], 3rd edition, Kolkata: New Horizon Book Trust.

Melzer, Patricia, 2009, '"Death in the Shape of a Young Girl": Feminist Responses to Media Representations of Women Terrorists during the "German Autumn" of 1977', *International Journal of Feminist Politics*, 11(1): 35–62.

Menon, Dilip, 2006, *The Blindness of Insight: Essays on Caste in Modern India*, Chennai: Navayana Publications.

Menon, Nivedita, 2000, 'Embodying the Self: Feminism, Sexual Violence and the Law', in Partha Chatterjee and Pradeep Jeganathan (eds), *Community, Gender and Violence: Subaltern Studies XI*, New Delhi: Permanent Black, pp. 66–105.

Menon, Nivedita and Aditya Nigam, 2007, *Power and Contestation: India since 1989*, London: Zed Books.

Menon, Ritu, 2004, 'Doing Peace: Women Resist Daily Battle in South Asia', in Radhika Coomaraswamy and Dilrukshi Fonseka (eds), *Peace Work: Women, Armed Conflict and Negotiation*, New Delhi: Women Unlimited, pp. 54–72.

Mishler, Elliot G., 1991, *Research Interviewing: Context and Narrative*, Cambridge: Harvard University Press.

Misri, Deepti, 2011, '"Are You a Man?": Performing Naked Protest in India', *Signs: Journal of Women in Culture and Society*, 36(3): 603–25.

Misztal, Barbara, 2003, *Theories of Social Remembering,* Maidenhead and Philadelphia, PA: Open University Press.

Mitra, Joya, 1989, *Hanyaman* [Under the Shadow of Death], Kolkata: Dey's Publishing.

———, 1994, 'Cholte Cholte' [In Passing], in Pulakesh Mandal and Joya Mitra (eds), *Shei Dashak* [That Decade], Kolkata: Papyrus, pp. 143–63.

———, 2004, *Killing Days: Prison Memoirs,* trans. by Shampa Banerjee, New Delhi: Women Unlimited.

Mitra, Saibal, 1993, *Manabputri,* Kolkata: Dey's Publishing.

Mody, Perveez, 2008, *The Intimate State: Love-marriage and the Law in Delhi,* India and UK: Routledge.

Monti, Alessandro, 2004, 'The Hero as Holy Man: A Plea for a Communal Hindu Identity', in Radhika Chopra, Caroline Osella, and Filippo Osella (eds), *Masculinities in South Asia: Context of Change, Sites of Continuity,* New Delhi: Women Unlimited, pp. 335–63.

Mohan, Rajeswari, 1998, 'Loving Palestine, *Interventions*', *International Journal of Postcolonial Studies,* 1(1): 52–80.

Mookherjee, Nayanika, 2008, 'Gendered Embodiments: Mapping the Body-politic of the Raped Woman and the Nation in Bangladesh', *Feminist Review* 88(1): 36–53.

Morgan, Robin, 1989, *The Demon Lover: On the Sexuality of Terrorism,* New York: Norton.

Moser, Caroline, 2001, 'Gendered Continuum of Violence and Conflict: An Operational Framework', in Caroline O.N. Moser and Fiona Clark (eds), *Victims, Perpetrators or Actors?: Gender, Armed Conflict and Political Violence,* London and New York: Zed Books, pp. 30–52.

Motsemme, Nthabiseng, 2002, 'Gendered Experiences of Blackness in Post-Apartheid South Africa', *Social Identities,* 8(4): 647–73.

———, 2004, 'The Mute Always Speak: On Women's Silences at the Truth and Reconciliation Commission', *Current Sociology,* 52(5): 909–32.

Mukherjee, Ishanee, 1999, 'Scaling the Barrier: Women, Revolution and Abscondence in Late Colonial Bengal', *Indian Journal of Gender Studies,* 6(1): 61–78.

Mukherjee, S.N., 1970, 'The Bhadralok of Bengali', in E. Leach and S.N. Mukherjee (eds), *Elites in South Asia,* London: Cambridge University Press, pp. 33–78.

Mukhopadhyay, Sirshendu, 2003, *Waiting for Rain: A Novel,* trans. by Nilanjan Bhattacharya, New Delhi: Penguin Books.

Mukta, Parita, 2004, 'The Attrition of Memories: Ethics, Moralities and Futures', paper presented at the Third International Oral History Conference, Rome, Italy, June, 2004.

Naaman, Dorit, 2007, 'Brides of Palestine/Angels of Death: Media, Gender, and Performance in the Case of the Palestinian Female Suicide Bombers', *Signs: Journal of Women in Culture and Society,* 32(4): 933–55.

Nag, Dulali, 1997, 'Little Magazines in Kolkata and a Postsociology of India', *Contributions to Indian Sociology*, 31(1): 109–33.

Nandy, Ashis, 1998, *Exiled at Home*, New Delhi: Oxford University Press.

Naqvi, Saeed, 1973, 'Interview with Mary Tyler', *The Sunday Statesman Magazine*, 30 September.

Nigam, Aditya, 2010, *After Utopia: Modernity and Socialism in the Postcolony*, New Delhi: Viva Books.

Niranjana, Tejaswini, 2007, 'Feminism and Cultural Studies in Asia', *Interventions*, 9(2): 209–18.

Noakes, Lucy, 1998, *War and the British: Gender, Memory and National Identity*, London: I.B. Tauris.

Nora, Pierre, 1989, 'Between Memory and History: Les Lieux de Memoire', *Representations*, 26(Spring): 7–24.

Olick, Jeffrey K. and Joyce Robbins, 1998, 'Social Memory Studies: From "Collective Memory" to the Historical Sociology of Mnemonic Practices', *Annual Review of Sociology*, 24: 105–40.

Omvedt, Gail, 1980, *We Will Smash This Prison! Indian Women in Struggle*, London: Zed Press.

———, 1993, *Reinventing Revolution: New Social Movements and the Socialist Tradition in India*, Armonk, NY, and London: M.E. Sharpe.

———, 1995, *Dalit Visions: The Anti-caste Movement and the Construction of an Indian Identity*, New Delhi: Orient Longman.

Orsini, Francesca, 2006, 'Introduction', in Francesca Orsini (ed.), *Love in South Asia: A Cultural History*, Cambridge: Cambridge University Press, pp. 1–42.

Pandey, Gyanendra, 2001, *Remembering Partition: Violence, Nationalism and History in India*, Cambridge: Cambridge University Press.

———, 2006, *Routine Violence: Nations, Fragments, Histories*, New Delhi: Permanent Black (originally published by Stanford University Press).

Parashar, Swati, 2009, 'Feminist International Relations and Women Militants: Case Studies from Sri Lanka and Kashmir', *Cambridge Review of International Affairs*, 22(2): 236–56.

Passerini, Luisa, 1987, *Fascism in Popular Memory: The Cultural Experience of the Turin Working Class*, trans. by Robert Lumley and Jude Bloomfield, Cambridge: Cambridge University Press.

———, 1992, 'Lacerations in the Memory: Women in the Italian Underground Organizations', *International Social Movement Research*, 4: 161–212.

Plummer, Ken, 1995, *Telling Sexual Stories: Power, Change and Social Worlds*, London: Routledge.

Portelli, Alessandro, 1991, *The Death of Luigi Trastulli, and Other Stories: Form and Meaning in Oral History*, Albany, NY: State University of New York Press.

Portelli, Alessandro, 1998, 'What Makes Oral History Different', in Robert Perks and Alistair Thomson (eds), *The Oral History Reader*, London: Routledge, pp. 63–74.

Punjabi, Kavita, 1997, 'Probing "Morality" and State Violence: Feminist Values and Communicative Interaction in Prison Testimonios in Argentina and India', in M. Jacqui Alexander and Chandra Talpade Mohanty (eds), *Feminist Genealogies, Colonial Legacies, Democratic Futures*, New York: Routledge, pp. 30–45.

———, 2002, 'Between Testimony and History: Interpreting Oral Narratives of Tebhaga Women', in Supriya Chaudhuri and Sajni Mukherji (eds), *Literature and Gender: Essays for Jasodhara Bagchi*, New Delhi: Orient Longman, pp. 241–70.

Puri, Jyoti, 1999, *Woman, Body, Desire in Post-colonial India: Narratives of Gender and Sexuality*, London: Routledge.

Puwar, Nirmal, 2004, *Space Invaders: Race, Gender and Bodies Out of Place*, Oxford: Berg.

Radstone, Susannah, 2000, 'Introduction', in Susannah Radstone (ed.), *Memory and Methodology*, Oxford: Berg, pp. 1–22.

Radstone, Susannah and Katharine Hodgkin (eds), 2003, *Regimes of Memory*, London and New York: Routledge.

Rajasingham–Senanayake, Darini, 2001, 'Ambivalent Empowerment: The Tragedy of Tamil Women in Conflict', in Rita Manchanda (ed.), *Women, War, and Peace in South Asia: Beyond Victimhood to Agency*, New Delhi and Thousand Oaks, CA: Sage Publications, pp. 102–30.

———, 2004, 'Between Reality and Representation: Women's Agency in War and Post-Conflict Sri Lanka', *Cultural Dynamics*, 16(2–3): 141–68.

Ram, Mohan, 1971, *Maoism in India*, New York: Barnes and Noble.

Ramphele, Mamphela, 1997, 'Political Widowhood in South Africa: The Embodiment of Ambiguity', in Arthur Kleinman, Veena Das, and Margaret Lock (eds), *Social Suffering*, Berkeley and London: University of California Press, pp. 99–117.

Ray, Manas, 2002, 'Growing Up Refugee', *History Workshop Journal*, 5: 150–79.

Ray, Rabindra, 1998, *The Naxalites and their Ideology*, New Delhi; Oxford: Oxford University Press.

Ray, Raka, 1999, *Fields of Protest: Women's Movements in India*, New Delhi: Kali for Women.

———, 2000, 'Masculinity, Femininity, and Servitude: Domestic Workers in Kolkata in the Late Twentieth Century', *Feminist Studies*, 26(3): 691–718.

Ray, Raka and M. Katzenstein, 2005, 'Introduction: In the Beginning, There was the Nehruvian State', in R. Ray and M. Katzenstein (eds), *Social Movements in India: Poverty, Power, and Politics*, Lanham, MD: Rowman and Littlefield, pp. 1–31.

Redman, Peter, 1999, 'Boys in Love: Narrative, Identity and the Production of Heterosexual Masculinities', Unpublished PhD thesis, University of Birmingham.

Rege, Sharmila, 1998, 'Dalit Women Talk Differently: A Critique of "Difference" and towards a Dalit Feminist Standpoint Position', *Economic and Political Weekly*, 33(44): WS39–46.

Ricoeur, Paul, 1991, 'Narrative Identity', in David Wood (ed.), *On Paul Ricoeur: Narrative and Interpretation*, London: Routledge, pp. 188–200.

———, 1999, 'Memory and Forgetting', in Richard Kearney and Mark Dooley (eds), *Questioning Ethics: Contemporary Debates in Philosophy*, London and New York: Routledge, pp. 5–11.

———, 2004, *Memory, History, Forgetting*, Chicago: University of Chicago Press.

Robson, Kathryn, 2001, 'Curative Fictions: The "Narrative Cure"' in Judith Herman's *Trauma and Recovery* and Chantal Chawaf's *Le Manteau noir*', *Cultural Values*, 5(1): 115–30.

Roper, Michael, 2000, 'Re-remembering the Soldier Hero: The Psychic and Social Construction of Memory in Personal Narratives of the Great War', *History Workshop Journal*, 2000(50): 181–204.

Rose, Jacqueline, 1996, *States of Fantasy*, Oxford and New York: Oxford University Press.

Ross, Fiona, 2001, 'Speech and Silence: Women's Testimony in the First Five Weeks of Public Hearing of the South African Truth and Reconciliation Commission', in Veena Das, Arthur Kleinman, Margaret Lock, Mamphela Ramphele, and Pamela Reynolds (eds), *Remaking a World: Violence, Social Suffering, and Recovery*, Berkeley: University of California Press, pp. 250–80.

———, 2003, *Bearing Witness: Women and the Truth and Reconciliation Commission in South Africa*, London: Pluto Press.

Roy, Arundhati, 1997, *The God of Small Things*, London: Flamingo.

Roy, Debal Singha, 1995, 'Peasant Movements and Empowerment of Rural Women', *Economic and Political Weekly*, 16 September: 2306–11.

Roy, Srila, 2009a, 'The Ethical Ambivalence of Resistant Violence: Notes from Postcolonial South Asia', *Feminist Review*, Special Issue on 'Negotiating New Terrains: South Asian Feminisms', 91(1): 135–53.

———, 2009b, 'Melancholic Politics and the Politics of Melancholia: The Indian Women's Movement', *Feminist Theory*, 10(3): 341–57.

———, 2010, 'Wounds and "Cures" in South Asian Gender and Memory Politics', in G. Hunt and H. Bradby (eds), *Living through Intended and Unintended Suffering: War, Medicine and Gender*, Aldershot: Ashgate, pp. 31–50.

Saldhana, Indira, 1986, 'Tribal Women in the Warli Revolt: 1945–47: "Class" and "Gender" in the Left Perspective', *Economic and Political Weekly*, 21(17): WS41–52.

Saikia, Yasmin, 2011, *Women, War, and the Making of Bangladesh: Remembering 1971*, Durham: Duke University Press.

Sanyal, Supriya, 2001, *Biplaber Sondhane ek Sadharon Meye* [An Ordinary Girl in Search of Revolution], *Monthon Patrika*, November–December: 13–20.

Sarkar, Sumit, 1983, *Modern India 1885–1947*, New Delhi: Macmillan.

_______, 1997, *Writing Social History*, New Delhi: Oxford University Press.

Sarkar, Sumit and Tanika Sarkar, 2009, 'Notes on a Dying People', *Economic and Political Weekly*, 44(26–7): 10–14.

Sarkar, Tanika, 1984, 'Politics and Women in Bengal: The Condition and Meaning of Participation', *Indian Economic and Social History Review*, 21(1): 91–101.

_______, 1987, *Bengal 1928–1934: The Politics of Protest*, New Delhi and Oxford: Oxford University Press.

_______, 1991, 'Reflections on Birati Rape Cases: Gender Ideology in Bengal', *Economic and Political Weekly*, 26(5): 215–18.

_______, 1996, 'Imagining Hindurasthra: The Hindu and the Muslim in Bankim Chandra's Writings', in David Ludden (ed.), *Making India Hindu*, New Delhi: Oxford University Press, pp. 162–84.

_______, 2001, *Hindu Wife and Hindu Nation: Community, Religion and Cultural Nationalism*, London: C. Hurst.

Saunders, Rebecca and Kamran Aghaie, 2005, 'Introduction: Memory and Mourning', *Comparative Studies of South Asia, Africa and the Middle East*, 25(1): 16–29.

Scarry, Elaine, 1985, *The Body in Pain: The Making and Unmaking of the World*, New York and Oxford: Oxford University Press.

Scott, Joan, 1986, 'Gender: A Useful Category of Historical Analysis', *The American Historical Review*, 91(5): 1053–75.

_______, 1992, 'Experience', in Joan Scott and Judith Butler (eds), *Feminists Theorise the Political*, New York and London: Routledge, pp. 22–40.

_______, 1999, *Gender and the Politics of History*, New York: Columbia University Press.

Sen, Kalpana, 2001, 'Paschim Banglar Naxal Andolane Meyera' [Women in West Bengal's Naxalite Movement], in Maitreyi Chatterji (ed.) *Esho Mukto Koro: Nareer Adhikar o Adhikar Andolan Bishayak Prabandha Sankalan* [Let Us Be Free: A Collection of Essays on Women's Rights and Movements], Kolkata: People's Book Society, pp. 159–86.

Sen, Minakhi, 1994, *Jeler Bhitor Jail* [Jail within Jail], *Vols 1 and 2*, Kolkata: Pratikshan Publications.

_______, 2002, 'Face' in *Her Stories: 20th Century Bengali Women Writers*, trans. by Sanjukta Dasgupta, Delhi: Srishti.

Sen, Manikuntala, 2001, *In Search of Freedom: An Unfinished Journey*, trans. by Stree, Kolkata: Stree.

Sen, Samar, Debabrata Panda and Ashish Lahiri (eds), 1978, *Naxalbariand After: a Frontier Anthology, Vols 1 and 2*, Kolkata: Kathashilpa.

Sen, Samita, 1993, 'Motherhood and Mothercraft: Gender and Nationalism in Bengal', *Gender and History*, 5(2): 231–43.

———, 2001, 'Histories of Betrayal: Patriarchy, Class, and Nation', in Sekhar Bandyopadhyay (ed.), *Bengal: Rethinking History*, New Delhi: Manohar, pp. 259–81.

Sen, Sunil, 1979, *Agrarian Relations in India, 1793-1947*, New Delhi: People's Publishing House.

——— 1985, *The Working Women and Popular Movements in Bengal: From the Gandhi Era to the Present Day*, Kolkata: K.P. Bagchi.

Sengupta, Promode, 1983, *Naxalabari and Indian Revolution*, Kolkata: Research India Publications.

Seth, Sanjay, 1997, 'Indian Maoism: The Significance of Naxalbari', in A. Dirlik, N. Knight, and P. Healey (eds), *Critical Perspectives on Mao Zedong's Thought*, New Jersey: Humanities Press, pp. 289–312.

———, 2004, 'Smashing Statues, Dancing Sivas: Two Tales of Indian Icons', *Humanities Research*, XI(1): 42–53.

Shah, Alpa, 2006, 'Markets of Protection: The "Terrorist" Maoist Movement and the State in Jharkhand, India', *Critique of Anthropology*, 26(3): 297–314.

———, 2011, 'India Burning: The Maoist Movement', in I. Clark–Deces (ed.), *A Companion to the Anthropology of India*, Oxford: Basil-Blackwell, pp. 332–51.

Shah, Alpa and Judith Pettigrew, 2009, 'Windows into a Revolution: Ethnographies of Maoism in South Asia', *Dialectical Anthropology*, 33(3–4): 225–51.

Singh, Prakash, 1995, *The Naxalite Movement in India*, New Delhi: Rupa and Co.

Sinha, Mrinalini, 1995, *Colonial Masculinity: The 'Manly Englishman' and the 'Effeminate Bengali' in the Late Nineteenth Century*, Manchester and New York: Manchester University Press.

Sinha Roy, Mallarika, 2011, *Gender and Radical Politics in India: Magic Moments of Naxalbari (1967–1975)*, Oxon and New York: Routledge.

Sjoberg, Laura and Caron E. Gentry, 2007, *Mothers, Monsters, Whores: Women's Violence in Global Politics*, London and New York: Zed Books.

Skeggs, Beverley, 2004, 'Uneasy Alignments, Resourcing Respectable Subjectivity', *GLQ: A Journal of Lesbian and Gay Studies*, 10(2): 291–8.

Silber, I.C., 2004, 'Mothers/Fighters/Citizens: Violence and Disillusionment in Post-War El Salvador', *Gender & History*, 16: 561–87.

Smith, Dorothy E., 1988[2002], 'The Everyday World as Problematic: The Standpoint of Women', in Tony Bennett and Diane Watson (eds), *Understanding Everyday Life*, Oxford: Blackwell Publishers, pp. 348–50.

Somers, Margaret, 1994, 'The Narrative Constitution of Identity: A Relational and Network Approach', *Theory and Society*, 23(5): 605–49.

Spivak, Gayatri, 2002, 'Breast-giver': For Author, Reader, Teacher, Subaltern, Historian...', in Mahasweta Devi, *Breast Stories*, trans. by Gayatri Chakravorty Spivak, Kolkata: Seagull Books, pp. 76–137.

Sreenivas, Mytheli, 2008, *Wives, Widows, Concubines: The Conjugal Family Ideal in Colonial India*, Bloomington: Indiana University Press.

Standing, Hilary, 1991, *Dependence and Autonomy: Women's Employment and the Family in Kolkata*, London: Routledge.

Steedman, Carolyn, 1988, *The Radical Soldier's Tale: John Pearman, 1819–1908*, London and New York: Routledge.

Stree Shakti Sanghatana, 1989, *We were Making History ... : Life Stories of Women in the Telangana People's Struggle*, London: Zed Books.

Sturken, Marita, 1997, *Tangled Memories: The Vietnam War, the AIDS Epidemic, and the Politics of Remembering*, Berkeley and London: University of California Press.

———, 1999, 'Narratives of Recovery: Repressed Memory as Cultural Memory', in Mieke Bal, Jonathan V. Crewe, and Leo Spitzer (eds), *Acts of Memory: Cultural Recall in the Present*, Hanover, NH, and London: University Press of New England, pp. 231–48.

Summerfield, Penny, 1998, *Reconstructing Women's Wartime Lives: Discourse and Subjectivity in Oral Histories of the Second World War*, Manchester: Manchester University Press.

———, 2000, 'Dis/composing the Subject: Intersubjectivities in Oral History', in Tess Cosslett, Celia Lury, and Penny Summerfield (eds), *Feminism and Autobiography: Texts, Theories, Methods*, London: Routledge, pp. 91–106.

———, 2004, 'Culture and Composure: Creating Narratives of the Gendered Self in Oral History Interviews', *Cultural and Social History*, 1(1): 65–93.

Sunder Rajan, Rajeswari, 1993, *Real and Imagined Women: Gender, Culture, and Postcolonialism*, London: Routledge.

———, 1999, 'The Story of Draupadi's Disrobing: Meanings for Our Times', in Rajeshwari Sunder Rajan (ed.), *Signposts: Gender Issues in Post-independence India*, New Delhi: Kali for Women, pp. 331–58.

———, 2004, 'Rethinking Law and Violence: The Domestic Violence (Prevention) Bill in India, 2002' *Gender and History*, 16(3): 769–793.

Tal, Kalí, 1996, *Worlds of Hurt: Reading the Literatures of Trauma*, Cambridge: Cambridge University Press.

Tambiah, Yasmin, 2005, 'Turncoat Bodies: Sexuality and Sex Work under Militarization in Sri Lanka', *Gender and Society*, 19(2): 243–61.

Tarlo, Emma, 2003, *Unsettling Memories: Narratives of the Emergency in Delhi*, London: C. Hurst.

Taussig, Michael, 1999, *Defacement: Public Secrecy and the Labor of the Negative*, Stanford: Stanford University Press.

Thapar–Bjorkert, Suruchi, 2006, *Women in the Indian Nationalist Movement: Unseen Faces: Unheard Voices, 1925–1942*, New Delhi and London: Sage Publications.

Thomson, Alistair, 1998, 'Anzac Memories: Putting Popular Memory Theory into Practice in Australia', in Robert Perks and Alistair Thomson (eds), *The Oral History Reader*, London: Routledge, pp. 300–10.

Todeschini, Maya, 2001, 'The Bomb's Womb? Women and the Atom Bomb', in Veena Das, Arthur Kleinman, Margaret Lock, Mamphela Ramphele, and Pamela Reynolds (eds), *Remaking a World: Violence, Social Suffering, and Recovery*, Berkeley: University of California Press, pp. 102–56.

Treacher, Amal, Hsiao-Hung Pai, Laleh Khalili, and Pam Alldred, 2008, 'Editorial: The Gendered Embroilments of War', *Feminist Review*, 88(1): 1–6.

Tyler, Mary, 1977, *My Years in an Indian Prison*, London: Gollancz.

Varon, Jeremy, 2004, *Bringing the War Home: The Weather Underground, the Red Army Faction, and Revolutionary Violence in the Sixties and Seventies*, Berkeley: University of California Press.

Verma, Meenakshie, 2004, *Aftermath: An Oral History of Violence*, New Delhi: Penguin.

Vindhya, U., 1990, 'The Srikakulam Movement', in I. Sen (ed.), *A Space Within the Struggle*, New Delhi: Kali for Women, pp. 25–49.

———, 2000, 'Comrades-in-Arms: Sexuality and Identity in the Contemporary Revolutionary Movement in Andhra Pradesh and the Legacy of Chalam', in Mary E. John and Janaki Nair (eds), *A Question of Silence? The Sexual Economies of Modern India*, London: Zed Books, pp. 167–91.

Walsh, Judith, 2004, *Domesticity in Colonial India: What Women Learned When Men Gave Them Advice*, Maryland and Oxford: Rowman and Littlefield.

Watson, Rubie (ed.), 1994, *Memory, History, and Opposition under State Socialism*, Sante Fe, NM: School of American Research Press, University of Washington Press.

Wetherell, Margaret, 1995, 'Romantic Discourse and Feminist Analysis: Interrogating Investment, Power and Desire', in Sue Wilkinson and Celia Kitzinger (eds), *Feminism and Discourse*, London: Sage Publications, pp. 128–44.

White, A.M., 2007, 'All the Men are Fighting for Freedom, All the Women are Mourning Their Men, But Some of Us Carried Guns: A Raced-gendered Analysis of Fanon's Psychological Perspectives on War', *Signs*, 32: 857–84.

Wilkinson, Sue and Celia Kitzinger (eds), 1995, *Feminism and Discourse: Psychological Perspectives*, London: Sage Publications.

Young, Iris Marion, 1990, *Throwing Like a Girl and Other Essays in Feminist Philosophy and Social Theory*, Bloomington: Indiana University Press.

———, 2003, 'Feminist Reactions to the Contemporary Security Regime', *Hypatia*, 18(1): 223–31.

———, 2007, *Global Challenges: War, Self-Determination and Responsibility for Justice*, Polity. Cambridge; Malden, M.A.

Yuval-Davis, Nira and Floya Anthias (eds), 1989, *Woman, Nation, State*, Basingstoke: Macmillan.

Žižek, Slavoj, 1991, *For They Know Not What They Do: Enjoyment as a Political Factor*, London: Verso.

———, 2000, *The Ticklish Subject: The Absent Centre of Political Ontology*, London and New York: Verso.

Zur, Judith, 1998, *Violent Memories: Mayan War Widows in Guatemala*, Oxford: Westview Press.

Zwerman, Gilda, 1992, 'Conservative and Feminist Images of Women associated with Armed, Clandestine Organizations in the United States', *International Social Movement Research*, 4: 133–59.

Internet Sources

Amnesty International, 1994, 'India: Archana Guha—16 Years Awaiting Justice: The Lack of Speedy and Effective Redress Mechanisms for Torture Victims', AI Index: ASA 20/08/94, March, available at http://www.amnestyusa.org/countries/india/document.do?id=900CA7C25DBC8313802569A60060485D (accessed August 2005).

———, 2001, 'India: Time to Act to Stop Torture and Impunity in West Bengal', AI Index: ASA 20/033/2001, 10 August, available at http://web.amnesty.org/library/Index/ENGASA200332001?openandof=ENG-IND (accessed August 2005).

Bag, Kheya, 2011, 'Red Bengal's Rise and Fall', *New Left Review*, 70, available at http://newleftreview.org/?view=2909 (accessed August 2011).

Banerjee, Sumanta, 2007, 'Naxalbari and the continuous rebellion', *Himal South Asian*, available at http://www.himalmag.com/read.php?id=2498, (accessed January 2010).

Baxi, Pratiksha, 2001, 'Sexual harasment', *Seminar*, available at http://www.india-seminar.com/2001/505.htm (accessed November 2005).

Charu Mazumdar Reference Archive, available at http://www.marxists.org/reference/archive/mazumdar/index.htm (accessed October 2005).

Chattopadhyay, Kunal and Soma Marik, 2004, The Left Front and the United Progressive Alliance, available at http:// www.socialistdemocracy.org/NewsandAnalysisInternational/NewsandAnalysisIntTheLeftFrontAndTheUnitedProgressiveAlliance.html (accessed October 2005).

Communist Party of India (Marxist–Leninist) Liberation, 2002, available at http://www.CPI(ML).org/index.htm (accessed August 2005).

'Commemorating the Naxalbari Anniversary of the Historical', 25th May 2002, available at http://CPI(ML).s4u.org/liberation/articles/4503.htm (accessed January 2006).

Guha, Ramchandra, 2004, 'On Samar Sen, Poetry and Bengali Marxism', *The Daily Star*, available at http://www.thedailystar.net/2004/02/28/d402282102103.htm (accessed October 2005).

Himal South Asian, 2007, Cover Feature on 'Echoes of Naxalbari' 20:12, available at http://www.himalmag.com/read.php?id=2495 (accessed February 2010).

Jafri, Syed Amin, 2004, 'Naxalites pay tributes to Charu Mazumdar', Rediff.com, October 12, 2004. available at http://www.rediff.com/news/2004/oct/12ap.htm (accessed January 2006).

Jha, Prashant, 2007, 'Naxalite Be Not Proud', *Himan South Asian*, available at http://www.himalmag.com/read.php?id=2494 (accessed April 2008)

Kannabiran, Vasanth, 2010, 'Scattered Truths, Bitter Seeds', *Seminar: Red Resurgence*, available at http://www.india-seminar.com/2010/607/607_vasanth_kannabiran.htm (accessed April 2012).

Kundu, Trideb Santapa, 2009, 'Partition Experiences of East Bengali Refugee Women', *Bangalnama*, 6 July, available at http://bangalnama.wordpress.com/2009/07/06/partition-experiences-of-the-east-bengali-refugee-women/ (accessed December 2009).

Mukherjee, Nirmalangshu, 2009, 'Open Letter to Noam Chomsky', *Kafila*, posted by Aditya Nigam, 21 October, available at http://kafila.org/2009/10/21/open-letter-to-noam-chomsky-nirmalangshu-mukherjee/ (accessed November 2009).

Nigam, Aditya, 2007, '"Kalbela", Naxalbari and Radical Political Cinema', *Kafila*, 31 July, available at http://kafila.org/2007/07/31/%e2%80%98kalbela%e2%80%99-naxalbari-and-radical-political-cinema/ (accessed November 2009).

———, 2008, 'Reflections on Revolutionary Violence', *Kafila*, available at http://kafila.org/2008/11/21/reflections-on-revolutionary-violence/ (accessed November 2009).

Nigam, Aditya, Apoorvanand, Kavita Srivastava, Nivedita Menon, Prabhash Joshi, and Satya Sivaraman, 2008, 'Maoist Disruption of the Non-violent Human Shields Movement in Chhattisgarh', available at http://kafila.org/2008/10/19/maoist-disruption-of-the-non-violent-human-shields-movement-in-chhattisgarh/ (accessed July 2011).

Nigam, Anirban Gupta, 2003, 'Moonwalking with the Comrades', Kafila, March 23, available at http://kafila.org/2010/03/23/moonwalking-with-the-comrades/ (accessed April 2003).

Pandita, Rahul, 2010, '100lb Guerillas', *Open Magazine*, available at http://www.openthemagazine.com/article/nation/100lb-guerillas (accessed August 2011).

Peoplesmarch, available at http://www.peoplesmarch.com (accessed August 2005).

Pettigrew, Judith and Sara Shneiderman, 2004, 'Women and the Maobaadi: Ideology and Agency in Nepal's Maoist Movement', *Himal South Asian*, available at http://www.himalmag.com/2004/january/essay.htm (accessed April 2006).

Roy, Arundhati, 2010, 'Walking With the Comrades', *Outlook India*, available at http://www.outlookindia.com/article.aspx?264738 (accessed July 2011).

Sarkar, Aditya, 2007, 'Nandigram and the Deformations of the Indian Left', *International Socialism*, available at http://www.isj.org.uk/index.php4?id=333andissue=115 (accessed December 2009).

Sen, Samita, 2000, 'Toward a Feminist Politics? The Indian Women's Movement in Historical Perspective', The World Bank Policy Research Report on Gender and Development, Working Paper Series No. 9, The World Bank Development Research Group/Poverty Reduction and Economic Management Network, available at http: //www.worldbank.org/gender/prr (accessed January 2002).

Singur Andolan: Amader Bhabna Amader Pratibad [Singur Movement: Our Thoughts, Our Protest], edited by Emancipation Publication, 2007, available at http://sanhati.com/literature/19/ (accessed September 2011).

Scrase, Timothy (2004) The Hegemony of English in India,Conference Proceedings of the 15th Biennial Conference of the Asian Studies Association of Australia in Canberra, 29 June-2 July 2004, available at http://coombs.anu.edu.au/ASAA/conference/proceedings/Scrase-T1-ASAA2004.pdf (accessed August 2005).

Simeon, Dilip, 2010, 'Permanent Spring', *Seminar: Red Resurgence*, available at http://www.india-seminar.com/2010/607/607_dilip_simeon.htm (accessed April 2012).

Vohra, Paromita, 2009, 'Prisoners of Conscience', *Open Magazine*, available at http://www.openthemagazine.com/article/documentaries/prisoners-of-conscience (accessed December 2009).

Women against Sexual Violence and State Repression (WSS), 2011, *Sexual Violence on Women in the Context of Anti-Maoist Operations in Jharkhand: A Fact Finding Report*, May, available at http://sanhati.com/wp-content/uploads/2011/08/jkhd_wss_report.pdf (accessed August 2011).

Visual Documents

(Courtesy: International Institute of Social History, Amsterdam)

Ashim Chatterjee, interviewed by Shahriar Kabir in Kolkata on 17 December 1996, Bengali.

Azijul Haque, interviewed by Shahriar Kabir in Kolkata on 17 December 1996, Bengali.

Kanu Sanyal, interviewed by Shahriar Kabir in Bagdogra, Shiliguri, on 20 December 1996, Bengali.

Shanti Munda, interviewed by Shahriar Kabir at Hatighisha in Naxalbari, Shiliguri, on 23 July 1997, Bengali.

Filmography

Anu, 1998, Dir. Satarupa Sanyal, SCUD.

Aranyer Din Ratri (Days and nights in the forest), 1970, Dir. Satyajit Ray, Priya Films (Asim Dutta and Nepal Dutta).

Kolkata 71, 1972, Dir. Mrinal Sen, D.S. Pictures.

Dooratwa (The Distance), 1978, Dir. Buddhadeb Dasgupta, Buddhadeb Dasgupta Productions.

Hazaaron Khwaishein Aisi (A Thousand Dreams Such As These), 2005, Dir. Sudhir Mishra, Pritish Nandy Communications.

Jana Aranya (The Middleman), 1975, Dir. Satyajit Ray, Indus Films (Subir Guha).

Jukti, Takko aar Gappo (Reason, Discussion and a Tale), 1974, Dir. Ritwik Ghatak.

Kalbela (The Omnious Hour), 1983, Dir. Gautam Ghose.

Lal Salaam (Red Salute), Dir. Gaganvihari Borate, Manas Communication, 2002.

Mahanagar (The Big City), 1963, Dir. Satyajit Ray, RDB and Co.

Meghe Dhaka Tara (The Cloud-Capped Star), 1960, Dir. Ritwick Ghatak, Chitrakalpa.

Padatik (The Foot Soldier), 1973, Dir. Mrinal Sen, Mrinal Sen Productions.

Pratidwandi (The Adversary/Siddhartha and the City), 1970, Dir. Satyajit Ray, Priya Films.

Zameer ke Bandi (Prisoners of Conscience), 1978, Dir. Anand Patwardhan.

Rang de Basanti (Paint it Saffron), 2006, Dir. Rakesh Om Prakash Mehra.

Seemabaddha (Company Limited), 1971, Dir. Satyajit Ray, Chitranjali.

Interview, 1970, Dir. Mrinal Sen, Mrinal Sen Productions.

Index